MW00423446

A
ROAD
OUT
OF
NAKNEK

Alaskan Salmon Fishing, Long-Distance Running,
and Life According to the Tide

RUNNING TIDAL
Publishing Co.

A Road out of Naknek:
Alaskan Salmon Fishing, Long-Distance Running,
and Life According to the Tide

Copyright © 2020 Keith Catalano Wilson

ISBN: 9781092295932

Some names and identifying details have been changed to protect the privacy of individuals.

Illustrations by Keith C. Wilson
Cover design by Chad Casper
Edited by Katrina Myers

Running Tidal Publishing Co.

Dedicated to Mom and Dad

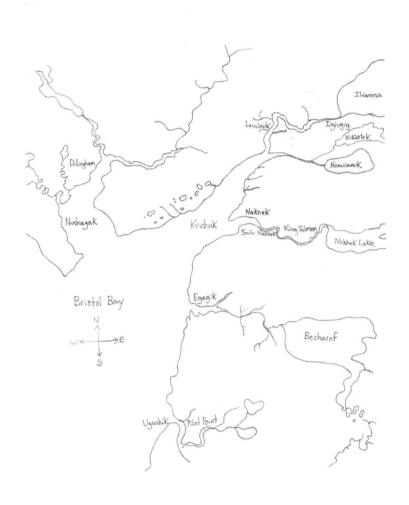

Iliamna

Levelock

Igiugig

Kokhlek

Dillingham

Nonvianuk

Nushagak

Naknek

Kvichak

South Naknek

King Salmon

Naknek Lake

Bristol Bay

N
W — E
S

Egegik

Becharof

Ugashik

Pilot Point

FOREWORD

By Luke Donkersloot

I've suspected Keith Wilson had superpowers since he was a child. Adventures, games, drawing, books, costumes, TMNT and cartoons on VHS—no two days were the same in that monumental A-frame house his dad built. He was a dragon, a knight, every hero and villain, a devil, a fairy... his mom tried to discourage that last one but Keith didn't care. All kids have the power of make-believe, but with Keith it's something more. He told me this book of his is non-fiction, but if that's true, he is superhuman. I'm not just talking about surviving as many seasons set-netting as he has with his dad, either, which defies probability. Keith imagines things—the impossible, I tell you—and makes them so.

And me? I was his babysitter.

We're both teachers' kids, growing up in Naknek. It's a small place but even in small places things do change. After a few years I wasn't the baby-sitter any more, but spent summers after high school fishing with Keith's dad, George, in a sublime place called Graveyard that is now more Keith's than mine in setting story. A few summers there I spent more time with Keith's dad than my own, working until we were rummy, picking fish and laughing to tears at recollecting SNL skits before we'd reached the punchline, or George's greatest books never written: *Brown Spot On the Wall* by Hu Phlung Poo, or *The Greatest Pain,* by Hai Kikki Dikki. Fine dining on a slow night was grilled Spam and Velveeta with onions, reading a book or writing letters by lantern light.

I sit here searching for a way to describe Keith's dad, who has shaped us both. I'll give just this—a memory from my first season, me fresh fifteen years old, our first big opener on July 4th and my first storm, the 22' open skiff rocking, hanging onto the rails, the net, trying to stay in the boat, pick fish, and decide if I would throw up.

"Are you scared?" George asked.

"Yes," I said. I was terrified. Bigger boats sunk. People died that day. I didn't know this yet.

"It'll be okay," he said. He looked me straight in the face, and his eyes are charged, electric blue. I believed him, that he could make it be okay. And it was. Hell, maybe George has powers, too.

I never got to fish a season with Keith. My family actually built a house in the A-frame's neighborhood after I went to college, just a short walk across the tundra away. Sometimes I'd swing in on a holiday to drop off a stack of comics. I got a job at the city dock, and then the barge company operating there—still working the tide, but now handling 40' freezers full of processed salmon with gigantic machines. I'd see Keith and George passing through with their purple skiffs, or sometimes just George, knowing Keith was out there on the beach, holding the boat. Sometimes we'd say hi, but usually in a hurry; seasons at a glance as Keith grew tall, then a beard, and now gray, lines in our faces.

The summer people, the seasons, Naknek, the sockeye—it's created something more than a lifestyle. A collective migration. That time between seasons, the settling period (Where will you go after this?), almost like feeding at sea. Something inside says you should be moving (returning), getting back on the road, even though essentially you're homeless, bouncing between friends or events, the trunk of your car organized like a chest of drawers. The journey is more than just the moment, but that's all our senses can give us, and it does feel good. It should, right? Everyone loves adventure. This may not be you, but if you've ever heard of a place called Naknek, I expect it's people you know. And not long from now, they'll be making their way back toward the rivers.

Every season, every opener, every journey, every race—for all things a beginning and an end, though a couple of the big ones are hard to fathom. Young and inexperienced, Keith and I were struck by the same thing while fishing: a totem, primordial underwater voices speaking to us en masse, of time stretching in both directions. It's prehistoric origins, our time, a brief stint in its history, and its end. If you've been a part of it maybe it's spoken to you, too, or will after you've read his book. If you have heard that voice, you know what an unforgivable thing its silence would be.

Enjoy the read. And Keith — Go Angels!

Luke Donkersloot
September 2020
Anchorage, AK

"The road must eventually lead to the whole world."

— Jack Kerouac, *On the Road*

A
ROAD
OUT
OF
NAKNEK

The tide waits for no one. I don't know how many times I've heard Dad say it, but he's right. It's both time and tide, as the adage goes, that stayeth for no man, but I've learned that time and tide are synonymous, and they wait for no woman, child, flower, furbearer, or fish either. I was never a stellar student, but I paid attention to the interesting parts — and as I understand it, gravity between the sun, our planet, and the moon pulls the ocean in a rhythm as reliable as night and day, summer and winter, or spring and fall. It creates ebbs and floods in a pattern that the rotation of a clock, the breath in a pair of lungs, or the beating of a heart could never match. The tide was turning long before life existed, and it will keep turning long after we're gone.

I've also learned that life on our planet began in the ocean, but I think it was the tide that brought it ashore. Then wind pushed microbes and flora above the shoreline. Seeds spread, and bacteria colonized. Amphibians started crawling and turned into reptiles. Some reptiles became birds. Others became mammals. Now snakes slither after frogs, frogs feed on flies, and seagulls scavenge for scraps. Great apes pick fruit dangling from trees. Species feed on one another, existing in one complex food web.

Not entirely separate, life in the ocean has developed its own similar system. On the surface, fish leap and splash, whales spew geysers, and birds swoop to scoop plankton and minnows, but although the ocean is not entirely separate from land, beneath the surface is unfathomable and alien to us. It teems with great white, black-eyed monsters, mammalian torpedoes speaking in sonar, water-breathing exoskeleton spiders, and eight-legged monsters with the ability to change color and texture. In the darkest depths and deepest canyons, anglerfish navigate with flashlights protruding from their foreheads. There are catsharks, seahorses, and lizardfish with luminous skin. Mountains range between poles, and life thrives at every level from the floor to the surface.

If there is any separation between land and the ocean, it is the shoreline, but it is indistinct and formless. The border between ripples and solid ground is ever-moving, ever-changing. It was only a matter of time before one of the land animals decided to push the boundaries.

First, some of the apes stood upright and walked on two feet and became people. We could walk and run farther than any other bipedal species, and we used the ability to exhaust our prey, club them to death, and have abundant sources of meat, allowing our brains to develop. With this development, we gained a sense of ownership of land, trees, other animals, and even each other.

With a new fascination with borders and lines, pushing beyond the shoreline was inevitable. At first, we waded, careful not to be caught in a current or eaten by a leviathan. Then we built rafts, kayaks, and canoes. We built baidarkas, boats, ships, and submarines. Vessels navigated between continents, and people conquered and eradicated each other, using waterways as transport. We scoured the ocean, harvesting shrimp, shellfish, sharks, and sardines — decimating populations. To people, the ocean was an endless void. Even now, after having left more footprints on our planet than any other species, we have explored less than five percent of the ocean floor.

The tide, however, washes away all footprints. It washes away a skeleton just as it does a tree branch. It washes away a village or a city the same as it does a sandcastle. The Atlantic, Arctic, Indian, South, Pacific, and all the smaller seas are one mass of water, ebbing and flooding into each other.

The Pacific is the largest portion of it, covering more of our planet's surface than all the continents combined. It was this way even during the time of a land we now call Beringia — a conglomerate of what is now Russia, Alaska, and land between them. It was a barrier between the Pacific and the Arctic, but as the water level climbed, it receded into an isthmus that we now call the Bering Land Bridge.

Before seafaring, people hiked the Bering Land Bridge from Siberia to the Norton Sound, following mammoths, muskoxen, and antelope. Then the water level got too high, and the tide was never again low enough to forge from one side to the other. The Bering Land Bridge narrowed until the Pacific met the Arctic, and the Bering Sea drowned it. Now as the tide ebbs and floods against the shores of Russia and Alaska, Beringia is but another part of the ocean floor, where there have been no footsteps in thousands of years.

Some people migrated north and gave themselves names like Inupiat, Sugpiaq, and Inuit. Others migrated east as Athabascans and southeast as Tlingit, Tsimshian, and Haida. Farther south, people became Cherokee, Anishinabe, Shawnee, Shoshone, and Sioux. Even farther south were Apache, Anasazi, and Aztecs. The Maya, Inca, and Aymara went almost as far south as they could get, their ancestral land as estranged as the deepest parts of the ocean.

Some people, however, stayed pressed against the Bering Sea. They were the Yup'ik, the Unangan, and some of the Athabascan people. The Unangan settled along the Aleutian Chain, a string of tiny islands that were once Beringia's tallest mountaintops. Maybe these Bering Sea people were left behind when others migrated south, but I think they stayed on purpose. They learned the power of the tide. They learned to harvest their sustenance from the Bering Sea with driftwood baidarkas, harpoons, hooks, and grass ropes. They hunted whales, clubbed seals, and caught trout, smelt, herring, and salmon. They had no system of numbers, no units of measurement, and they never had to worry about catching too many fish.

The Bering Sea narrows into Bristol Bay, north of the Alaska Peninsula and south of the Kuskokwim mountains. It is a body of water where the difference between ebb and flood changes the shoreline more drastically than sunrise, sunset, or the changing seasons changes the amount of warmth and light.

Starting in the late spring, millions of salmon gather to Bristol Bay from the Pacific to fulfill their final purpose. First, they mill and swirl in the saltwater like the tick around the face of a clock, each one waiting for the right wind, the right temperature, the right moment in the tide. Then they disperse into freshwater rivers, forging toward the headwaters. In schools and surges, they make their run toward their natal lakes and streams. They forge against the current, moving straight ahead to spawn, die, and continue a pattern that was in existence before the first twine was woven, before the first baidarka was built, and before the first human hand ever touched the water.

Yup'ik people established the village of Naugeik at the mouth of one of these rivers flowing into Bristol Bay. They named the village after their word for a muddy place, where the tide climbs to cutbanks on either side, distilling the sand into swirls and flows of thick, brown ebbs and floods. The Yup'ik were the first people to catch the salmon there. They fileted and cooked them, or they cut them into strips to dry over a rack in the open air. They saturated these strips in the smoke of slow-burning birch and alder, beads of oil dripping from deep red meat with a strip of skin with its golden luster shining in the near-midnight sun.

However, it wasn't too long before Russians invaded Southwest Alaska. Yup'ik were overtaken. Unangan were called Aleut, mistaking the word for *island* as the name for people. Athabascans migrated away. Russians mispronounced Naugeik, and it was put on the map as Naknek.

Soon enough, Russians claimed all of Alaska as their property, and later they exchanged it with other invaders who had claimed another mass of land far to the south. They traded it for bits of paper and metal called currency, an invented ebb and flood of numbers. Some of that metal had brought people rushing to other parts of Alaska like Nome and the Yukon, villages turning into towns of roughneck saloons and bearded sourdoughs.

In Bristol Bay, the promise of currency was in exchange for salmon. People from all over our planet arrived in places like Naknek, Egegik, Togiak, and Dillingham. Like the Yup'ik, Unangan, and Athabascan before them, they learned to work with the ebb and flood. They depended on the tide to launch sailboats, release nets, and catch millions upon millions of salmon. Canneries were erected, ports were constructed, and villages sprouted into towns where salmon were caught, gutted, shoved into cans, and shipped on barges along the coast and across the ocean.

The village of Paug-vik, on the north side of the Naknek River, was soon connected by a dirt path to King Salmon, the site of an Air Force Base put in place during World War II. During the Cold War, it was ready and able to defend against any sudden-second attack from the Soviets. With the advent of air travel and the King Salmon Airport, more newcomers flocked to Paug-vik than to Naknek, and Paug-vik was deemed the new Naknek. The old Naknek, once Naugeik, became South Naknek. The three towns together became the Bristol Bay Borough. The dirt path between Naknek and King Salmon was named the Alaska Peninsula Highway.

Meanwhile, down the continent, across the Pacific, and across the Atlantic, salmon populations were disappearing. Most people didn't know or care, but some people wanted to prevent it from happening in Bristol Bay. Some of these people organized and called themselves the Alaska Territorial Fishery Service. Like invading Russians, they were self-proclaimed. Unlike invading Russians, few people believed in their claim. First, Alaska had to be called a state. Then the Alaska Territorial Fishery Service could become the Alaska Department of Fish and Game. Only then could their rules be established, and their suggestions could be put into practice.

Now, based on escapement, nets are allowed in the water during designated times coinciding with the tide. It's not perfect, but it's an instance where people have learned not only to accept the ancient pattern of the tide and the annual influx of salmon, but to work with it, and to limit the harvest and enable the salmon's return again and again. Bristol Bay holds the last, most sustainable fisheries on our planet.

In Naknek, we can witness the power of the tide with the naked eye. At the ebb on the Naknek River, the water is not much more than a trickle through ever-shifting mudflats. Skiffs and subsistence nets slope downward with the beach. Canneries reach out onto docks on top of crooked, splintering pilings. Driftboats tie together in a line of vessels stretching into the channel. Flocks of seagulls gather, flapping and squawking, pecking at guts and grime from processors. Skiffs lay in the mud with their anchors stabbed into the beach. As the water flows out into the ocean, pilings are like trunks of trees rising. Tributaries as thin as the bones of fingers trickle down the mud into what's left of the channel.

After the water has disappeared into the forever of the ocean, movement ceases. Twigs, leaves, clumps of grass, and bubbles aren't drifting along the surface, but they remain in the stillness of slack tide. Then, as though a table were tilted, the tide begins to shift direction. It moves faster and faster, and white water gushes over the mudflats as boats rock and thrash as the waves chop like madmen with axes. Pilings sink into the water.

Outside the mouth of the Naknek River is the Naknek-Kvichak District of the fishery, where commercial fishermen use gillnets. Salmon swim into these nets anchored between buoys placed there by setnetters like Dad and me. In the deeper water, they collide into nets floating behind driftboats with spacious decks and cockpits and onboard sleeping quarters. Aluminum and fiberglass hulls smash each other in the battle for the optimal spot at the border, where fish swim thickest. Cork lines splash with heads and tails on the surface. Corks bob from hits below it. Salmon are caught, delivered, processed, and disbursed to small family operations, Pike Place Market in Seattle, restaurants in Tokyo, street vendors in London, and all corners of the continents, in places where salmon used to return, and places where they have never swum.

Above the water, above the cutbank, most traffic downtown is the cannery workers on foot, between meals at Peter Pan, Red Salmon, Silver Bay, or whatever cannery employs and houses them. They linger along the paved shoulder of the Alaska Peninsula Highway, traveling in tribes. There are Japanese workers with knee-high, gray, rubber boots, Ukrainian teenagers with dreadlocks and bandanas, white trash with neck tattoos and face piercings, mustached Mexicans blaring music from smartphones, and lanky West Africans appearing as tall as phone poles. These living, breathing stereotypes are the perfect demonstration of the diversity of who gathers to Bristol Bay.

Fishermen linger out of Naknek Trading with plastic bags of Kraft Macaroni, cans of Bush's Baked Beans, and bananas as brown as the beach. They head back to their boats, back to their camps, back to their bunks at the cannery before they can fish again. People stumble off the steps of Fisherman's Bar, Hadfield's, and the Red Dog, hoping the money they've made this season hasn't disappeared into the Barmuda Triangle. Boxes of leftover pizza leave D&D Restaurant in cars and onto the backs of fourwheelers, held down by bungee cords. The aroma of grease and scraps attract tagless dogs that wander town like the silent homeless population that they are.

By the end of July, salmon numbers taper and fade to the occasional splash or bob of a cork. Fishermen and cannery workers load planes taking off from King Salmon. Then there are none.

Boats fill the boatyards and canneries board their windows. Seldom is a car on the road, and foot traffic is no longer people but the occasional dog or brown bear searching for scraps. Off in the distance, a sudden shout or a gunshot might echo across town without question. The gate in front of every cannery closes, and Naknek is still, like the Naknek River in the moments of slack tide.

500 or so people stay in Naknek, picking berries, hunting moose and caribou, chopping firewood, and winterizing pipes. Many of these people are direct descendants of people who walked the Bering Land Bridge. Many of them are not. No matter their ancestry, people who stay in Naknek see yellow leaves fall from birch and alders as cold air creeps its way across the tundra like a ghost, leaving it brown and dead in its wake. The days get shorter. The nights get darker. It will be months before the salmon return again. It will be months before the masses again arrive at the King Salmon Airport. Meanwhile, out in Bristol Bay, the Bering Sea, and the depth and expanse of the ocean, the tide ebbs and floods as our planet and its moon orbit around the sun.

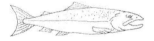

When I was a student at Northern Michigan University, I ran for hours on the wooded trails and paved bike paths along the shores of Lake Superior in Marquette, Michigan where driftwood accumulated on the sand. One foot in front of the other, in a rhythm of heartbeats, breath, and sweat, I ran on any route I could find.

Don't get the wrong idea. I wasn't a collegiate athlete or even a competitive one. Running had nothing to do with school other than keeping me from studying. I wasn't a slow, clumsy runner or a terrible, lazy student, but my motivation for either of these endeavors had nothing to do with a career path or some kind of idea about personal development or personal growth. All I wanted to be was someone who didn't live in Naknek, and besides going back every summer for the fishing season, I was living my dreams.

I had discovered running my senior year of high school as a means to physical fitness, an outlet for teenage frustrations, and an escape from the reality of living in an Alaskan fishing town isolated by tundra and ocean. Then, for some reason, when I was far away from that tundra and ocean, I never stopped running.

I had no idea how fast or how far I was going, but I didn't care either. It was more about getting outside and moving forward than a test of physical prowess. It was about breathing in and out, letting salt escape my pores, and sweat evaporating into the clouds. It was about looking out over what looked like the ocean, but it wasn't the ocean. It was Lake Superior, a lake larger than any other enclosed inland body of water, save the Caspian Sea.

Superior seemed as endless as career choices, places to live, the pavement path, or the dirt trails. Like Forrest Gump, if I had decided, I could run clear across the contiguous United States. There was no finish line until I'd decided to stop, and even then, I still had to make my way back home to whatever cramped dorm room or musty apartment with shag carpet it happened to be at the time. Every semester, I took full loads of classes, including plenty of them that I didn't need. I studied politics, philosophy, psychology, anthropology, and environmental science. I drew portraits, practiced yoga, shot arrows, played tennis, and choreographed routines of flipping and tumbling over mats. I half-assed my way through all of it.

My major was in English, but only because someone in some office said I needed to declare one. I didn't know what I was going to do with it, but when I was coerced into making a decision, I shrugged my shoulders and added Secondary Education to that major.

Growing up, most of the adults in my life were teachers, and I suppose they had influenced me. Sure, they had an influence on me when I was in their classes, but I mean that teachers were the adults that I knew the best. They were in my parents' social circle. They came to the house for parties. We went on camping trips together. Mom was a teacher, Dad was a fisherman, and I had fallen into both paths.

They had even gone to the same University. Because of their alumni status, I paid in-state tuition, one of the determining factors in choosing Northern. Like Bristol Bay salmon, I had found my way to a freshwater lake by following the same path as my parents. The salmon in Superior were planted. I guessed I was, too.

Mom and Dad had moved to Alaska in the 70s, seeking excitement and adventure. It drew them in with magnificent landscapes, majestic wildlife, and interesting people with fantastic stories. They went North to the Future, to the Last Frontier, to the wild west beyond the Wild West. There was Kodiak and its tidal pools of starfish. There was Denali, a mountain taller than Everest from base to summit. There was the lush Tongass Rainforest and totem poles of the Southeast. Mom and Dad chose the muddy river.

They grew up within eight miles of each other, but Mom and Dad didn't meet until college. Mom was from Birmingham, a suburb of Detroit, where she lived with her parents and two sisters, played with dolls and wrote in her diary about boys like Dad. Dad grew up in Ferndale, another suburb of Detroit, with his deaf parents, one younger sister, and three brothers who all went to the same Catholic school and fought over food at the dinner table.

Mom was working on a degree in Special Education, dreaming about a knight in shining armor who would sweep her off her feet. Dad was a tall, strong, handsome conservation major with a shiny Harley, curly brown hair, handyman skills, and repeated jokes like, "Just because your head is pointed doesn't mean you're sharp." Mom told me it was love at first sight. Dad told me that she gave him her number, but he never called. After all, he had a girlfriend, and she had a boyfriend.

Sometime after the girl I know from Mom as Dogbreath broke up with Dad, he left to work for the forest service between Colorado and Wyoming. There he lived his dream of pretending to be Clint Eastwood in a cowboy hat, puffing Swisher Sweets, climbing mountains, and hunting and fishing for food. Back in Marquette, the guy I know from Dad as The-Guy-Who-Stole-the-Skis used Mom's car as a getaway vehicle after loading as many pairs as he could from the shop at Marquette Mountain. The relationship didn't last.

Out west, Dad returned to his trailer after work one day, and his roommate said some girl had been looking for him. The girl had hitchhiked all the way there from Michigan, he told him. *Kitty*, he thought she said — a name Mom had been given by kids she taught as a student teacher in Oconto Falls, Wisconsin, who couldn't pronounce *Catalano*. "Kitty?" he said. He went out and found her. Then she went on with a trip farther into the west, and he kept doing his job.

It was later, back in Michigan, when Mom's date at a mutual friend's wedding didn't dance. Dad did. It still makes me laugh when he dances around our fish camp to oldies on KDLG. Within months, Dad accidentally proposed under a tree in the backyard of his childhood home in Ferndale by asking Mom what her answer would be if he did propose. Her answer was yes. After one maiden voyage to Alaska, they had their wedding in the backyard of the Catalano household in Birmingham in the summer of 1979, their friends floating down the river behind the house, pot smoke billowing behind them. Mom and Dad loaded a van with their wedding presents and two dogs, and they began their journey.

They established a base of operations in Anchorage where Dad worked at a tire store and Mom waited tables and tended some dive bar. She applied for jobs teaching Special Education in rural Alaska, and she was offered several jobs on the same day. Out of all of them, she took the position at the Bristol Bay Borough School in Naknek. Dad started working for the Alaska Department of Fish and Game, studying salmon, taking samples, regulating the fishery.

They lived in a rickety house on the cutbank where running water, as Dad would say, was when one of them ran with the bucket. Insulation and heat were scarce, and on one winter morning, he awoke with his hair frozen to the wall behind the bed. Despite the frazzle-haired photos of him on a motorcycle, I've never known Dad with a full head of hair. I attribute it to this story.

They lived next to Mo, who had moved to Naknek from Buffalo, New York, and Smiley, whose bloodline went back directly to the Bering Land Bridge. The pair would become my godparents as a priest dumped water into my eyes at Saint Teresa's Catholic Church in Naknek. Although I never embraced Catholicism, or religion for that matter, in some surreal memory of a memory, looking through eyes full of holy water is the first time I recall having consciousness.

Mom and Dad had been married six years when I was born in 1984. It was a dark, cold night in October and the clocks were striking midnight. Ronald Reagan was President, the Soviets were testing nuclear weapons, and some pissed-off Irishmen had just bombed a hotel where Margaret Thatcher was staying. Major current events, however, were irrelevant in Naknek. There was no cable TV, no internet, and no household telephones, let alone handheld cellular devices — but I was born in Anchorage, the big city of a quarter-million people. It didn't have just TV but Costco, Taco Bell, traffic lights, and most important this time, a hospital with a birth center.

When they moved to Naknek, Mom and Dad learned Anchorage to be the hub for loading totes, boxes, and coolers of groceries to send home through the post office and checked baggage. Naknek Trading, our home grocery store, did the same thing, but they tripled and quadrupled the prices. *Anguish*, Mom and Dad called the city. It was the place to shop, visit a dentist, check in with an optometrist, or in this instance, deliver a baby.

In October of 1984, Mom and Dad loaded totes and coolers and shipped them home as usual, but this time they took their midnight son onboard as carry-on luggage. Bundled in blankets, in a turbulent little plane, I flew for the first time over the jagged, snow-capped peaks of the Aleutian Range, the endless expanse of tundra and ponds, approached the Naknek River, and rolled down the runway at the King Salmon Airport. Then Dad drove us down the Alaska Peninsula Highway to a house he was still finishing. There, I was raised on wild salmon, wild caribou, wild blueberries, vegetables from Mom's greenhouse, and boxes of Kraft macaroni and canned corn from Costco.

The Wilson household was in Gottschalk's Subdivision, a plot of tundra with gravel leading to various homes. It was a neighborhood where many of the teachers lived, a community within a community where everyone knew everyone, but the houses were far enough apart for privacy. When Bob Swanson, the principal, put a corner of his own house on our property by accident, Mom and Dad didn't mind much. It was when little Kasey Swanson pushed me out of my highchair, and when little Chris Swanson took a bite out of my orange Nerf ball, that if I had any concept of property or boundaries, I might have said something about that corner.

Our house was a kit from Lindal Cedar Homes, and Dad built it from its concrete basement to its triangular roof almost entirely by himself. Before he built a garage, the basement was a place for sawhorse benches, power tools, and a seasonal caribou or two, skinned, hanging over the drain in front of the furnace room. The main floor had two bedrooms at the end of a hallway with a bathroom across from the kitchen. My room was the blue room, with blue carpet and blue walls, on the side of the house by the driveway. My sister, Erica was born when I was nearly four, and she kept me awake by talking in her crib. The yellow room, as we called it, with its yellow walls and green carpet, was a guest room until Erica moved into it. I could still hear her forming complete sentences across the hallway in her sleep.

Red carpet rolled through the hallway, past the kitchen, into the dining room, and it expanded into the living room where there was a woodstove on a brick platform. I used to grip the handles like they were a bike or a fourwheeler, and I'd drive the house. The living room had four big windows overlooking the tundra, the Naknek River, and the porch. When Dad found an old ship wheel, he attached it to a pedestal on the front corner of the porch, and I drove the house from outside. The house was a triangle, and Mom and Dad's bedroom loft narrowed into the corner.

Dad said he had always imagined building his own house for himself and his family. It was a safe structure for a new generation of Wilsons, which confused me when he would throw me up toward the fan while it was spinning. It was thirty feet up, but Dad was the strongest man on our planet, and I could have been chopped like fish guts. It wasn't until I was eight that my brother, Luke was born, and Dad threw him toward the fan instead. It was okay, Mom assured everyone, because now she had an extra boy.

Wilson was a name Mom had been reluctant to take with their marriage. As the name of one US President, Dennis the Menace's grumpy neighbor, the title character of a Mark Twain novel, and a volleyball that would someday keep Tom Hanks' character company on an island, the name was a symbol for the mundane, the antithesis to moving to Alaska.

It wasn't Dad's fault. As I understood it from a class at Northern, the fault was of a man named Will who was the proud descendant of Vikings. His ego was so big that he made sure to conquer England in the Battle of Hastings. Then Rufus was Will's son, and everyone knew him as such. As the name drifted across the Atlantic, into Hudson Bay, and trickled down tributaries to the Great Lakes, it morphed into one word and Grandpa George Wilson was named after his Grandpa George Wilson, and he named his son George Wilson. Grandpa Wilson died when I was too young to remember, so Dad is the George Wilson that I know.

Catalano, on the other hand, is a name originating from refugees of the Spanish Inquisition. All three of us — Luke, Erica, and I — were given the middle name. It comes from a time when Jews, Muslims, other non-Catholics, and suspected non-Catholics were gathered for conversion, torture, and execution, and masses of people escaped from Catalonia, the region of Spain farthest to the east, bordering France and the Balearic Sea. Even then, Catalonia wanted independence from Spain, and the Inquisition no doubt aggravated the feeling. Catalans poured into Italy and assimilated into a culture of pasta, olive oil, and, in a wicked twist of irony, Catholicism, as Catalanos. This name also drifted across the Atlantic, but it washed ashore on the Chicago River in Little Italy of the Windy City. Carmine and Tomasina Catalano raised Joe and his siblings, and Joe married Marvelle Gunderson who had descended straight from Vikings, maybe even from the same village as Will's ancestors. Joe and Marvelle raised Cynthia Catalano, who I call Mom.

Mom and Dad had no intended meaning for my first name, but Keith is Scottish, and some kind of deviation of a word for wood. Generations of translation changed the word the way water changed those fallen trees washed onto the shores of Lake Superior. Each branch breaks away, floats in the wind, ebb, and flood, and drifts to one shore or another, washed away, again and again, bark peeled, flesh rounded by time. The wood transforms into something unrecognizable from the tree from which it came.

My Viking ancestors told the story of Odin creating the first people from driftwood. He found them on the beach and breathed life into their lungs. They stood upright and branched across our planet, growing, breaking apart, and growing again, twisting, and meeting again on some distant shore.

With no true roots in Alaska, I was born a broken branch. In the isolation of a southwest Alaskan fishing town, I was raised not by Yup'ik or Aleut, but by Michiganders who saw others like them driven out of Naknek by the cold, the dark, the cost of living, the isolation, or a combination of any of the above. Some of them returned for the fishing season every year. Some never came back.

Mom and Dad were taken with rural Alaska, and there they stayed. Naknek was a good place to be raised by good parents. It was a small community with an involved school, a subsistence lifestyle, and a thriving commercial fishing industry making our family, like others, fortunate. I could have grown up anywhere with my introverted nature and my imagination. Still, by the time I was a teenager, I was running back and forth on the shoulder of the Alaska Peninsula Highway like I was trying to run away on a road with no way out. By the time I no longer lived there, and I was running along Lake Superior with driftwood accumulating on the shoreline, it was like I was still trying.

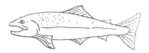

On my way back to Naknek for the summer, I start noticing other Bristol Bay fishermen on the flight from Portland to Anchorage. I can tell by the beards, sweatshirts, and a collective musty smell lingering as though these guys have all been on a boat since last summer. As I scratch my own beard, I guess they look like me, but I hope I smell better. Many of them are wearing their XtraTufs, the rubber boot known as the Alaskan moccasin. Wearing them on the plane leaves room in their luggage, which is usually an empty cooler or plastic tote to carry fish back home in frozen filets after the season is over.

The flight from Anchorage to King Salmon is almost exclusively fishermen. All three towns in the Bristol Bay Borough have airports. Most cities, towns, and villages in Alaska have them, because most of the state is without interconnecting roads. The Bristol Bay Borough School District flies students from South Naknek to King Airfield in Naknek every school day except for inclement weather. The King Salmon Airport is a public, state-owned, commercial airport where Alaska Airlines jets fly in and out during the summer months. The rest of the year, it is only provided with the services of Pen Air.

The plane to King Salmon flies southwest, over Cook Inlet, the north edge of the Kenai Peninsula, the Aleutian Range, and Lake Iliamna. I stare out the window at the left wing and a thick, gray shroud below us. We soon dive into the shroud and become enveloped by it until we descend, and it dissipates. Then I see mountains turn to tundra broken only by ponds freckling its endless expanse. The first signs of civilization are houses surrounded by pine trees, alder brush, and birch along the Naknek River, curving and turning where it is still thin and blue near Naknek Lake. The runway is the largest construct made by people. We land fast and hard against it, and I'm home again.

It's early June, but it's forty degrees, and it rains on the walk from the plane into the airport terminal, which is crowded shoulder to shoulder with fishermen who wait for luggage. As bags circulate, workers in their orange vests set dozens of identical plastic coolers, totes, and cardboard boxes on the floor. Fishermen flock to them like seagulls flock to a fish on the beach, but there is no pecking order.

Mom and Dad are here. Mom asks me about the trip. Dad is already using his six-foot-four stature to search for my luggage.

"It's a cooler?" he asks.

"Yeah," I say. "It's a red cooler that looks just like every other red cooler."

Dad smiles. Mom rolls her eyes.

The rest of my luggage is on my back. When we walk into the parking lot, I throw it into the bed of the truck along with the red cooler full of oranges, grapefruit, watermelon, and pineapple — produce with thick enough skin to protect it from injuries during travel. The truck is a Dodge Ram, and Dad has had it for years now, but it's still odd when it's not the red F-150 of my childhood.

Behind the King Salmon Airport is the Air Force base with its airplane hangars, artillery storage, radar surveillance center, and bowling alley. It's closed now to civilians, but sometimes I wonder how many bombs, bullets, and bowling balls are still hidden on the premises. Beyond the base, there is a gravel road forking to Rapids Camp, along the Naknek River, and Lake Camp, Naknek Lake's entry point.

For now, Dad drives us in the opposite direction, over the curve in the road on the bridge over Eskimo Creek. The Alaska Peninsula Highway is about sixteen miles of pavement connecting Naknek and King Salmon — but King Salmon is just an extension of Naknek as far as I'm concerned. It's on the Naknek River, it's much closer to Naknek Lake, and it's powered by the Naknek Electric Association just like Naknek and South Naknek. The official border between towns is somewhere around Paul's Creek, where Karl told us in kindergarten that his dad had found sunken treasure after wrestling a great white shark. It was while he was scuba diving, he had explained.

We pass Paul's Creek, and we're surrounded by what looks like specks of snow on the tundra. It's cottongrass, and it's said to signify the numbers of returning salmon. I don't know who first said it — Yup'ik, Unangan, or white people — but it always seems to be accurate, and it looks like it will be a decent season. The cotton, however, has nothing to do with price. A dollar a pound is a decent amount for sockeye, but I've been paid as low as forty cents. Before my time, Dad was paid as much as $2.40.

Homes to our left are spread far apart along the Naknek River, but the right side of the pavement, to the north, is tundra and only tundra until we pass the cemetery. If we were to stop, I would recognize the names carved in stone, where I could reflect on the mysteries of life and death or wonder once again who would want their body overlooking the landfill. I think about how be bury both our dead and our trash and contemplate what it says about us.

After the landfill, Dad drives up a slight incline in the road, and we can see our old house for a moment when bushes aren't in the way. The house we are headed to now is in downtown Naknek, after the bridge over Leader Creek, and past SeaMar, Icicle Seafoods, Silver Bay Seafoods, Red Salmon Cannery, Cedar Village, Snob Hill, HUDville, City Dock, and Napa Auto Parts. Our house is next to the old Kue Klub, where adults used to play pool. Now it's surrounded by brush, derelict and abandoned besides the snowshoe hares burrowing beneath it.

Other than fishermen, busy people in Naknek are teachers closing the school year, post office employees sorting boxes, and employees stocking shelves at Naknek Trading, Ace Hardware, or Napa Auto Parts. They're serving pizzas at D&D or handing six-dollar cans of Budweiser over the bar at Fisherman's, Hadfield's, or the Red Dog.

The first week of June is when the canneries come to life when gates open and windows are uncovered. Cannery workers begin their walk back and forth on the side of the Alaska Peninsula Highway. With all these idle hands, it isn't uncommon to hear of a vehicle stolen and abandoned in the bushes, a stabbing behind the Red Dog, or a game of Russian roulette gone wrong.

During my first few days back, the clouds are gray, and I am running again by D&D, the restaurant that still holds my definition of a pizza. When I'm not in Naknek, my diet consists mostly of whole grains, tubers, vegetables, beans, nuts, seeds, and other items of what my family calls "health food" to optimize running, but I will forever have a weakness for pizza. Anywhere other than D&D, even Italy or Greece, I can eat an entire pie by myself before ever feeling satisfaction. I think it's because I'm trying to relive the generous slather of red sauce, the thick white crust, and the multiple layers of oozing cheese of a D&D pizza of my youth.

As I run by D&D, I take note once again of its wooden sign, painted white with black letters: *NAKNEK HOTEL*. The rooms are tucked into a corner of the building, and I always wonder who the hell ever stays there, but I know better. There are thousands of people who come to Naknek every summer.

There are many ways that Naknek defies logic. It's as though it exists in a realm outside of time and space — like the gray shroud the plane descends into is a portal to another dimension. After D&D, I'm on the edge of the Alaska Peninsula Highway, where the pavement ends at Fisherman's Bar. Maybe I don't need to run to escape. Maybe I could jump right here, fly into the gray sky above me. I imagine I'd reach the water, or some invisible boundary on the tundra, or I would drift through the clouds and magically appear back on the ground as though it's some kind of anomaly in space-time. I think again of the pictures of Meteora, the tall rock formations in Greece named for the Greek word for "high in the air."

I know that Naknek is the same planet, but only because the tide is proof of it. In Naknek, we can see the rhythm of the tide, the pattern of spawning and returning salmon, and the patterns of life and death. The sun and our planet's moon are both up there even if I can't see them on most days. Marquette, Seattle, Anchorage, Madrid, Rome, Athens — just because I can't drive there, ride a bike there, or run there doesn't mean they're on some other planet. I can stand on a cutbank in Naknek and see into windows in South Naknek, but I've been there as many times as I've been to Rome. The absence of a road makes all the difference.

A familiar Bronco pulls alongside me. Riel, my childhood friend who I used to see nearly every day, is driving. He is part Aleut, but he's big and white so no one would ever know it. In the passenger seat, Shoosh is my friend who can't be mistaken as anything but full-blooded Inupiat. I call him Shoosh because he's quiet and never corrects anyone for mispronouncing his last name, Nashookpuk by replacing that first *k* with the shooshing sound.

Someone has found mammoth bones in the cutbank, Riel tells me, and they are heading down there right now. I keep jogging in place, and he tells me to quit bouncing around and get in the car, but I'm feeling the endorphins, the rush of sweat, and my pulsing imagination, so I turn him down. He rolls his eyes and drives away. He knew better than to interrupt me during a run.

There isn't much of a crowd when I do finally stop at the foot of the cutbank. With the tide behind me, the distant barking of dogs, and the breeze chilling my bones, I'm too late to see those of the mammoth, but I'm never too late to ponder my own life. I was in highschool when our history class watched a documentary about the Jarkov mammoth discovered by some kid in Siberia. Riel was a grade below us, and Shoosh was an angel in class, but my friend Joey and I couldn't help but giggle at the mammoth's name over and over again. Now, as I've returned once again to Naknek after another failure to settle my feet into one place elsewhere, I hope my life hasn't been one big Jarkov session.

My right foot lands below my left foot on the slope of the beach, but if I stay high enough, where there are pebbles, I won't sink into the mud. Out here, beyond the mouth of the Naknek River, rickety cabins line the top of the cutbank. The beach expands into a mudflat with the ebb, and it contracts back with the flood. My run leads first to Pedersen Point, an operating cannery, and then to Libbyville, now just a line of tattered pilings protruding from the mud. Its buildings are long-since collapsed. Cabins are scarce now, and there aren't many more of them until heading far enough from Bristol Bay, and into the Kvichak River, the flow of water from the largest lake in Alaska, Iliamna. For now, I turn around.

There are no buoys on the beach yet, and screw anchors have no lines attached to them. Plywood sheets cover the windows on cabins, but a few of them are opening now. The edge of the cutbank creeps closer to these little shacks every summer, and sometimes they have to move back, away from inevitable erosion.

I know how much this scene will change in a week. Fourwheelers and trucks will blaze back and forth, running lines and buoys will be set every 300 feet, and it will be busier down here than downtown. All canneries, with their bunkhouses, cafeterias, and processing facilities nestled between the Naknek River and the Alaska Peninsula Highway, will be busier than the town itself.

When I get back to the house, I don't stop. I keep running until I cross the bridge over Leader Creek and climb the hill to where houses and buildings are few and far between, I reach a gravel road called Shore Street, where the school bus used to leave me to walk home. I run left onto more gravel called Michael Street, named after Michael Gottschalk of Gottschalk Subdivision, but to me, it's Memory Lane. The Naknek River is just below the brush on the bank and a gravel turnaround for the school bus, from when the school district decided a half a mile was too far for a kid to walk.

There is a hill up Michael Street, and the gravel ends at the top of it, brush grown over it as if it were road barrier, but there is no more road beneath it. There is a white cabin behind the brush, where no one has stayed in decades. Its door is wide open, and inside the furniture is broken, the refrigerator is open and empty, and the electricity has been cut for years. On the right side of the gravel is Riel's old house, long abandoned since the days I walked down its sloping driveway to knock on the door and ask if he wanted to come over.

Birch and alders Dad transplanted no longer just line my old driveway, but they have overtaken the property as a jungle. No one trims them anymore. When I stop at the end of the driveway, I can't even see the gazebo-shaped greenhouse Dad built across the gravel from the three-car garage where Mom parked her Jeep and our family kept the StarCraft camping boat. In the back was Dad's workshop where he built and sawed and hammered and fixed things. I can't see any of these things

I could say that Naknek isn't home anymore, but home isn't just a house like Naknek isn't just a town. When I'm here, I look forward to the time I can leave again, but when I'm not here, I am often reminded of it. I see Naknek in a salmon filet at the grocery store, a straight pavement road, a curving river flowing alongside it, or the tide moving up or down a shoreline. Sometimes, when I'm somewhere between dreams and my surroundings, I expect to open my eyes and be in my bed in that old house. I expect to look up and see the sloping cedar ceiling above blue walls, or I expect to hear footsteps above me in the dining room after Dad built my bedroom in the basement. I expect to walk outside to the sprawling expanse of tundra alongside a brackish river. No matter where I live as an adult, I always expect to open my eyes to see that I'm back in Naknek.

As a three-year-old, I wasn't the least bit aware that our town on the edge of the tundra was any different from any other town. I don't know if I was aware of it at any age. Instead of buying steak at a supermarket, Dad hunted caribou. Instead of a movie theater, we had video rentals at Fisherman's. Instead of changing traffic lights, we had a changing shoreline. Mud extended and receded from the water as sticks, twigs, and grass drifted in and out, but I'd never paid attention to it. Instead of a fascination with hunting, fishing, or a lifestyle people might find unique, I kept myself occupied with books, toys, TV, and my limitless imagination.

Mom and Dad read me books like *Where the Sidewalk Ends*, *Where the Wild Things Are*, and *Green Eggs and Ham*. Sometimes Mom added green food coloring to my scrambled eggs, but she told me it wouldn't work with ham. I could still pretend.

Stories could bring me to places I'd never been, and I could do things I'd never done. Before I learned to read, I memorized the words to go along with the pictures. I could be in a box with a fox, or on a train, in a tree, or in a car, so let me be! When Mom and Dad's friends asked if their three-year-old was really reading, I didn't know the difference between reading and reciting. I looked at them like they were idiots and told them that yes, I was reading. Couldn't *they* read?

A story or poem may not have remained verbatim, but the meaning and message of it remained as consistent as the tide. *If You Give a Moose a Muffin*, still taught me about insatiability, as I'd be reminded with pizza. *The Cat and the Hat* still got across the idea not to mess up the house when Mom and Dad were gone, and the idea was reinforced by a babysitter who always made us clean.

One Alaska-specific story that I remember in particular came from a time before the tide. After Raven had created our planet by collecting sticks, twigs, and grass and rolling it into a ball with mud as an adhesive, there was still no light to see, because a shaman kept its three sources in three separate boxes. Raven, ever the trickster, was compelled to set them free.

The shaman, however, knew of Raven's wily ways, and he was always one step ahead of him. That was until Raven took the form of a pine needle and plunged into the shaman's daughter's tea. She swallowed the needle, and thus commenced the immaculate conception of Raven in the form of man.

"Uppa," he said, putting down his toy firetruck. "Can I open one of the boxes?"

"No way, José," said the shaman, even though little Raven's name was Timmy or something cute like that.

"Ah, come on Uppa! Just let me take a peek," little Timmy said. "You'd be way cooler than Uppa Charlie."

The shaman hated Uppa Charlie, that good-for-nothing Unangan shaman up the Kvichak River in Levelock. He shrugged, thought *to hell with it*, and handed his grandson the key.

"Gee golly willikers!" Timmy ran to one of the boxes.

"Be careful," said the shaman.

"Don't worry," said Timmy, finagling with the lock. The lid flew open, and trillions of stars shot like sparks into the cosmos, sticking to the blackness.

"Oh, shit," said the shaman. "That was not just a peek."

The shaman didn't babysit for his daughter for another couple of years. Timmy was mischievous, and finding a babysitter was tough. Between working at the bank, trips to Costco, and attending PTA meetings, the shaman's daughter was busy, distracted, and desperate enough to beg the shaman to watch Timmy just this one time for a few hours. He reluctantly conceded.

"Uppa," Timmy said, looking at the remaining locked boxes.

"Uh-uh. No way. No how," the shaman said. "I remember what happened last time, and I'm no sucker!"

"It'll be different this time, Uppa. I promise."

"We can't risk it. This one is way more dangerous."

"I learned my lesson last time, Uppa," said Timmy. "I'll be careful. Please?"

"Nope."

"Pretty please?"

"Not a chance."

"Pretty please with a cherry on top?"

"No chance in hell."

"I'll never ask again."

Timmy kept at it, wearing down his grandfather like thousands of years of current over a stone in the river.

"Fine!"

This time our planet was graced by a big, bright moon.

"Oh, for chrissakes," the shaman said.

It was almost six years before the shaman's dared to ask him to watch Timmy again. There was a younger brother now, who had asthma and early-onset diabetes and needed more attention. She just needed a little extra help this one time. Besides, Timmy spent most of the time with his nose in a Gameboy. The shaman sighed and agreed to watch Timmy for just an hour.

"Uppa," said Timmy sheepishly.

"No! I know what you're going to ask, and you're out of your damned mind."

"Come on, Uppa," said Timmy. "I know better now."

"No," said the shaman. "The last one is way, way, way too dangerous."

"You can open it yourself, and I'll watch," said Timmy. "I'll stand way over here, across the room."

"It's been in there forever," said the shaman. "Even I don't know what will happen if it gets out!"

"If it's been forever, it needs air," said Timmy. "Don't you even want to see what it looks like, Uppa? Do you even love me?"

He looked at his grandson, looked at the box, and sighed. "Okay, but you have to stand way, way the hell over there."

Timmy walked to the other side of the room, where the shaman was pointing, and shoved his hands into his pockets. The shaman inserted the key, twisted, and the lid unlatched. Black feathers sprouted from every one of Timmy's pores as he morphed into his true form, flew over to the shaman, pushed him to the floor, and popped the lid wide open. The brightest light either of them had ever seen shined its way into the sky, illuminating the trees, the land, and the water. Raven flew away, laughing. The shaman knew at last that he had been fooled by the old trickster, and he shook his fist in the air.

Both Mom and Dad would say that I was an easy kid, not like Raven at all. I was quiet and introverted, and adults often commented on how I never said much, how they never knew what I was thinking, and how I didn't scream and cry without constant attention. I responded to questions with a shrug of my shoulders, unable to conjure an explanation as to why I didn't feel compelled to say much. At my first birthday party, I was sound asleep in my crib while Bob Swanson smeared chocolate frosting on my portrait in my highchair. The portrait, everyone agreed, talked about as much as me.

I wasn't an unhappy kid. I was just a loner, off in my own world. I spent time outside, playing with rocks and sticks, running on the lawn, and jumping into fox holes in the tundra. Inside the house were books, toys, a living room with a dark red carpet I knew for sure was lava. Fisher-Price people, Disney characters, Ninja Turtles, and trolls with up-combed, colorful, crazy hair hopped across pillow and Lego islands surrounded by lava. Later, the basement had a cool blue vinyl land of ice.

Some toys were presents from Mom and Dad, Grandma and Grandpa, my godparents Mo and Smiley, and other adults. Other toys were collected from McDonald's in Anchorage and other places where McDonald's could be found. Mom called these toys the junkies, and the plastic tote full of them was labeled as such with a piece of masking tape. Sometimes I opened the tote of Legos. Sometimes I opened the tote of cars and trucks. Other times, I opened the tote full of junkies.

I never had to fool an old shaman, but when all the totes were opened, my world came to light. Plastic people checked the mail, filled their vehicles with fuel, and shopped for groceries. Pirates raided in a ship Dad had helped me put together, and soldiers fought them. When Shredder, Bebop, Rocksteady, and Foot Soldiers attacked, the Ninja Turtles could always defeat them with the aid of their Turtle Van and Turtle Blimp. No one starved, no one ran out of money, and when they died, they could always come back to life.

Die, they did of course. Destruction, there was. Trolls plummeted from the peaks of a Disney castle. Lego homes were smashed, sometimes as soon as they were erected. An old woman dissatisfied with her haircut beat the barber to death. A mailman was mauled alive by a Tyrannosaurus Rex. Cars soared over the edge of the wooden rocking chair, leaving scratches across the seat. Dad had to haul the chair into the garage and refinish the surface at least once.

Then I discovered another means of creation. All it took was some paper and my newfound ability to hold a pencil, marker, or a crayon. By holding the tip of the utensil to paper and moving it, I could create anything that I imagined. If I could conquer this ability, the possibilities would be endless. No longer would creation be limited to physical material. Plastic would be obsolete for my imagination on paper, reserved for buckets of Play-Doh, packages of pasta, sippy cups, and islands of petroleum-based goo swirling in the ocean.

Buildings, clouds, flowers, trees, and even entire families ended up as scribbles. Then I was able to focus on drawing different parts to make a whole. Concentration was strenuous. Ideas flowed and my hand struggled to match the speed at which they came. With my imagination pulsing and my hand yearning to move in different directions across the page, I managed an oblique circle. Then I put another one adjacent to it. One more circle was needed, but it had to be smaller for my idea to work. The effort was taxing, but when it appeared on the paper, it was indeed smaller. Then I added a corncob pipe and a button nose. It was Frosty the Snowman. Mom and Dad had made snowmen with me in front of the house, but now I could make myself.

After mastery of Frosty, I progressed to more complicated characters like Mickey Mouse, whose basis was also a group of three circles, but in a different arrangement. Circles were atoms. By arranging them in various possibilities, atoms made molecules. Molecules made life forms.

I didn't learn about molecules quite yet, but preschool soon started. It was in a modular building in the school parking lot. I was excited when I saw that there was a different set of toys in every corner. There were shelves of blocks, stacks of books, and a sandbox with scattered toys in the grains far from any shore.

I remember when Mrs. Feriante dressed as a witch for Halloween, in a black gown and tall pointy hat. She stood in front of a mirror, painting her face green when some classmates and I approached her. Then she turned around, cackled a scary witch cackle, and we ran away. It was easy to forget she was the nice lady who read us stories and not a wicked hag who wanted to turn us into frogs.

I also remember when little JJ Gardner launched interconnected red blocks across the room. Kids ducked behind a bookshelf as the blocks broke apart and scattered upon impact.

"No throwing blocks," Mrs. Feriante said.

"They're not blocks," JJ explained. "They're bombs!"

"Then no throwing bombs," she said.

I remember the box of costumes, including a firefighter's outfit, a police uniform, a doctor's gown, and a tutu. One of the costumes was a set of white, fabric horns and a black-and-red cloak. I needed help tying it, but once I was transformed, I could chase my classmates around the room. I ran from the wooden teeter-totter boat to the block center to the Play-Doh table, other kids scattering like those red blocks. Then again, maybe it was just the girls who ran away, and I would attest to this fact as a teenager.

Heidi Jo was entertaining herself with plastic horses and dolls in the sandbox, and maybe it was JJ's influence when I recognized the opportunity to plague this little desert civilization with a sandstorm. With my hand full of sand, I brought upon my wrath by flinging it across an otherwise peaceful realm before laughing and scurrying away.

I didn't see the sand spray Heidi Jo's eyes, but she was frantically brushing at them, her face scrunching tight and flushing red. As much as I wanted to deny it, I knew exactly what was about to happen. I had seen too many other kids go through these same stages, including Erica. First, there was a moment of shock. Then there was a critical decision to make. I studied each of her minute movements, hoping it wasn't about to happen, but it was too late. The decision had been made. Heidi Jo began to cry, and even though she wasn't particularly loud, her cries reverberated inside my skull.

Mrs. Feriante rushed over to her, and the other kids froze mid-movement, devoting their complete, undivided attention to this unspeakable tragedy. Grains of sand ground against the insides of Heidi Jo's eyelids. My gut sank. Time stood still. Standing dazed, I lifted the horns from my head and watched them drop in front of me, landing flaccidly on the floor.

"So, what happened today with Heidi Jo?" Mom asked later at the dinner table.

I put down my fork. "How do you know about that?"

She said nothing. I looked over at Dad.

"Mom knows," was all he said.

Mom worked at school. She knew everything that happened there. When I was the last kid to tie his own shoes, she knew about it. When I had a poor grade on a test, she knew about it. When I giggled about the Jarkov Mammoth sophomore year, she knew about it.

It was that same sophomore history class when we had been discussing the role of toys and the imagination in society. When the teacher asked what it meant if a culture had left behind sculptures of female figures, I suggested that it meant the adults liked to play with toys, too. It was a joke he repeated to Mom, and she knew what happened at school once again, but even by that time, I still understood the importance of imagination and creativity as I kept drawing into my teenage years.

Like any kid, I got into trouble, but I never got into major trouble. Maybe I dropped those horns when I was four years old because it wasn't in me to be a little devil — but I was never really an angel either, which was our school mascot. Maybe I would have felt more like I belonged if the wings had been plumed with black feathers.

Dad starts the F-150 with faded red paint, and Mom watches me while I buckle my seatbelt. Mom recently told me I was acting five, even though I haven't had my birthday yet, and I want to live up to the compliment. Mom is holding Erica, who has stopped crying her gargley cry for the first time in at least an hour, which Mom says is the time it takes to watch two Ninja Turtle cartoons. It's not far from the house to the pavement, and from there, we aren't going much farther to the Labamba, the wooden, purple-painted skiff.

Sometimes we find Mosie, Auggie, and Bonkers down there at the beach, wandering, wet with dead fish smell. Dogs get everywhere on foot, following smells of caribou carcasses, table scraps, and shots of urine on bushes. They follow each other, and they follow their instincts to wander toward the water. They're like all furbearers, but they have collars and names and some are allowed inside houses. We go looking for our dogs when they wander away and disappear, but when we find them, they never seem like they're lost.

Mosie is named after jazz and blues musician, Mose Allison. She is tiny and spry, and she is more interested in fetching a stick than a steak. She lives the longest of any dog until she gets into some antifreeze left out by a neighbor. Auggie, her offspring named after a cartoon, is hit by a car, which is the demise of most dogs in Naknek. Dad tells us that the police chief decided to put him out of his misery, but he missed all the vitals. Dad laughs, and Mom tells me he's laughing to make it seem like it's not sad. Dad tells us he found him alive, bleeding, suffering, and had to shoot Auggie himself. Later, he tells us how, at the Red Dog, the chief told Dad that he owed him a beer for taking care of his dog.

"No," Dad tells us that he said. "You missed."

He also tells us that he had to hold back his fist.

Bonkers is the dog who wanders away and disappears.

There are no dogs in the back of the truck before we leave on our camping trip. There are only blue plastic totes, a red cooler, cookware, sleeping bags, a tent, and the same tan suitcase Dad carries when we get on a plane. We're not getting on a plane. We're going to the Bay of Islands, below the Aleutian Mountain Range on the far end of the North Arm of Naknek Lake. Dad says we'll do some fishing while we're up there. It's the kind of fishing where we use a pole, Mom explains, and not the kind where Dad makes money. We're going camping to get away, and to be outside, which I've gathered to be anywhere not in the house. *Outside* is in the front yard, on the porch, or the tundra behind the house, but adults like to drive trucks and boats to an outside much farther away.

Dad cranks the stick shift in front of me once, twice, three times as we roll down the driveway, rocks kicking into the undercarriage. Dirt has gathered between the black swirls of texture on the floor, and I can see bear faces in the pattern. Mom and Dad are confused when I point to the faces. They tell me that looking out the window would be much more fun. I can't see that high, so I stare at the faces and wonder if the cab of this truck counts as inside or outside. If it is inside, I wonder if the back of the truck counts as outside because there is no roof.

The truck moves down the gravel, onto the pavement, and onto a hill down to City Dock where red, orange, yellow, and white metal storage containers tower into the sky. The Dock stands on pilings, some of them crooked, some of them straight. The pilings are never the same height from the water's surface. Down on the beach, the Labamba is floating near the shoreline. Like the back of the truck, the Labamba has no roof. Dad uses a pair of chestwaders to get to it, pull the cord on the motor, and come to shore to get us. Mom and Dad load the camping supplies. Then we all put on life jackets and rain gear, and Dad drives us up the Naknek River.

Naknek Lake feeds the Naknek River, which passes King Salmon on its north side, not far downstream. To get there, we forge against the current, beyond the reach of brackish water, beyond the soft, brown river bottom shrouding a salmon's line of sight. We go beyond the mud beaches and eroding banks. We drive past grassy walls and green reeds carpeting the edges. This route is how we get to Naknek Lake, across the saltwater from Kodiak Island, at the base of the Alaska Peninsula, where water pours from the mountains and accumulates into a deep, blue, pristine pool.

The North Arm is vast and wild with its Bay of Islands at the east end of it. A peninsula separates it from the Iliuk Arm, which would be just as wild without Brooks Camp, where tourists land in float planes to flyfish and walk a wooden boardwalk to take pictures of brown bears at Brooks Falls swatting at salmon returning to spawn. The end of the peninsula that separates the two arms is a sandy beach with a sand spit. Driftwood and pumice accumulate against the layers of shorelines. We call this spot Decision Point. We have lunch here, and I throw dozens of pumice into the water and watch them float against the blue surface reflecting the clouds and the mountains.

We always go to the North Arm, where people won't bother us, where the surface of the water is a mirror, reflecting no houses, buildings, or any sign of people other than us. The only other movement on the water is fins circling, sometimes splashing in waves when the Labamba approaches. I think this place is why Mom and Dad stayed in Naknek for so long.

The island where we like to camp is called Horseshoe Island because of its shape. We park in its cove, protected from any upcoming wind. Our campfire and our tent are somewhere in the middle of the horseshoe. We can hike through the trees to either side of the island to fish for lake trout. Sometimes there is moose poop on the island, but Mom and Dad say that bears won't swim out here, even though we can hear them growling at each other from a beach we can see on the mainland. It's safe enough that Mom and Dad let me wander both sides of the island. I don't get lost, and I bring back firewood.

I like to dig beneath the moss and find ash from the Mount Katmai eruption. Decades ago, Nova Rupta erupted, Mount Katmai imploded, and ash killed plants and animals. Then new plants and animals took their place. For all we know, the same has happened to people somewhere. We could be the only people alive on our planet right now, and we wouldn't know it.

There are other people out there, and not all of them have a place like this one. They wouldn't know what to do without a road. When I'm eight, Mom and Dad buy a fancy blue StarCraft boat in Marquette, not long after Luke is born there. They test drive it on Lake Superior, which reminds me of the Bay of Islands, but with buildings and roads and cars and people nearby. The boat has a windshield and blue carpet and a roof that snaps on and off.

Dad hauls the boat on a trailer across the United States with Mom's new Jeep. Erica rides in a carseat, and I ride in the front, watching towns and cities woven together by an intricate system of roads of pebbles or pavement, one lane or six, with speed limits, weight limits, and Dad's limit of patience for other drivers. Cars and trucks cruise along the roads, heading to our different destinations, seemingly unaware of each other. Semi-trucks haul Doritos, Coca-Cola, Butterfingers, and Budweiser, as I see painted on the sides of them.

Dad puts the boat and the car on a barge in Seattle, we get on a plane, and the car and the boat both arrive at City Dock in a month. Mom and Dad keep this boat inside the garage, and we launch it from Lake Camp, skipping the journey up the Naknek River. Instead, it follows the truck on a trailer.

Alongside the Naknek River is the Alaska Peninsula Highway — a straight, pavement course to Fisherman's Bar, but the Naknek River dumps into the Kvichak Bay, a corner of Bristol Bay. The Alaska Peninsula Highway connects two towns without alleys, detours, intersections, or traffic lights. When driving to King Salmon from Naknek, there are miles of moss, lichen, and clumps of grass growing to the left, just inches above the layer of permafrost. To the right is more of the same, but there is also the Naknek River. On a clear day, the mountains appear in the distance, but the road ends long before they are anything but tiny blue ridges on the horizon.

Naknek, King Salmon, Marquette, and Seattle, I realize, are each the end and beginning of a road. Each of these places is a collection of cars, boats, TVs, and grocery stores. A town is a lake collecting water from tributaries, but the tributaries are pavement. In the Bay of Islands, foot traffic of moose, bears, foxes, lynx, and wolverines tread over terrain to water, food, and shelter, making pathways in the dirt. People do the same thing, but the pathways have turned to roads. Villages turned into towns that grew into cities with streets, sidewalks, and pipes sending smog into the sky.

Before the first pavement, before the advent of asphalt, and before other concrete examples existed, oceans and waterways were the first means of mass transportation. For this reason, Seattle is between Puget Sound and Lake Washington, where barges arrive from Asia. Marquette has its ore docks along Lake Superior, trading with Canada to the North. King Salmon is near the Naknek River's freshwater spawning grounds, and Naknek is along the Naknek River where the salmon first arrive.

Other than the Alaska Peninsula Highway, Naknek isn't connected to roads, but it has its waterways. In Naknek, freight barges arrive at City Dock with the cargo. At the end of the fishing season, barges head back to the Pacific with container vans of cans and frozen fillets. Salmon arrive on their own, without a ride on a barge or a truck along a highway, bringing food and fertilizer to Naknek where people live inside, telling themselves that they are separate from outside.

In the morning, in the Bay of Islands, on a peninsula we call Double Beach, the tent is set on the sand on the calmer beach. Mom is nursing Luke when she hears two bears wandering toward the tent. She wakes Dad, who says it will go away. Then one of the bears approaches the tent. With one step closer, another step, and another, he presses his nose against the window below the rainfly, peering in at three children, a mother, and a father planning his next move. In the tent, the layer between inside and outside is a thin wall of fabric.

Inside a house, inside a vehicle, or inside the school, people go about our routines day to day as though outside isn't there. In what we call outside, bears follow the same paths they have always followed — but the separation between inside and outside means nothing to them. Bears have been in our garage. They have shattered windows. They have even torn apart layers of wood and sheetrock to enter a living room in our neighborhood. One time, a bear was found in the kitchen behind the school cafeteria, raiding the frozen corn dogs and tater tots. In the tent, the layer between inside and outside is so thin, it is almost imaginary. Maybe it *is* imaginary.

The bear takes one last look at us and turns to walk away and join the other bear at the boat.

"George," Mom says. "The bears are on the boat."

Dad shoots upright. "The boat?"

He yells, claps his hands again and again and again. Two pairs of bear paws drop from the carpet on the edge of the bow and take a glimpse at the tent. Both of them stare one more time into the layer between inside and outside. I wonder if they even see it. Then they turn and meander away, down the beach, into the bushes, disappearing into the paths they've always followed.

Clark Kent spent his childhood in Smallville, Kansas, wondering why he was so different from other kids. Soon he learned that he was Kal-El from the planet Krypton. Kryptonians had evolved under the radiation of a harsher red sun, and Kal-El's extraordinary powers were a reaction to our planet's less-intense yellow one. Clark Kent, Kal-El, assumed an additional identity as Superman, a hero and savior for the people of our planet.

In third grade, I learned about the first planet discovered outside of our own solar system. I wondered if it had ebbs and floods of water or if it had people or life of any kind. If there were people, I wondered if they had teleportation devices and flying cars. I wondered if they were still cavemen, learning to start fires with rocks — but most of all, I wondered if this planet was anything like Krypton.

Grandma Catalano sometimes recorded the cartoon channel, Nickelodeon, with her VCR in Saint Petersburg, Florida. She'd mail us eight-hour tapes of *Rugrats, Doug, the Adventures of Tintin,* and *The Ren & Stimpy Show.* Nick at Night, from the later hours, had TV programs like *I Love Lucy* and *the Dick Van Dyke Show.* It was after *Get Smart* when the introduction to the next classic show would begin in a black and white blur of stars and planets, a shooting star crashing into center screen, transforming into the title.

"Look! Up in the sky!" the TV said. "It's a bird! It's a plane!"

My red-yellow-and-blue pajamas had the 'S' insignia on the chest just like actor George Reeves. I ran down the hallway in those pajamas from my bedroom, leaping up in the sky for just a second before landing onto the couch, bouncing a time or two, and running back up the hallway to do it again.

Sometimes I climbed over the railing on the porch to leap over the lawn. I landed with a thud, feeling the impact from my feet through the rest of my body, but for the moment, I was flying — red cape floating behind me. Then I ran back and forth on the lawn from one end to the next, or I'd run a full lap around the house, behind the fuel tank and firewood pile behind the house, over the gravel driveway, and back onto the lawn. In my imagination, I wasn't running. I was flying.

I don't know what happened to the cape. Maybe a tree branch pulled against the Velcro, or maybe it was caught on the metal slide next to the monkey bars at Martin Monsen Park. Maybe it entered the Phantom Zone through the washing machine, and it's still there, floating among Metallo, Brainiac, General Zod, and lost underwear and unmatched socks. Then Santa Claus replaced it with a cape more crimson than red. It was a sturdier material and had a black 'K' sewn to the back of it. Super Keith was back in action, ready to fly anywhere on our planet or beyond it.

If I could have one wish, I wrote in my third-grade journal, it would be to have all Superman's powers. Questions on the chalkboard like *What famous person would you want to meet?* bored me, but for a wish, the sky was the limit. I wanted powers and abilities far beyond those of mortal men, to change the course of mighty rivers, and bend steel with my bare hands. I wanted to be faster than a speeding bullet, more powerful than a locomotive, and leap tall buildings in a single bound — but most of all, I wanted to fly. I wanted to leap into the sky above me with my arms out front, and land anywhere I wanted — somewhere beyond the couch, the lawn, or the Alaska Peninsula Highway.

When I had to read my wish aloud, my class erupted into laughter. I was a loser, a nerd, and an idiot. I couldn't even touch the net hanging from a basketball hoop. How was I supposed to leap a tall building? The appropriate response, as my classmates had asserted, was to wish for world peace. I'd missed the memo. I had no clever comeback. Their wish was the same as Superman's wish, and the answer was bulletproof.

Whenever I went to Anchorage, I came home with action figures and comic books. When other kids went to Anchorage, they wore new clothes to school and played the latest CDs loud through headphones attached to Discmans. It felt like my classmates were always taking trips to Anchorage, maybe once or twice a month — but I took solace in knowing that sometimes I got to fly far away.

Our family used to spend every other Christmas in Florida with Grandma and Grandpa Catalano. It was there where Mom and Dad had rented *Superman: The Movie* for me, and I watched the hero grow up in Smallville and leave for the bigger and better Metropolis to work at the Daily Planet. With Christopher Reeve in the lead role, Superman stopped thieves, saved a cat from a tree, and rescued Air Force One from crashing. Toward the end of the movie, Margot Kidder as Lois Lane was dropped in her car into a crevice created by an earthquake and she suffocated to death.

Saddened and furious, Superman leaped into the sky and flew around our planet at super-speed. He flew around it over and over again until he reversed the direction of its orbit and thus reversed time itself. He flew until time returned to the moments before Miss Lane's death. It might have been the first time I thought my classmates were right. Being Superman was impossible.

When our family flew, we spent most of the trip inside airport terminals. When we went to Florida, I had no idea what cities we were in. It could be Portland, Seattle, Salt Lake City, Phoenix, Atlanta, or Dallas. We could be in Metropolis for all I knew. The only difference between airports was the colors of t-shirts and coffee mugs for sale.

Sometimes we were there for hours. We slept on hard floors. We wandered stores with candy and magazines with pictures of famous people on the covers. Sometimes we had no time, and we ran to our next flight, awkward steps from backpacks bouncing, Dad shouting to the gate people to keep the damned door open, Luke yelling to Mom behind us, "You can do it!" We found our seats, sweaty in the cramped space between strangers.

Tampa was the last stop, where we walked outside for the first time in over a day. Then Grandpa would drive us to St. Pete Beach, the old person's colony that he and Grandma called God's Waiting Room. They lived in a three-story pink condo on a white-sand beach where the tide was small, but the sunset was big, and surfers rode back and forth on the waves. I made sandcastles with plastic buckets, but sometimes they were too close to shore, and I'd watch a wave wash it away. Once, some kids stomped on my castle. When I exclaimed that it was my sandcastle, they confirmed that yes, it *was* my sandcastle, stomping on the remains again. When I told Mom and Dad, they said that it wasn't very nice of those kids, but the tide would have gotten it anyway.

I didn't let it get to me. Florida meant a trip to MGM Studios, the Epcot Center, and the Magic Kingdom, where I could see a castle not made of sand. Mickey Mouse, Peter Pan, Robin Hood, and the Ninja Turtles were there. We rode the current surrounded by pirates, blasted off aboard ships with aliens, and took an underwater voyage aboard the Nautilus. Captain Nemo navigated our voyage to the North Pole, to the ruins of Atlantis, and to the Abyss where bizarre lifeforms lived. Along the voyage, there were clawed crustaceans, turtles without masks, shipwrecks, sharks, and of course, all kinds of fish. There were mermaids and sea snakes and a giant squid that attacked our submarine with menacing tentacles. We lived in a small world after all, but the ocean below the surface, like the sky, was big enough for all our imaginations and more.

I had seen *Jaws* at least a dozen times, a movie that had shown me that the less people know about life in the ocean, the more terrifying it is to us. When Erica and I dug in the sand on Venice Beach with strange, distant cousins, looking for shark teeth, I wondered how many of them had belonged to creatures still lurking just offshore, waiting for me to step a little too deep. Even in Lake Superior, the theme music to *Jaws* played in my head.

During the warmer months, Grandma and Grandpa lived in Marquette. Aunt Christine, Uncle Bruce and cousins and friends of Mom and Dad lived there, too. Friends and relatives lived across

Wisconsin, Minnesota, and Michigan along the shores of the Great Lakes where the tide was so small that it went unnoticed. It was where the water was never salty, where the salmon were stocked by people, and the fish were small and weak.

Marquette is where Mom and Dad took me to *Batman Returns*, and I saw a hero who couldn't fly foil the plans of the Penguin, a monster of a politician put in position by a corrupt businessman named Max Shrek. Superman was an icon of truth, justice, and the American way, but Batman worked in the shadows to take down villains. Superman was all-powerful, but Batman was resourceful. Although he couldn't fly, he was more like Raven — imperfect, using the guise of darkness while in truth he worked toward the greater good.

The contrast made sense to me. Sometimes a bat would swoop in front of our house on the Alaskan tundra, swallowing unsuspecting enemies like mosquitoes, whitesocks, and no-see-ums. Bats were quick and mysterious, their darkness blending into the night. They didn't crash into our windows like the bright, colorful birds found lifeless on the front porch.

When the question *What is a hero?* was written on the third-grade chalkboard, I wasn't sure how to answer. I had written a report about OJ Simpson for Black History Month, and my partner for the project called OJ a hero. First, I was confused, because he had never saved anyone. By fifth grade, OJ was on trial for murdering his wife. We watched the acquittal on TV in our classroom, and my classmates whispered a collective "Yessss..." That's when I knew for sure how different my ideas about heroes were from theirs.

What is the American Dream? was another hard one. In my dreams, I could fly like Superman. In my dreams, I could do whatever I wanted — but sharing my dreams had dire consequences like being laughed into submission and pushed down at recess and asked why I didn't use my super strength to fight back. Then I learned about Martin Luther King Jr, and how having a dream got him shot.

In the continuity of the comic books, Superman had been killed, but he had also been resurrected. The villain Bane had lifted Batman over his head and broke his back over his knee. He too had recovered. Those were comics. In the real world, people died and stayed dead. In the real world, people had injuries from which they would never recover. A classmate told me that George Reeves had shot himself in the head, sending him gone with the wind more than 30 years before we were born. Then on my last day of fifth grade, Christopher Reeve was thrown off a horse and paralyzed from the neck down. He would never walk again.

That summer, Ted Kaczynski threatened flights into LAX with his infamous bombs. It was during the fishing season, so just Mom was taking me, Luke, and Erica to California. Kaczynski's true identity was still unknown. Instead, he was the Unabomber, with a disguise of aviators, a mustache, and a wad of curly hair under a hood. The sketch was all over the TV screen as news anchors told us to be afraid. He was a real supervillain, and there was no real Superman to stop him. Erica and I cried on the couch, begging not to fly into LAX. The news had become relevant in Naknek.

We got off the plane safely, and Uncle Ed took both Erica and me to Universal Studios, where we met Zsa Zsa Gabor and other famous people I didn't know or recognize. I was more excited by King Kong rocking our tram and Jaws splashing from the water. Then Uncle Ed took me to see the new Batman movie starring Val Kilmer. In the film, the hero had haunting dreams of a bat flying toward him. Batman couldn't fly or bend steel with his bare hands, but he could move in the direction of his fears and aspire toward the unachievable — which in his case was to eradicate all crime. In the movie, I watched him vow to quit his role as Batman. Then, in the interest of stopping a district attorney gone bad and a man who asked too many questions as part of his evil plot, he ultimately decided to be Batman forever.

The first time I drove a car, I was nine years old, and I pretended it was the Batmobile. It was from a place called Rent-a-Wreck in Marquette. The car rumbled down a thin dirt stretch of dirt down to my Aunt and Uncle's house in the woods. Trees towered over us from both sides, and the car shook and gyrated, splashing in the occasional puddle rippling over the dark brown surface, Mom screaming, "Brake! Brake! Brake!"

The next time a teacher asked me to share my dreams, caution told me to pump the brakes again. Superman didn't need a car, and the sky was the limit on what he could do. Batman was a character grounded by reality. Dreaming was something I could do, but it wasn't heroic. Moving forward in a plane, a car, on a bike, or with my own two feet was something I could do. Moving forward through life was something

I could do. Despite what my classmates thought, being famous didn't make someone a hero, but they were right when they said flying was left to birds and planes — and only the tide, not time, could reverse directions. The tide, however, would never give me extraordinary abilities. The tide would never put grains of sand back together into a castle.

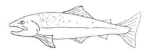

Mom and Dad make me finish every last green bean on my plate. On TV, there is a Jolly Green Giant who doesn't seem like he'd burst into a fit of fury if I don't enjoy the contents of his cans. He might wave a finger, or he might fold his hulking arms over his leaf-clad chest, but I don't imagine him eating me or turning me into a green bean. Mom and Dad tell me the green beans will make me big and strong, but it doesn't make them easier to swallow. I never have a hard time finishing my salmon though, and I always want seconds. Salmon is a different story.

I was read a story about a boy who, instead of finishing his meal, chucked hunks of meat and bones into the bushes, disregarding the life sacrificed to nourish his own. One day, he went swimming in the river with the other children and was caught in the current. He drowned, and salmon swarmed his soul, taking him deep into the ocean where he learned that the salmon were people.

The salmon people explained to the boy that only if all their flesh was eaten, and all their bones were returned to the water, would they come back to life and return to feed the village. When it was that time again, the boy went with them. He was caught by his mother who recognized him and took him home to become a boy again. He spent the rest of his life sharing what he'd learned about the experiences, patterns, and the cycle of the salmon.

While there is one species of Atlantic salmon, there are five species of Pacific salmon, which are chum, humpy, coho, chinook, and sockeye, or they are dog, pink, silver, king, and red, depending on who is talking about them. Either way, all species of Pacific Salmon return to Alaska. They all return to Bristol Bay and into the Meshik, Igushik, Egegek, Togiak, Ugashik, Nushagak, Kvichak, and Naknek River, feeding towns and villages like Naknek along their shores — but the majority of what returns to Bristol Bay is the sockeye.

A sockeye's life begins in a lake when a red bead opens and a new fry wiggles in the stream. Water slides across skin without scales, without a silver shine, smooth like the surface of the lake on a calm day. Spots act as camouflage against the gravel. Two years is a typical time it takes a fry to escape downstream into the river's brackish water, where it meets Bristol Bay. There is enough salt to transform them into smolt with harder, silver scales as their armor for life in the ocean.

When they return, they pour from the Pacific, the Arctic, and all the waters in between by the millions, into the rivers of Bristol Bay. Sockeye are the lifeblood, and when they reach the headwaters, the red astaxanthin of their flesh migrates to their skin to reflect as such.

Pinks, or humpies, are Alaska's most abundant species. They are the smallest salmon and have the shortest lives. Almost every pink returning to spawn is two years old. One year a river has millions of them, and the next year there are almost none. They spawn in the late summer and early fall, and their eggs lay buried in gravel before they emerge in spring. A pink doesn't linger. A pink is born and migrates right away into the ocean. They run shorter distances, but they do go as far north as the Arctic. When it's time to spawn, males develop a hooked jaw and a humped back.

Chums, or dogs, also migrate to the ocean soon after emerging from the gravel, but chums spend two or three years in the ocean, depending on their food and how fast they grow. They run as far north as Siberia and as far south as the California coast. They will spawn lower in a river, sometimes as low as where brackish water will reach. They'll live for weeks after they spawn, as they turn green and purple with teeth big and sharp like canines. Their flesh is pale and soft, and they are more likely to be fed to Mosie, Auggie, or Bonkers before they make it to a plate.

Coho, or silvers, swim toward Russia and Japan through the year and return to Bristol Bay on the tail end of summer, their silver streaks shining in their scales. They spawn, die, and new ones hatch late in the winter and into spring. They spend up to two years in a stream, sometimes mistaken as trout. Then they live in the ocean one year before they return late in the summer.

Chinook, the king of the salmon, spend a year in the freshwater before roaming the expanse of the ocean up to seven years, gaining size and strength as massive creatures thick with rich oil and powerful muscle. They are the most coveted by sport fishermen and have been as big as 100 pounds. The largest I've ever seen was 45 pounds. The largest Dad has seen was 62. Once, there was a king caught on the Kenai River that weighed 97 pounds.

There is a function and purpose to every salmon's life, no matter the species. Whether or not they make it, every one of them heads toward a specific spot where water distills into a rich gush of oxygen for fertile eggs. A female lays her roe of little red beads, a male sprays them in white clouds of milt, and one generation begins the next. The old salmon die, decay, seep into the soil, and fortify trees climbing into the mountains. The mountains range to the edge of the ocean, and their peaks cut into the sky. One way or another, they return to the rest of what is out there.

Every salmon is an individual vessel of consciousness, no matter how basic. People try to understand and make meaning out of life and our surroundings, but salmon don't care. It all exists with or without recognition, distortion, interpretation, or any attempt to categorize and systemize with symbols and language, spoken and unspoken, literal or figurative. The tide ebbs and floods, whether or not we see it. Breath flows in and out whether or not we think about it. A live heart beats whether it is inside a salmon or the chest of a person.

When a fry is born, it already is susceptible to raptors swooping down, clutching their bodies in tightened claws and beaks. Then there are the trout that swallow them whole. Some of them are chomped in half by seals. Even more of them are pulled into a boat, caught by the gills in a nylon web. Many of them are captured by ocean trawlers. Of three thousand eggs, only hundreds of them hatch. About a tenth of them make it to the ocean. Three, four, maybe five of them become adults. Like sperm through fallopian tubes, it's uncommon for more than one male to swim far enough upstream to fertilize eggs. Only the survivors get to spawn. Then they die.

A human embryo is more fish than human, engorged in fluid, with slick skin and a tail. Then the embryo transforms. Instead of fins, arms and legs form with fingers and toes. Instead of a tail, a nub of bone remains under the skin. A baby is born with blurry vision and no ideas about distinguishing objects. There is no separation between the body and the rest of what's out there. Sometime during our first two years is when observation begins to translate into meaning. A king is different from a sockeye, a river is different from a stream, a male is different from a female, and Naknek is different from other towns. Existence without distortion is lost to language and symbols. Attempts to replace that type of existence leads to conquest, consumption, invention, and production.

The first people to catch salmon used spears and bone hooks. They caught them in the rivers of Bristol Bay and around the entire world. The source seemed endless, because they would always return no matter how many were speared and hooked. We respected fish. Then we invented nets and types of weirs, cutting circulation of the salmon upstream. Whoever was upstream could only attain their catch only after the people downstream caught enough.

Now there is never enough, because we have invented supermarkets, sidewalks, and a global market. Filets appear not just near coasts and riverbanks, but in landlocked freezers and refrigerators. Aside from Alaska, and Bristol Bay in particular, salmon have disappeared from rivers and fish farms have been constructed to compensate. The farmed salmon are pumped with dyes and synthetic fertilizers, and they spew feces laced with altered chemicals leaching into the ocean. All the while, smaller fish used for their feed are annihilated.

The Alaska Department of Fish and Game prevented that kind of disappearance in Bristol Bay, but it is not an exact science. There is plenty about the patterns and habits of salmon in the ocean that people don't know or understand. We know where they are going, and we know that they need to get there to maintain a pattern in existence long before the interference of people.

The reality is that we need to eat to live, and to eat, something else has to die. Nutrients are pumped through our bloodstream. Carbohydrates and fat are burned as fuel or stored or later use. Protein rebuilds our structure. Vitamins, minerals, phytochemicals, and bacteria work to make our system operate.

Mom and Dad tell me that green beans will make me big and strong, and if I don't eat them, I'm wasting green beans someone else could have had. I would prefer those people to have them instead of me, but we would have to find those people first. We might have to fly or drive a boat or send them away in a container van on a barge, but those people are out there. It's not fair of me to just throw away food, so I choke down every last soggy bite, cursing the can they came from. I want to be big and strong.

Uncle Stan wasn't my uncle. He was Joanne's uncle. She and her husband, Gary, owned and tended Fisherman's Bar, and she introduced him as Uncle Stan to everyone. Uncle Stan lived alone in an old house in the bushes behind Fisherman's. He rolled his own cigarettes, smoked his own fish, and the only thing religious I ever heard him say was, "God only made so many beautiful heads. The rest, he covered with hair."

There was a radio tower on his black-shingled roof, and he would sit behind a switchboard in the living room, fiddling with buttons and knobs, communicating with voices from around the globe. It looked like the cockpit of a plane, from where he could navigate anywhere on our planet — but Naknek is where he had come, and Naknek is where he stayed.

Short, plump, bald, and with ears like Yoda, Uncle Stan told us about the conversations he had through his radio tower. Mom and Dad were more intrigued by stories of trapping and subsistence fishing in a time of sailboats and post-World War II wariness. They listened and conversed while I wondered about voices from the sky. I wondered what it was that they had to say.

Whenever Uncle Stan thought I looked bored at his small table in the kitchen, he pulled out an envelope of noisy rattlesnake eggs, a peanut jar with a loaded projectile, or a chicken egg from the fridge that refused to break.

There was always a bowl on the kitchen table full of smoked salmon from a recipe that he had learned upon his arrival to Alaska. We chomped on the salty smokefish, trying to satisfy an instant addiction. Uncle Stan had a walk-in smoker behind the house where the next batch was always hanging, soaking in the rising flavor, and Mom badgered him for the recipe. He did end up giving it to her.

When Stan died, Naknek lost an uncle. Mom delivered the eulogy at Fisherman's, and it was the first time I had seen Joanne there in front of the bar instead of behind it, where she had served me Shirley Temples and slipped me handfuls of quarters to dump into PacMan, Terminator Pinball, or the Ninja Turtle arcade game. I fought Foot Soldiers on the streets of New York while Mom drank beer with my teachers. I picked often picked Ninja Turtle cartoons from Fishermen's assortment of rental tapes, and I often watched them at Joanne's house when she babysat me. Sometimes she would bring me a new action figure from trips she took to places where stores sold toys, and she handed them to me over the bar.

Toward the end of the eulogy, Mom assured us that, despite his opinions about religion, Uncle Stan was in heaven. I wondered if he even wanted to be up there, sitting around on a cloud, wings spread, strumming on a harp, a home-rolled cigarette between his lips. If he had his own celestial fridge, God probably wouldn't let him fill it with beer or magnet pictures of naked ladies on its door.

Joanne was always at church when we went, and we went whenever Mom felt the urge. If I protested, she asked me where I wanted to go when I died, and I thought that maybe Mom wasn't so sure about Uncle Stan's fate after all. I sighed, dragged myself away from whatever character I was drawing, comic book I was reading, or TV show I was watching, and I avoided eternal damnation one more week. Then the family packed into Dad's red F-150 with the cracked windshield, and we squeaked, rattled, and rolled down to the community's Catholic establishment.

St. Theresa's Catholic Church was part of the Holy Rosary Parish in Dillingham, a town about 60 miles across the Kvichak Bay, on the Nushagak. The church was a derelict building from a cannery, moved and mounted on top of a hill near Tibbets Airfield in Naknek. It was a short walk for Father James Kelley, one of the parish's flying priests who would pilot a Piper Cherokee from Dillingham to smaller towns like ours. He alternated churches on Sunday, which is why sometimes mass was in the morning, and sometimes it was in the evening. If it was in the morning, I didn't know we were attending it until Mom was in my room to get me out of bed.

St. Theresa's was painted sky blue, and I was sure that there were more lead-based chips scattered on the ground every time we went. Whenever we went to church, I imagined the sky was falling. There was no heat inside, and rain dripped from the ceiling into buckets. Familiar faces towered above me — teachers, neighbors, friends from town — but they seemed not themselves as they recited words in unison, sang songs, knelt, sat, stood, and knelt, sat, and stood again as the bald man in the dress conducted them.

Father Kelley was a retired Navy pilot who told us stories of his military days, and he punctuated them by telling us something God or Jesus would want us to do.

"Do you want to hear a story?" he would begin.

"Yes, father," he coerced us to say with a hand cupped around an ear. Like Uncle Stan, his stories were entertaining and full of wisdom, but unlike Uncle Stan, he couldn't make us hear the voice coming from the sky. Instead of a radio tower on top of the building, there was a white steeple, and when I was bored, Father Kelley didn't pull out a rattling envelope, an exploding jar of peanuts, or an unbreakable egg to throw on the floor. I kept track of time by asking Mom how many songs were left, and without a word, she showed me her fingers, teaching me to count backwards.

By the time I was eight, the parish had built a new church between King Salmon and Naknek to join Catholics from both towns in a warm, dry place to gather and worship together. It was a beautiful building with wide windows, a spacious floor, and front platform. It also had a clean basement for us to stay after mass for baked goods every so often, when it was Social Sunday.

The building was new while I was studying for my first communion, the part of service for churchgoers to get in line to accept the body and blood of Christ. The Eucharist, which I called the cracker, became the body. A dry merlot became the blood. The adults called it transubstantiation. I called it hocus pocus. I was to take part in the hocus pocus after learning enough passages and prayers. It was like school, but instead of worrying about bad grades, I worried about going to hell.

There were prayers to recite upon rising, before eating, before going to bed, after sinning, and more prayers I guessed were just for extra credit.

Father Kelley visited the house on occasion to guide me. He wasn't a bald man in a dress then, but a bald man in a black shirt with a white collar. He was a casual kind of priest, and Mom always thought it was funny to offer him a beer. He chuckled, smiled, and politely declined. Instead, he always settled for a glass of Ocean Spray Cranberry Juice Cocktail from a plastic bottle, whether or not it had been refrigerated. Then he and I got to the tasks at hand. If I had to pause during a prayer, he wasn't angry or frustrated. He smiled, took a sip of Ocean Spray, recited it for me, and let me try again.

Mom and Dad helped me practice, too. Mom, a declared Lutheran, wasn't allowed to take communion with Catholics — but she said that the stories were the same. Dad was raised Catholic, but most of what he had to offer were stories about nuns smacking him with a ruler for asking questions. No one ever hit me, but I did have some of the same questions.

Where did all the other people come from after Cain killed Abel? Were Adam and Eve cavepeople? When did the dinosaurs come in if God made all the animals at once? The animated feature film, *the Land Before Time* had offered a glimpse of fish-looking things turning into lizard-looking things, and I asked Mom about them, too.

"It's okay not to believe *some* things that are in the Bible."

"Yeah, I don't believe *everything* the Bible says," Dad added. "I'm not just some big, strong Catholic."

I didn't understand.

"So don't go asking Father Kelley, 'what about the dinosaurs,'" Mom said. "The cavemen and the dinosaurs are a whole 'nother story."

I still didn't understand. I had seen books with pictures of dinosaur bones and pictures of people skulls that looked more like gorilla skulls.

"Then is it okay if I don't believe in Adam and Eve?"

Mom started borrowing Bible cartoons for me from the public library. I didn't complain. I loved cartoons. Noah built an ark and saved two of every species from the flood. Jonah lived inside a whale. Moses parted the Red Sea. Jesus fed the multitudes with five loaves of bread and two fish. Four mutated turtles in New York City's sewer system were trained in the art of ninjutsu by a talking rat named Splinter.

Kids at school went to the Bible Church, the Church of Jesus Christ of Latter-Day Saints, and the Russian Orthodox Church — or at least when Russian Orthodox Christmas fell on a school day. Some kids didn't go to any church. They were the kids who said there was no God and there was no Santa Claus. One man couldn't go to every kid's house in one night, they said, even if it is just the good kids. I listened to those kids. It took us at least a day to get to Florida, and we had much less ground to cover than Santa. Those winters, we celebrated Russian Orthodox Christmas, too. When we got home in January, we opened presents with Mo and Smiley. That way, Mom and Dad had fewer presents to haul to Florida and back. Those were the years when Jesus had two birthdays.

After Russians arrived on Alaskan shores, no longer had Raven created our planet. No longer had he brought light to it either. In the Russian stories, God is who let there be light before our planet was around. He separated the waters below and the waters above with the firmament. Then he created birds from the waters, which meant Raven couldn't have been there in the beginning. Then, in the same story, God created birds from the ground. At school, I learned that birds came from dinosaurs. I was all sorts of confused.

My middle school science teacher taught us about stars, atoms, changing climates, Galileo, and Darwin. He taught us that the universe is a complex system of galaxies, solar systems, black holes, subatomic particles, and dark matter — ever-changing, ever-shifting, ever-expanding. The Bible had a man in the sky who killed first-born sons and made it rain frogs. I was in my twenties when that teacher died, but not without opening for me a whole universe of questions.

Accepting the cracker and wine as the body and blood of Christ was how to prove I believed — but as much as I tried, I couldn't do it. I couldn't make myself believe that a stale white disk was the flesh of a two-thousand-year-old messiah. I couldn't make myself believe that a dry Merlot was a combination of plasma, hemoglobin, and red blood cells. I clenched my eyes and repeated to myself that I believed, I believed, I believed, but it was like trying to convince myself that two plus two was five. It was a sin not to believe, but it was a sin to lie. I was damned if I did and damned if I didn't.

Before my first communion, I met with Father Kelley one
more time for my first confession. It was in his office at Saint Teresa's,
which was more of a glorified broom closet.

"Forgive me, Father, for I have sinned," I said. "This is my first
confession."

He nodded.

"I don't think I can make myself believe in this stuff," I didn't
say. "I don't believe in God, Santa, Superman, Odin, Raven, or the
Teenage Mutant Ninja Turtles either. The patterns of the universe, the
rotation of our planet, synapses responding to a brain, the beating of a
heart, and the life cycle of salmon might all exist and correspond by pure
chance — or there might be an intelligent force behind it all that we
don't understand, but just because we don't understand it doesn't mean
it's supernatural. Choosing a certain dogma or deity out of an infinite
number of possibilities is just making a wild guess. I'm not satisfied with
guesses as answers. I know I don't have the answers. I can live with that,
and I can die with that."

I didn't say any of these things, of course. I didn't articulate
thoughts this way until I was a teenager running alongside the Alaska
Peninsula Highway. What I said to Father Kelley was that I didn't listen
to my parents. I didn't think to mention any specific incident, and he
couldn't help but smile.

"Maybe there's something you did to your little sister?"

I shrugged.

After absolving me of my sins, he walked me through the
details for the following Sunday. He reminded me how to approach the
cracker, which hand went on top of the other, and how to sip the wine.

"Then that's the part where we say it turns into the body and
blood of Christ, but that's not really what happens," he said. "That's just
a story." I was bewildered when he said it. I realized later in life that the
Catholics didn't take the Bible as literally as I had been led to think, but
still, transubstantiation was uncompromisable.

Maybe it was a final test. Maybe it was Father Kelley's way of
telling me that it's okay not to believe *every little thing* the Bible says —
or maybe it was a trap, a subtle way to get me to ask questions. I didn't
say anything, but I wish I did.

After what happened next, I always wished that I had asked.
He handed me a coloring book. It was a dinosaur coloring book. Mom

had said not to ask about them, so I stayed quiet, but I've wanted to ask Father Kelley about the dinosaurs my entire life.

It was Palm Sunday of 2001 when Father Kelley crashed his Piper Cherokee into Tuklung Mountain, a peak southwest of the village of Manokotak. He died on impact. He had spoken at Joanne's funeral not long after Uncle Stan's memorial service at Fisherman's. He had reminded us that we'd see her again if we stayed faithful. It offered no comfort, because with all the infinite options, I couldn't make myself believe in one specific, supernatural idea to explain the complexities of what's out there.

I still pondered a place where we go after death, memories intact, where we sprout wings and play harps on top of clouds. If there was such a place, maybe I could get some answers. Maybe Uncle Stan would be there, talking to people through the sky. Maybe Joanne could hand me a roll of quarters to put into the Ninja Turtle game. Maybe I could still ask Father Kelley about the dinosaurs.

During the winter, I have to wear snowpants to and from kindergarten or else I can't ride the bus. Other kids get off the bus on the side of the Alaska Peninsula Highway. Our house is too far up the gravel for a five-year-old to walk, so the bus driver takes me all the way to the end of the driveway where Dad shovels snow and piles it to the sides. Icicles dangle from his mustache and beard, white from frost accumulating in his whiskers. Crystals accumulate in his eyelashes. He walks with me to the house, sets the shovel upright in a snowbank, and we go inside where he makes me a sandwich that I hope is peanut butter and jelly. I like to watch the splatter of purple plop onto my plate. By the time *Sesame Street* is on the tiny black-and-white TV with antennas, Dad's beard has become brown again.

When there are warmer temperatures, and no more snow falls, I step off the bus, and Dad comes inside from transplanting another tree around the lawn. The sun casts their shadows long after bedtime, and I don't have to go to school anymore. Soon, Dad goes fishing. Mom tells me it's the kind of fishing where he makes money and not the kind with a pole. My money comes from the tooth fairy, and I wonder if it's created in the same place.

Mom makes my sandwich in the summer, but she doesn't use as much peanut butter and jelly. Nothing spurts out onto my plate. It's okay. I get to go out to the greenhouse with her, where there are flowers and vegetables. I help pick green beans and put them in a basket. It means one more night they won't come from a can. Dad comes home sometimes, but he isn't around long. He spends most of the time sleeping in the bedroom loft above the living room. Mom says to stay quiet. Dad doesn't get to sleep much when he's fishing.

Then there are times we go with him. We load into the Labamba at City Dock and go to a place Mom and Dad call Fish Camp. Sometimes they call it Graveyard. It used to be a town called Koggiung, they tell me. Now just fishermen live there, and only in the summer. At Graveyard, there is no TV or refrigerator or lights or running water. There is just the cracked white paint, the pans on the wall, and the sink that doesn't work where Mom and Dad wash dishes by heating rainwater with a propane stove. They tell me the building used to be a hospital.

To get here, we take the Labamba out the mouth of the Naknek River into the Kvichak Bay. Waves curl toward us as we splash across them. To the right, there is land. To the left, there is water that goes on forever.

Most of the time, we are in the Labamba. It has ribs like the ribs I see in the caribou hanging in the basement over the drain after Dad cuts off their skin. The Labamba has square ribs, and they shake when a wave crashes from underneath, and a splash sprays into the side. The water is salty when I taste it. Water in the bottom gushes from one side to the other, and it pours into the stern where it pools. When we move again, Dad pulls a wooden plug, and the water pours back into the Kvichak.

When we stop, it's so Mom and Dad can lift one net or another over the bow. It has a line of corks on the surface. A heavier line of lead stays below it. The web is in between them. That's where the fish are tangled or dangling toward the ribs in the floor. Dad is in front of the corks. Mom stays behind the leads, with her back to Erica and me. They pull along the lines and the net moves over the bow. With every pull, more fish emerge from the water in the web between the lines.

"One!" A fish flies from Mom's orange glove. It lands into a big bag tied between two metal bars across the skiff. Mom and Dad call the bag a brailer.

"Two!" Dad tosses another one. His gloves are blue, and his fish is in the air before the first one lands.

"Three!" I shout as the next one is on its way, and I keep counting until the numbers are too high for me to remember. Mom and Dad start shouting them to help me.

"Eleven, twelve, thirteen…" I repeat. When Erica is old enough to count, she repeats the numbers with me, but I think she learns them quicker. Adults say I do well in school, but she does better. She knows how to talk to adults. She knows how to get more peanut butter and jelly on her sandwich.

She and I stand in a gray, plastic tote with a blue, plaid picnic blanket that we crawl beneath when it gets cold, when it rains, or if the waves start splashing over the sides. Mom and Dad fold a tarp over us. The tote is shoved between two ribs.

Fish are shoved into the brailer, and after counting to numbers that I'll never remember, Dad drives the Labamba away from the nets. The ribs bounce again. Splashes spray from the side until we pull up to a big, black-and-yellow boat with a white cabin. Mom and Dad call it a tender. A crane lifts the bags of fish as a man pulls two levers. Then Dad climbs aboard.

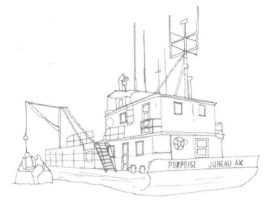

"This is the part where Dad makes money," Mom says.

I imagine a metal machine, steam shooting from whistles as coins and dollars project into piles on the floor. I imagine people aboard scooping it into their arms and collecting it into big bags with big dollar signs printed on the sides of them. Instead, Dad climbs back into the skiff with a pink slip of paper he tucks under his raincoat. Mom tells me that it says how much the fish weigh.

Dad keeps a pile of these pink slips of paper on the shelf next to the table at Graveyard. At the end of the season, Dad gets another slip of paper from the cannery. He puts it on the counter at the kitchen next to the pink papers to see if the numbers match. I ride with him when he takes the truck to King Salmon. Then he hands the paper to the lady behind the counter at the bank.

"Where's the money?" I ask.

"It's in the bank," he says.

I wonder how much money is in the bank, and what fish have to do with it. I wonder if there are more fish on our planet or more dollars, but I know that I have seen more fish. Most of the money I've seen is in a basket of coins Mom and Dad keep on the windowsill in the dining room. Sometimes they take out the coins and put them in paper rolls.

Dad talks about how the prices aren't what they used to be, like they were in the heyday of the 80s. That was before the drunken captain of the Exxon Valdez handed the steering console over to a shipmate. That shipmate crashed the tanker into a reef on their way out of the Prince William Sound. Millions of gallons of crude oil dumped into the water, suffocating fish, whales, seals, otters, birds, and the Alaska seafood market. Although that water is across the Alaska Peninsula, across Cook Inlet, and across the Kenai Peninsula, and oil didn't seep into Bristol Bay, the reputation of Alaskan seafood brought down prices all over the state. Subsequently, Japanese CEOs of the companies owning canneries put their money into fish farms in Chile, and farmed salmon boomed, bringing prices down even further.

As I understand it, oil is a thick, black liquid from below our planet's surface that we use to make the fuel for our cars, our trucks, and our outboard motors. When it diffuses as a grey-blue puff into the air, Mom and Dad say to stay away from it. They say not to breathe it because it's bad for me, and it's bad for our planet.

We need it, though, for the outboard motor used to set the nets and catch the fish. Oil is also used to make plastic.

In Anchorage, Mom or Dad swipe a piece of plastic they call a credit card. At Costco, Sam's Club, and Fred Meyer, boxes of oranges, oatmeal, raisins, peanuts, Tang, and a toy if I'm lucky, pile onto the cart. Then the cart gets pushed through a line, and Mom and Dad don't give anything to the lady behind the counter in return for it. Mom explains it's not stealing. The credit card means they pay later. The lady behind the counter waits for her money like Dad waits for his money. I study my new, plastic, Batman action figure in its package.

Mom and Dad pay when an envelope comes in the mail with a number on a folded sheet of paper. Dad gets out a leather booklet, writes the same number, tears it out, and puts it in his own envelope with a stamp. There is only one envelope, and it goes into the blue mailbox outside the post office. I don't know how it goes to Costco, Sam's Club, and Fred Meyer all at once. It's just one piece of paper.

There are fish fillets at Costco like the ones we have in our big freezer in the garage. They are like the fillets that Dad cuts and Mom puts into freezer bags. Mom and Dad never buy fish. They don't give it a thought. They push the shopping cart as though the bright red filets aren't there. I wonder if we've seen any of these fish before. Mom and Dad pick up grapes, grapefruit, Grape Nuts, roasted peanuts, peanut butter and take it home. We get fish from the nets.

Dad picks the fish, the fish go to the cannery, the cannery sells cans to the store, and someone at the store takes it home to eat. Could we, I ask, find the fruit people, cereal people, peanut people, Tang people, and toy people, and trade them for fish? Wouldn't it be easier? Instead, fish swim into the net, Dad brings the fish to a big boat, the big boat gives him a pink paper, he gives the pink paper to the cannery, the cannery gives him a white slip of paper, the white slip of paper goes to the bank, he goes to the lady at Costco, and he gets to take home a box of oats, because the bank will give her the money later. Could we just take fish to Anchorage and hand it over the counter? Could we just eat fish, caribou, berries, and vegetables from Mom's greenhouse?

Dad laughs at my questions and says what's on a t-shirt he likes. "Pull the net to make the money to buy the bread to gain the strength to pull the net."

Most of us run when we're still kids. Driven by impulse, we race across our streets and yards, maybe jumping through a sprinkler. We chase each other, laughing and smiling. Then we are taught, usually by a coach or a teacher, that running isn't any fun. Running is a punishment. It's to make us in better shape. Running becomes an intentional undertaking, in controlled bouts of exercise — but even after hundreds of races and thousands of self-prescribed workouts, I still remember running in clunky basketball shoes over grass tufts on the tundra and the gravel road of our neighborhood.

Dull rocks, colorful rocks, and rocks with a crystalline or metallic luster flew beneath my shoes. Some of them in the driveway were rocks I had found camping and on the beach in the mud. Sometimes a collection of them was lined across my bedroom windowsill. From time to time, the collection disappeared, but I'd see them again in the driveway. My friend Nick recognized one of them as a fossil. It made sense, he said, because Naknek was once covered in water. He knew this fact, he explained, because his fourth-grade teacher told him. Riel said that Nick was full of it. Naknek was covered in ice.

Nick was a couple of years older than me. Riel was a year younger. They lived across the gravel street, down a sloping dirt driveway surrounded by bushes. Their house was once a cannery bunkhouse that Norm, their dad, had hauled to their property. The summer before I started third grade, Mom made me go over there and introduce myself. I shuffled my feet, scattering rocks the entire way. Both Nick and Riel, both heavyset guys, were in the back of their dad's little red truck. Riel said he'd come over. Nick stayed seated over the wheel well without saying a word. Riel explained that Nick was mad because he was going into fifth grade, and he wanted to stay in fourth grade. Riel became my closest, most longtime friend. Nick became a good friend as well, but there were different sides to him that I would later find fascinating.

We played SEGA Genesis games like *Mortal Kombat III* and *NHLPA Hockey '93* on the box-shaped TV in the basement. We played both of these games for the fighting, and both of these games included warnings for graphic violence for blood that spilled from characters and disappeared on the ground. Mom would have loved if blood worked that way. Whenever someone was hurt or crying, the first thing she asked was if there was any blood on the carpet.

Sometimes we pretended we were superheroes and supervillains and chased each other around with our powers, but Riel and I often just wandered around on the lawn or the tundra, talking, joking, and teaching each other new ways to swear. On occasion, Riel would walk up to Mom's flowers or chives and kick at a bumblebee buzzing around it. Then we'd run away as fast as we could. Sometimes Nick, Riel, and I played pitcher, batter, and outfielder on the patch of tundra between our houses. Our bases were uneven tufts of grass that we seldom made our way all the way around. With endless tundra as our field, there were no home runs. We either had to run the bases quickly or leave a ghostman on first, second, or third. Nobody ever ran quickly. Nobody ever won.

Bikes were our regular mode of transport around the gravel streets of Gottschalk Subdivision, and venturing away meant riding down the hill, gravel crunching under our tires. Our favorite part was slamming the brakes at the bottom, scattering rocks, leaving another streak exposing finer, damper dirt. I was the only kid who could pedal back up. I always kept my butt on the seat, hiding the picture of Rainbow Brite and her unicorns. Like my clothes that were always too big, the bike was a hand-me-down from another Naknek family.

Maybe that's where I got my first thoughts of running along that gravel, or maybe it was from the time I was almost run over by a truck. Riel was still riding the kindergarten bus, so just Nick and I were dropped where the pavement met the gravel, about a half-mile away from our house. I thought it would be funny to lay down and ask Nick, "Don't you wish a car would come by?" A truck did suddenly turn the corner onto the gravel, and I sprung to my feet, running. I kept running after the truck had swerved and passed me.

The Borough eventually put in a gravel turnaround for the bus a quarter mile from our houses, and if I got off the bus alone, sometimes I tried running home from there. It didn't seem as daunting as the entire half a mile. Of course, I was always stopped by a side stitch or the pack of neighborhood dogs surrounding me, barking, circling me as I slowly shuffled home. Dad told me to throw rocks at them, or at least pretend to throw rocks, which kept them away for the most part. Between the dogs and my own stamina, I didn't have the charisma I wanted to have.

Then I saw it in one of my friends. When Nick, Riel, and I were 15, 13, and 12, there were younger kids in the neighborhood who liked to throw rocks at all of us. We were at a loss. Those rocks hurt, but we would be the bad guys if we threw them back. By that time, Nick said that he wanted to be called Norm, his first name. He was Norm the Second, and not Norm Junior, he said, because, as he put it, there was nothing junior about him. It was Norm who took the brunt of the rocks with no reaction whatsoever.

Nick, I realized, had been goofy, shy, and insecure. Norm, however, wouldn't need rocks to keep away barking dogs. He was a rock. I could envision him bitten in the arm, maybe even mauled, and he would stare the dog in the eyes until the dog got bored and walked away.

Sometimes Norm, Riel, and I had Super Soaker fights, which always escalated into garden hose battles on the front lawn. One of us had the hose from the faucet on one side of the house. Another one of us would stretch over the other hose from the opposite side of the house. Then the lawn would be the venue for an ultimate showdown. It ended quickly with Norm around. He would first move straight toward Riel, directly into the spray, accepting blasts to the face and even the crotch. Then his grip wrapped tight around the hose before he tugged it out of his hands. Then he came for me. When he had both garden hoses, we ran like hell.

I was under no delusion that I was the fastest kid. At school, PE class always started with running laps around the gym. I wasn't the last one done, but I was never the first one done either. Mr. Bakun, the PE teacher, lived in the house across the tundra from us, in the old Swanson place. My class likened him to a drill sergeant, but he was a drill sergeant we respected. I liked Mr. Bakun, but PE was often a source of anxiety for me. Making a basket was impossible, catching a football took a miracle. In a game of dodgeball, I was often the first one out. As much as nobody, including me, looked forward to running three laps around the gym, I wished running laps could last all day.

After laps, there were calisthenics and stretches. Then Mr. Bakun led us through drills for whatever game we were learning. He scrutinized our movements and criticized our form, making us perform them again and again and again. It was during our swimming unit, when we'd walk across the school parking lot to the pool that he told me, after several tries, that my dive was the best dive he'd seen me perform. Then he told me to keep working on it.

I didn't think Mr. Bakun would ever be satisfied, let alone impressed. Then he told me that he sometimes saw me making it to the top of the hill on my bike. He was the first person other than Mom or Dad to give me anything close to a compliment about any kind of athletic ability. Maybe that's when I first thought about trying to run up that hill.

When we undertook the President's Physical Fitness Test in PE, it might have been the first time I embraced running. The test had requirements for strength, flexibility, speed, and endurance. Whoever passed all feats would receive a sew-on patch at the awards ceremony in the auditorium at the end of the school year, but I liked the Fitness Test because no one else was good at it either. Kids dangled from the pull-up bar, farted with their sit-ups, and faked asthma before any of the running even began.

Everything was tough for me, but the shuttle run, for speed, and the mile run, for endurance, were the toughest. I was never fast enough at either of them, but Mr. Bakun told us if we wanted to try any of these feats again, he'd be around after school. No else ever showed up but me. Mr. Bakun set up the wooden blocks in the gym to sprint to, pick up, and run back. He set up orange cones in the field behind the school, and he stood with a stopwatch while I huffed and puffed and ran on lumpy dirt and patchy grass.

I'm still not sure exactly why I kept going. Laughing and smiling and being driven by impulse was long gone. I wasn't driven by a desire for glory either. It was frustration. The first time I ran the mile after school, I was over a minute too slow. Then I was under a minute from the qualifying time. Then I was just four seconds too slow. I tried again and again, but I could never finish the damned course fast enough. The shuttle run teased me with fractions of seconds every time. After the kids who received the award were called onstage at the end of that school year, Mr. Bakun spoke to the audience about a kid who tried and tried and tried. He never said my name. He retired when I was in middle school, but I never stopped trying.

If there was any peer who influenced me to propel my own body over long distances, it was a kid that we'll call Little Johnny who moved to Naknek in fifth grade. LJ talked about life and school in Montana, in a place with theaters and malls and roads. He was another kid Mom forced me to invite over to the house, and we became friends.

We were an odd pair, because he was athletic and into basketball. His favorite team was Orlando Magic, and he knew what music was cool, like Coolio, LL Cool J, Nirvana, and Bush. Girls flocked to him, and boys wanted him on their team at recess. It didn't take him long to figure out he was one of the cool kids, and our friendship was no longer for the public eye.

When we were still friends, LJ and I used to ride our bikes to each other's houses, which was always his idea. By then, I had a new Huffy and didn't have to hide unicorns and Rainbow Brite. We lived four miles apart, and I didn't think kids could ride bikes that far, let alone that Mom and Dad would think it was okay. It turned out they didn't mind as long as I asked permission. Then LJ had the idea to ride our bikes from my house all the way to downtown Naknek. Mom was home, but I didn't want to ask permission because then LJ might not think I was cool enough to make my own decisions. We mounted our bikes, and two kids hit the gravel shoulder of the Alaska Peninsula Highway.

Unlike the thousands of times I'd been in the cab of an enclosed vehicle, in one direction or the other, I'd never seen it up close at this slow pace. For the first time, I noticed the boats in every driveway, the derelict cars and trucks in the bushes, and the garbage littering the side of the pavement. We met wandering dogs, waving drivers, and stopped to talk to other kids riding fourwheelers.

LJ's mom worked at the Camai Clinic where we stopped in to say hello, what *camai* meant in Yup'ik. That's where I called home to tell Mom I'd gone into town and had "forgotten" to ask permission. She wasn't upset until I said where I was. LJ's mom snatched the phone from my hand to explain that I was not hurt and not to worry. I just hoped she would remind her that Camai didn't have any carpet.

I started riding my bike to school in the morning on nice days in the spring, and I kept at it long after John had disappeared into the cool crowd. It gave me something to look forward to in the morning besides sitting at a desk, being ridiculed for my lack of athletic ability, and worrying about test scores. I didn't realize it yet, but there was something about moving myself across a long distance that wasn't synonymous with athletic ability.

I was reminded of it by Norm. When I was amidst any kind of sport season, practice often involved running "Angel Laps" around the gym. Angel Laps included running along three walls of the basketball court, up the stairs, up the walkway to the top-floor bleachers, a passage behind them, and down the stairs back into the gym. I lapped Norm in a Native Youth Olympics practice, playfully taunting him as I bounded up the stairs. That's when he chased after me, stumbled, and broke his leg. There was no cry or scream or even a grimace. He reached down to touch it and said, "Oh, that's broke." He didn't immediately stand up and start moving again, but something was fascinating about his total lack of acknowledgment of pain.

I didn't yet see that ability in myself. I would never possess it to the level that Norm did, but I eventually learned to develop it. Through running, I learned that I could develop my ability to withstand discomfort. *Endurance* was the term that I'd learn.

I would like to say that there was some kind of an epiphany soon after failing the Fitness test. I'd like to say that I started running long distances on my own after I started riding my bike to school. However, my relationship with any kind of athletic activity remained complicated for a long time. I don't know if it's ever stopped being complicated. I hadn't even begun my career as a commercial fisherman, and that part of my life is the same way.

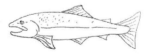

After a vacation to Los Angeles, Mom sends me fishing with Dad for the last week of this season. He's been at it since before we left. While Mom, Erica, Luke, and I rode paved streets in the back of a van, Dad was driving the skiff back and forth on the Kvichak River. While Luke stepped off the sidewalk to pee in a neighbor's lawn, pants to his ankles in two-year-old fashion, Dad was whipping it out over the side of the skiff. While I slept in the guest room bed at Uncle Ed and Aunt Claire's house, creeped out by the doll sitting on a chair in the corner, Dad was getting quick shots of sleep at Graveyard. While I was on the tram at Universal Studios, while I sat in a movie theater watching *Batman Forever*, and when I was sprawled over a blanket in a field under Fourth of July fireworks, Dad was pulling the nets to make the money to buy the food to gain the strength to pull the nets.

Mom says fishing is something I might want to do next year if I want to make money. If I make money, I can buy an even newer bike, because I've outgrown the Huffy. When I'm old enough, I can buy a car. Later, I can go to college. In other words, fishing is my way out of Naknek.

For now, I'm ten, and my raincoat is big enough to fit a hooded sweatshirt and a puffy coat underneath it, and it reaches over my hip boots to my knees. A pair of orange gloves dangles from my hands. My raincoat sleeves are cut in half and still too long. The wind is cold, rain hits my face, and waves splash me. I think I've seen real Fourth of July Fireworks for the last time.

Dad stands in the stern, helming the motor as I sit on the bench between Luke and John. Luke has been fishing with Dad for three years now, but it is John's first time in Alaska. They were roommates in college, and John still lives in Marquette. All three of them have been fishing long enough this summer for scales to speckle their raingear, and for whiskers to grizzle their faces. For the first time, I notice white streaks in Dad's beard. John doesn't have them, even though he is Dad's age.

Luke is Mrs. Feriante's son. When I was younger, he was the babysitter who watched the *Teenage Mutant Ninja Turtles* with me and brought comic books and handheld video games to the house. Mom says my brother isn't named after him, but she also says my brother wouldn't be Luke if Luke were a crappy kid.

Corks and lines and webs are heaped in the skiff, and I don't see how any of it will make it into the water without tangling into a wadded mess. Then I watch John leap out, ankles splashing in the water. He ties the end of the net to a screw anchor augured into the beach. Luke holds the skiff, John hops back into it. Dad drives the skiff out toward the channel as the net unravels flawlessly into the water, a line of corks on the surface, splashing and bobbing with heads and tails from fish gilling themselves in the web.

John ties the outside end the net to a buoy. It's attached to another screw anchor on the bottom of the channel. Then I watch the three men go through this process three more times, a leadline sinking and a corkline keeping the mesh stretched to the surface. A net looks like a curved line of white corks between two round, salmon-colored buoys. I watch the tide rise and pull the nets into this curve. I watch white water rush faster against the corks. Then there are more splashes.

Dad pulls the skiff to the corks, and Luke and John lift them over the bow. Then they lift the lead line. All three of them pull along the net, picking out fish and throwing them into brailer bags. It's my job to tie them. Dad says to tie them tight, as tight as I can get them, and to tie the knot like I tie a shoelace, but not really the way I tie a shoelace, because my shoes always come untied. Four brailers fit between the bulkhead behind the bow and the bulkhead in front of the stern. Each of them can hold 1,000 pounds. When the skiff is full, we go to the tender parked in the channel. A hook and a big metal scale lowers from a crane, lifts the bags, and the crane operator records the weight. Dad goes on board and comes back with a pink slip of paper.

Then we head to Graveyard, a place that holds too many memories for my sanity. Graveyard was once the village of Koggiung, a village at Graveyard Point, where the Kvichak Bay meets the Kvichak River. It's the site of both a Native burial site and a cemetery for workers at the cannery built in 1910. There have been times when the tide has eroded Graveyard's edges, pulling coffins from the bank, the occasional skeleton reaching toward the shore. When the cannery burned down in 1959, leaving charred pilings and piles of metal rusted by the tide, the village was abandoned. Its last year-round residents are those skeletons.

Our family started staying at the old hospital in 1984. Dad sits in his spot across the table by the window and explains that it was Mom who started the family fishing operation in the early 80s. She, Bob Swanson, and another partner wanted to experience the seasonal industry Naknek revolved around. They took out loans, bought gear, leased sites, and staked their claim in the doctor's office at the hospital for their shelter. They painted the outside of their skiff purple and described the operation as a *Cheech and Chong Go Fishing* movie never made.

In 1984, Mom finished the season with a broken arm. She had fallen from the ladder on her climb to the top bunk. A fellow fisherman splinted her arm with a stick and a t-shirt, and I was born three months later with no obvious defects. Dad soon quit his job with the Department of Fish and Game so he could take care of me at home during the school year and take over the fishing operation. Mom kept teaching, watching me during the summer.

When Dad moved in, he chainsawed a doorway between the doctor's office and the medicine closet, and it's where we walk through to the patient room, now the bedroom. A sink installed into the makeshift counter drains water into the ground through a piece of PVC pipe, and behind it are hanging pans, spatulas, ladles, and insulated mitts.

When we wake up in the middle of the night, as the tide goes out, Dad lights a propane lantern hanging from the old light socket in the doctor's office. Dad, Luke, John, and I spread peanut butter on pilot bread, brush our teeth in the sink with cups of water, and walk into the hallway. Its halls are covered in handprints from vandals who discovered the contents of the medicine closet years ago. The hallway is where we keep the totes, the cooler, and spare rain gear hanging from nails in the wall. The porch slants downward, and on it, we put on lifejackets, raincoats, and gloves. The other guys have neoprene chest waders. I have hip boots and rain pants with the bottoms rolled up.

The planks of the boardwalk are loose and splintered. Some of them are missing. Fishermen have nailed boards and sheets in a vain attempt to salvage it, or at least to avoid being slapped in the face or falling into the dirt. Telephone poles lay broken and rotten, staircases covered in moss crumble, and old plumbing protrudes from the dirt. Charred pilings line Graveyard Creek where we park our skiff, and rusted pipes, furnaces, canning equipment, and other artifacts lay strewn all over the shore.

On Dad's birthday, John finds a wooden cork, gives it scrap metal fins, and he paints an eye. He nails the fish to a board in the middle of the outer ring of an old dartboard. Dad affixes it to the wall at our camp. It is the first piece of artwork hung there. Some of my sketches go up later. Dad's birthday, July 17th, marks the end of the regulatory season. The beginning of the regulatory season is Father's Day. Fishing season is Dad's own special season.

It's Luke's last year, and John won't come back either. The wooden cork fish remains on the wall, among mosquitoes with the year of the kill inscribed in pencil. Luke and John's names remain written on the wall by the cast-iron pans, next to the year they began and the year they finished. They are next to names like Pat Wilson, Don Stambeck, and Allen Levinson. Next year, 1996, my name will be there with them, but I will have no end date in sight.

Even after running the mile over and over again, I had no sudden interest in running long distances. I was still not an athletic type by any means. I still would argue that I am not. I've always attributed my ability to run long distances to my introverted nature, but running is not how it was channeled when I was growing up.

My introverted nature truly began to fester when I was 12, when Dad installed two walls in the basement for me to have a new bedroom down there, and for Luke to take my old room. Mom and Dad soon thought it was a mistake. The TV room was in the basement, and as basic cable in Naknek accumulated more channels, I accumulated more interest in the world outside the tundra. On the other side of the screen was a civil war in Rwanda, an earthquake in the San Fernando

Valley, and a talking chihuahua telling me to buy a chalupa. The nearest Taco Bell was of course about 800 miles across tundra and mountains.

To be honest, it wasn't news or current events that had me interested. I watched shows like *Quantum Leap, Forever Knight, and SeaQuest DSV* on the Sci-Fi Channel. I loved the Sunday afternoon lineup on Fox with its cartoons like *King of the Hill* and *the Simpsons.*

Movies, however, were my favorite medium. I remember many times in my life based on what movies I had seen in a theater. Trips to Anchorage meant the Toys 'R Us, the Dimond Center Mall, Taco Bell, Bosco's Comics, and Barnes and Noble, but the best part about visiting Anchorage was seeing a movie on the big screen. I was in sixth grade when Dad took me to Anchorage to have braces grafted to my shark-like, overlapping teeth. He groaned at the thought of *Beavis & Butt-head Do America,* but he took me to see it anyway, and I saw the lead characters begin their journey across the United States after waking up to discover their TV missing. I laughed at the immature sex jokes only a twelve-year-old should find funny, and Dad fell asleep by the time they got to the Hoover Dam.

A year later, I was in Anchorage to get those braces adjusted, and Mom left me at the theater at the Dimond Center Mall to see *Titanic.* It was Mom who had taught me how to finish one movie and sneak into the next one without buying a new ticket. We had first seen *the Nutty Professor* and then we watched most of *Black Sheep* — but this time, Mom had no time for movies. She had her own appointments and had to continue the ongoing quest for groceries, so I saw Kate Winslet's bare breasts all by myself.

Another time in Anchorage, our whole family went to see *A Bug's Life* — an animated movie for kids about a talking ant who lives in a world of other talking ants and other talking bugs, including evil talking grasshoppers. Dad groaned at this one, too. Our layover in Anchorage was long enough to take a cab to the theater, watch a movie, and take a cab back to the airport. *A Bug's Life* fit our schedule, assuming a cab would get to us on time, but after the movie, we waited in the entryway for at least a half an hour, watching people trickle into the next presentation and leave in mobs from the last one.

"Fifty bucks!" Dad yelled. "Fifty bucks to anyone who will drive us to the airport!"

People walked by with their faces in their jackets, moving fast past the six-foot-four man assaulting them with a loud voice.

"Hey!" Dad jumped in front of a young couple, likely on a first date. "Will you drive us to the airport for fifty bucks?"

"George," Mom said. "You're scaring people."

Dad said in a softer, calmer manner, "Will you take us to the airport for fifty bucks?" The younger guy, who was by himself, just shook his head and walked out the door.

"Will you take us to the airport for fifty bucks?" Dad said to a group of four that looked like they were on a double date. They apologized without pausing to stop.

"I'll drive you." The voice was from an older gentleman. He was with his wife.

They took us to the airport, and Dad, Mom, Erica, Luke, and I made another trip to Florida for Christmas with Grandma and Grandpa Catalano at their Condo.

Dad, Erica, and I saw *Armageddon* together another time in Anchorage. I hadn't cried at the end of *Titanic*, but when Bruce Willis's character sacrificed himself to save the planet, I couldn't hold back my single tear. Ben Affleck's character married Liv Tyler's character, and they lived happily ever after as it cut to credits. I heard the same Aerosmith song I'd hear at school dance afterwards, where I'd lean against the wall and wish I had the courage to approach the girls from whatever visiting volleyball team was there. Student council always held dances when a visiting team was staying the night at our school.

Then the steady stream of superhero movies started with the first *X-Men* movie in 2000. I didn't get to see it in a theater, but one of the older guys had the VHS tape on a wrestling trip, and we watched it in our room three times. Then there was *Spider-man*, starring Tobey Maguire. It was the only movie I had ever seen twice on a big screen. I saw it first in Kodiak when our family went for the Crab Festival, and I saw it again in Anchorage a couple of weeks later.

Luke and I were in Anchorage for a dentist appointment when we went to see *Daredevil*, another movie starring Ben Affleck. A blind man would have known it was a terrible movie, but I was a geek of a comic book geek, and these were the days before a superhero movie was in theaters every month. Besides, I would be back to watching reruns of *The Flash* soon enough.

The basement was partway above ground, and the slits of windows looked at the front yard from beneath the porch. There was a door to a stairway leading to a boardwalk toward the front of the house. The back room had food storage. The furnace room had the water heater and the washer and dryer. It was behind the futon, and we shut the door when the sounds drowned the volume on the TV.

Aside from TV and movies, I read Stephen King novels, trash vampire books, and issues of comics accumulated from trips to Anchorage. I spent hours drawing super-powered characters at my desk. The pictures wallpapered the room where music was always playing. I gathered CDs by peeling stamps from a catalog, licking the backs, affixed them to a sheet, putting the sheet in an envelope, dropping the envelope into the big blue mailbox at the Post Office, and waiting six to eight weeks for delivery. I paused the music when Mom barged in to ask if I'd like to invite a friend over.

"All you do is sit in this dark basement all day," she said. "It's not normal!"

There was only one time Mom didn't let me go to a friend's house. My class was sitting on top of our desks, watching *FernGully* when the bell rang. It was time to get in line and walk to recess. Instead of scooting off my desk, I stepped to the next one, the next one, and the next, walking across an entire row of desks, and jumped down into line. Mrs. Gasca sent me to the principal's office. Of course, Mom knew about it. In fact, she saw me in there.

After school, LJ asked if I could come over.

"I don't think so," I said.

"Come on," he said. "Ask your mom."

With my head down, I shuffled my feet into her classroom.

"Can I go to LJ's?" I couldn't look her in the eye.

"I think you better go right home," she said.

Later in the year, I sat in the office, pretending to be in trouble, waiting for Mom to see me. When she didn't come, I sent a classmate to her classroom, two doors away. She still didn't come. I gave up and told her she ruined the joke. She said she was glad it was a joke, because she was just about to call Dad and tell him she had second thoughts about giving me my birthday present.

I did get that present. Mom and Dad had wrapped a gigantic box. They smiled with anticipation as I unwrapped it to find another box inside another box. Inside the smallest box was a booklet with diagrams of a fourwheeler, and different chapters on safe driving and troubleshooting. I had no idea it was an owner's manual as I flipped through it, and I feigned excitement about a book of tips about how to be a more skilled driver. Then Mom and Dad told me to dig for the key and led me to the garage where I had my new fourwheeler.

It was a Honda 200, a small fourwheeler for a small kid. It was a basic design — red, with a storage compartment in the back, and most important, and electric start. With one push of a button, the engine started. There was no ninja-kicking or tearing at a pull-cord required. It changed gears with a lift up or push down with my left foot. Soon, I was riding my fourwheeler to friends' houses and to school. Many kids did, and we took off at lunchtime to ride down the Beach Access Road to the platform overlooking the River. As other kids had fourwheelers of their own, it was a main form of recreation.

When I was fourteen, Dad took me and some friends up the King Salmon Trail, outside of King Salmon, on threewheelers and fourwheelers and we spent the night in a cabin at the end of it. On the way back, one of those friends flipped a threewheeler and it landed on his leg, breaking it. He was one of the star basketball players and the season was about to start.

The summer after my freshman year of high school, Mom and Dad encouraged me to buy my own vehicle with the fishing money I'd been saving. Dad had won and sold a Ford Ranger at Fishtival, and it seemed to have been a decent enough vehicle. What I cared about most was when I went to college, I could throw my things in the back. I wanted four-wheel drive for obvious reasons, and a stick shift because it was cool to drive a stick shift, even though it was tough for me to learn. I don't know how I didn't blow out the clutch of Mom's Jeep.

Before the fishing season, Dad and I went to Seattle and went truck shopping. Men in ties swooped like seagulls at every dealership and pecked at us until we either left or made a purchase. First it was one tie. Then another would join. Soon, three, four, or five ties ganged up on us, sweet-talking us toward signing papers. If I were by myself, I would have run as quickly as I could down the sidewalk, never to be seen again. Dad, however, was a guy who would take the time to talk to telemarketers during dinner unless Mom screamed at him to hang up and get back to dinner for chrissakes. I didn't want to be sweet-talked by a telemarketer. I wanted to buy a truck I wanted to buy.

We were just about to leave another dealer when I saw a cherry red Ford Ranger with a stepside, an extended cab, stick shift, and three-liter, six-cylinder engine. I knew what four of those six details meant, but it was a truck I liked, and I saw it first. It's the truck I bought, and Dad directed me through the stoplights and intersections of Seattle traffic, my muscles tense and every movement outside amplified.

Mom, Luke, and Erica arrived in Seattle after I'd bought the truck, and they took it on a cross-country trip while Dad and I returned north for the fishing season. That was the deal. Mom got to borrow the truck, and she and Dad would pay the shipping costs to get it to Naknek. Of course, she loaded it with dry goods from the Costco in Seattle before sending it on the barge. I was 15 and couldn't drive on my own yet anyway. I still rode my fourwheeler to school.

After the truck arrived on the barge, it sat in the garage for months before I was sixteen. I took the driver's test, which was a lap around the Air Force Base, and I was given a card with a license to drive. I was free to travel in my own truck, in one direction down the Alaska Peninsula Highway and the other. I was one step closer to beginning a journey on a road out of Naknek.

I lasted about a month before I filled the truck with diesel fuel. I didn't know anything was wrong until morning when the engine died after I backed out of the garage. I pushed the truck back into the garage and took Luke to school on the fourwheeler. Mom and Dad couldn't believe how stupid I was, I didn't know how stupid I was, and I didn't want anyone to know how stupid I was, so I told kids at school I did something bad and that my truck had been "taken away" by my parents.

"What did you do?" kids asked. "What did you do to get your truck taken away?"

"Something bad," I said. "Don't worry about it."

Dad needed a new fuel filter to fix it, and when he ordered one, the wrong one arrived. He ordered another, and it repeated. It was the wrong one. The truck was such a new design that no one needed a new fuel filter, so he had to order directly from the factory. After two months, my truck was on the road again.

Then I put two scratches in the sides parking in the garage. They weren't small scratches, but long, deep scratches down all the panels, front to back. Every time I'd parked, Dad had told me I wasn't close enough to the wall for Mom to park the Jeep. I was lucky to be parking in the garage in the first place, and if I didn't learn how to park close enough to the wall, I'd need to park outside.

I came home from wrestling practice like any other day, hungry and exhausted, but this time, I turned the wheel hard, and the side of the truck grazed the side of the garage door. I got out, inspected it, saw it was unscathed. I figured the rubber lining on the door must be for this purpose, so I pulled forward and put the scratches in the truck. I spent the evening screaming, throwing things, and scaring the hell out my little brother.

I conjured a story that I was parking and couldn't hear the scratching because the stereo was up too loud. Then I walked out and saw that, oops, I had tarnished the shiny cherry red paint, deep into the metal. Neither the story nor the real one could keep my stupidity secret. When I scratched the truck, it was still wintertime, and it was dark before school and after school, but by springtime, when daylight shined early, people started asking about the scratches. The winter wasn't enough time to come up with a good story. I paid to have it fixed, but I would always know the mistakes beneath the surface.

I moved back and forth on the Highway in an enclosed space, separating the wind, the weather, and the elements from myself. The cab of a vehicle was inside, as opposed to outside, and the windshield was a mere screen, like the screen I stared into at news stories and movies and commercials. My introverted nature would never change, but I guess it still needed a different channel.

"This is the Alaska Department of Fish and Game in King Salmon with an announcement for commercial fishermen in the Naknek-Kvichak District."

The words from KDLG are surrounded by soft static, and they hold as much tension as a net when the tide is running the hardest. Conversations end in the middle of a boatyard. A game of cards in a cabin comes to a standstill. An afternoon of trying to start a stubborn motor stops. Aside from the voice on the radio announcing our fate, Naknek pauses.

"The time is 3:00 PM. and the date is Monday, June 24th, 1996. In the Naknek-Kvichak District through 2:00 PM today, Naknek River escapement was 95,000 sockeye for a cumulative of 111,000. The Kvichak River escapement was 264 sockeye for a cumulative of 2,400."

The run is here, and Dad scribbles the numbers down in his *Capt'n Jack's Tide & Current Almanac.* The fishing districts of Bristol Bay are some of the last sustainable commercial fisheries in the world, and they have remained sustainable with the regulation of the Alaska Department of Fish and Game since the 1950s. An opener is decided based on escapement, and escapement is measured by sample fishing, prediction, and someone standing on a counting tower up the river decide our fate. Then the decision is relayed to the radio station.

"The Naknek-Kvichak District will open to set gillnet gear for an eight-hour period from 5:00 AM until 1:00 PM Tuesday, June 25th. Drift fishermen in the Naknek-Kvichak District should stand-by at 9:00 AM Wednesday, June 26th."

Fishermen, both setnetters and drifters, gather to Bristol Bay every summer from faraway lands, seeking glory and gain, harvesting millions of pounds of wild-caught Alaskan salmon and collecting a check at the end of the season. Some fishermen spend one summer, live out an authentic Alaskan experience a little too authentic, and never come back. Some of them buy a boat, lease a site, and it becomes a lifestyle. Then there is the spawn of those people. There are those of us who start fishing because of a dad who asks, "Want to go fishing next summer?" which means, "You're going fishing next summer."

In his early 30s, Dad fished by himself, not something done by any mere mortal with a wooden skiff, Evinrude outboard motor, and a couple of 25-fathom nets. Like raising kids or building a house, he learned to fish on his own. He made his fair share of mistakes, of course. For instance, there is his story about getting caught in the anchorline after setting a net. As the tide tightened the line around his shin, he knew he'd either pass out from pain or be pulled overboard and drown. He cut the line with the knife in his pocket. The reason it took him so long was all the fish he was catching.

He had only one permit back then. He'd hired different crew, like the music teacher from Oklahoma, nephews of friends, and his Vietnam-weathered brother Pat who stopped coming back because Dad was "too mean." When he got the second permit, however, he could put in another 50 fathoms of gear. Luke held it last year, but now the permit is mine.

When I start fishing, Dad recruits Cameron Porter whose Coast Guard training ended with a faulty oxygen tank ruining his lungs. He has a hacking cough, but he's a non-smoker, non-drinker, and he's built like a small bear — perfect attributes of a quality deckhand. Dad put an ad in the classifieds, and Cameron responded to it from Oregon. He met our entire family at the Ted Stevens Airport in Anchorage during a trip to Florida this winter. Cameron's wife was a flight attendant, so it wasn't a major expense to hop on a plane from Portland to Anchorage.

"He looks good and strong," Mom said. Dad agreed.

I'm eleven, and I stand four-foot-nine, weighing 87 pounds, according to the photo ID that I'm required to have onboard along with my permit card. Beneath my layers, my cards hang from my neck on a piece of the same twine that holds the corks on the nets. The gloves on the ends of my arms can't even reach the cork line from the bow.

Cameron and I stand in the water on the beach in Naknek below City Dock, holding the purple skiff. It's not a dark purple. It's a lighter, lavender kind of purple, like a forget-me-not, the Alaska state flower. It's not the original Labamba. It was thrashed by waves and it's been replaced just like another purple coat of paint. Although the change is undetectable to most people, the shade of purple has ranged from *Extravagance*, *Flowered Tundra*, to my personal favorite, *Pansy*. We simply call this skiff the Purp.

Cameron shoves the Purp off the beach as I hop into it, tumbling over the side. Dad starts the motor, and we head out of the Naknek River and turn into the Kvichak toward Graveyard. Dad takes us into the creek, and Cameron jumps out with the anchor and carries it up the steep incline of the beach. I jump out and sink into the mud. It holds me by the thighs, and the more I struggle, the harder it is to pull myself out. Cameron stands to my left. Dad stands to my right. They hoist me up by the armpits. I scramble up the bank on hands and knees, onto hard dirt. Dad and Cameron laugh, unload the totes, the cooler, the heater, the stove, the propane tank, the water jugs, and our bags, and we all haul them across the dirt path through the trees.

After our first trip back to Naknek, Cameron drives the green skiff out to the Kvichak behind Dad. We keep it parked by one of the nets in case there are too many fish to handle before the closure. My jobs are tying brailers, throwing fish into them, holding the skiff off the beach as the tide goes out, holding the skiff in as the tide comes in, and bailing out water, bailing out water, and bailing out more water. The Purp has a leak somewhere in the bottom of the stern.

After we load the Purp with fish, Dad pulls back his raincoat sleeve to look at his watch, which I have learned means the closure is soon. Fish and Game will see our nets from a chopper and pull no punches in punishment. The least they'll do is give us a fine. The most they'll do is take the nets, put the delivered fish on their own tab, and take away our fishing privileges.

Dad pulls it up to the green skiff and Cameron throws out the bow anchor to keep it in place. They hop into it and Dad starts its motor. He tells me not to let the Purp sink, and that there is a Butterfinger candy bar and a Barq's Root Beer in the orange, plastic snack box. Then Dad and Cameron disappear into the distance, their wake rocking the skiff side to side. It fades, but it never stops.

All around me is gray sky and its rough reflection on the water. It's the first time on the water I'm alone, and I stay hunched in the stern, scraping the square edge of a plastic bucket against the bottom, between the ribs, scooping water, brackish with salt and blood. The blood thins as the fish stiffen. They are all sockeye, and the aquatic green in their skin dulls to a dead gray. Every splash is clearer than the last splash. Every splash means more water to leak back into the floor. The fish are no longer bleeding, but the skiff still does.

Soon, Dad and Cameron will come back, and we'll deliver two skiffloads to the tender. Weeks from now, the season will be over, and I can go back to the comforts of my basement room, but I don't think this is my last season. I don't think this is the last time I'll stand alone in a sinking skiff.

I always thought most school mascots in Southwest Alaska were fitting. There were the Pilot Point Lynx, the Togiak Huskies, the Newhalen Malamutes, the Kokhanok Warlords, the Bethel Warriors, and the Dillingham Wolverines. It seemed that the Bristol Bay Sockeye would have been the most fitting mascot for our school, but we were the Angels, purple and gold, with Angel Power, Angel Pride, Go-Angels-Go attitude, and other Angelriffic chants and Angeltastic slogans. At least it was more appropriate and politically correct than the Aniak Halfbreeds.

It was never competition or Angel Pride bringing me to the games. Contributing factors were the raw appeal of a physical challenge and maybe the fear of missing out, but it was mostly the chance to fly somewhere other than Naknek that kept me active in sports. A load of us kids packed into a nine-passenger Cherokee, or sometimes something even smaller, soared over the tundra, and spent the night on a classroom floor before competing in the morning. Wrestling was in the fall, basketball was in the winter, and Native Youth Olympics was in the spring. Volleyball was during the wrestling season, for just girls.

Like any Naknek kid, I played basketball from the time I was in third grade, in the youth program. Then, as it was expected of me, I continued into highschool. I looked at the ball to dribble, drills were hard to remember, and my shot was atrocious. In other words, I sucked, everyone knew I sucked, and kids at school reminded me how much I sucked by saying things like, "You suck." I'd say they were making fun of me, but I never thought they were having fun. When other kids criticized my basketball skills, they had anger in their eyes and hate in their hearts.

"You fucking suck, Keith," I heard often.

"You're a piece-of-shit player, Keith," I heard more.

"Why don't you kill yourself, Keith?" This one, I heard once.

Confident enough in my reasons to live, I went through the motions, even though my motions were clumsy and unskilled. In the youth program, kids were split into teams to scrimmage on the weekends. One team grabbed blue mesh jerseys from a bag, and the other team had the luxury of running up and down the court without the smell of accumulated sweat hitting us in the face.

"Stay between your man and the basket," was easy enough to follow, and I was so determined that I would stay between my man and the basket even when my team was on the offense. My mind was elsewhere. I don't know where it was, but it was somewhere far away from a basketball court. I dreaded the moment someone might pass me the ball, and I yearned for someone from the bench to take my position. It usually didn't take long. I was told to be more aggressive, but I felt if I ever had my hands on the ball, the scrutiny over what I did with it was never worth the trouble.

In middle school, I went on my first overnight trip to Dillingham. Nine kids climbed into a Cherokee at King Airfield in Naknek, and it sputtered down the runway toward the Naknek River, and we took off over the Kvichak Bay and the Nushagak River. The engines hummed in my ears the entire way before we landed on the paved runway at in Dillingham. We took a bus to the school and slept on the floor of the Science room on the second level of the building. It was across a similar room, next to the elevator, and down the hall from the KDLG studio next to the bathroom. I would take this same trip at least a dozen times.

We rearranged desks into fortresses for our sleeping bags. The better players fought over the spot behind the teacher's desk, and Pete, our coach, slept by the door. Even now, if I happen to sleep on a floor, I still expect Pete to start dictating pushups to silence troublemakers during the night. I woke up sore and stiff, ran a lap with the team in front of the crowd, and reported immediately to the bench, listening to cheers for Dillingham and jeers for us. My bouts on the court during an actual game were no more than 30 seconds.

Wrestling was different. In wrestling, there was only one Angel in the spotlight at a time, making it all the more terrifying. The outfits were even more revealing than volleyball shorts and rolling around in purple spandex with sweaty guys didn't appeal to me. Norm and Riel were into wrestling, and they liked watching the professional matches, even as many times as I pointed out that they were fake.

"So?" Norm said, "Comic books are fake, aren't they?"

I didn't wrestle until ninth grade, when Joey joined and Shoosh joined. It was the year the twins my age lived in Naknek, and they had good talking points like, "Only pussies don't wrestle."

While the volleyball team practiced in the New Gym, an addition of the building in 1992, we were in the smaller and more rustic Old Gym, running laps, performing calisthenics, practicing drills, learning new moves, and sprinting across the gym, sprinting across the gym, and sprinting across the gym again. Then we'd sprint across the gym. When we thought it was the last sprint, we'd have one more sprint. Back and forth across the mats, we sucked wind, insides screaming. Every other part of practice was just as long and just as draining, but it was the last part that made it longer and tougher. I'd go home dizzy, famished, dehydrated, muscles full of acid, and collapse onto the couch for hours.

On occasion, we ran outside. We started from the school, ran down the decline after the Post Office, and up the incline to Fisherman's Bar. Then we ran onto the gravel Beach Access Road and up another hill before turning back. I dreaded the run like everyone else, but once we got going, I fell into a rhythm I never seemed to embrace when running laps around the mats.

The class two years older was all boys. They were three-quarters of the team, and they didn't make practice any easier. They liked to throw basketballs at freshmen during laps. They shoved us behind the mats when they were rolled against the wall. They held us down and pounded our foreheads with their knuckles until we could name ten kinds of candy bars. When I could name them without pause, they started asking for car manufacturers or brands of spark plugs.

My first match was at our home gym, the New Gym, the rectangular Angel Dome where I stood inside the white circle in front of the bleachers in front of the community. I knew everyone in the audience, and they all knew me — this little purple bullseye in the middle of a giant target.

My opponent's arms dangled like a gorilla's arms, and he had the kind of hands meant for strangling angels. With his foot on a strip of red tape and mine on the green, we shook hands, and I could feel his raw strength. At the whistle, everything I'd learned in practice blew clean out of my head. Single leg? Double leg? Sprawl? What was my coach shouting? What were they shouting from the bleachers?

My entire body tensed like I was trying to summon an exoskeleton or Iron Man armor, but the only physical layer between reality and my body was purple spandex. With my arms and legs locked in a hold that I couldn't name, there was nothing I could do but flop like a fish underneath the weight of an Aniak Halfbreed until my back was flat against the mat. After the whistle, I scurried to the locker room.

I got better, but I was never particularly good. Practice pushed my physical limits, and I was curious to find out what they were. The older guys were brutal, but I never felt hated or threatened. They offered knowledge and guidance just as soon as they would smash me behind a rolled mat or tap their knuckles on my forehead. When we took a trip somewhere, we were comrades, brothers, soldiers on the same side. We were less angels and more warriors with acne and purple spandex. Wrestlers were the tough guys, and I wanted to think that I was a tough guy.

Native Youth Olympics is the sport where I proved my toughness by hopping across a hardwood gym floor in a pushup position on my knuckles. This teenage version of the Arctic Winter Games and the World Indian Olympics was in the spring. Although not a drop of Aleut blood flowed through my veins, and not a Yup'ik bone held the structure of my scrawny body, I started in seventh grade, as soon as I could start. The State Tournament was in Anchorage, and almost everyone on the team got to go.

The events included the Kneel Jump, the Wrist Carry, the Stick Pull, Leg Wrestling, the Scissors Broad Jump, the One-Hand Reach, the Alaskan High Kick, the Two-Foot High Kick, the One-Foot High Kick, and at the end of any tournament as a grand finale, the Seal

Hop — my event. Athletes jumped, carried, pulled, wrestled, leaped, reached, kicked, and hopped all over the basketball court, but by eighth grade, I realized that I was the only kid in school who could make it any significant distance in the Seal Hop.

For the Seal Hop, athletes started facedown at one end of the gym in a pushup position. Then we hopped with flat backs and straight bellies on our knuckles and toes. If and when we reached the other end of the gym, it was time to hop in a circle and start our way back. It wasn't a race. It wasn't about who got anywhere first. The winner was whoever made it the farthest.

As basketball had proven, I was not prone to learning an athletic skill, but as a Seal Hopper, I didn't need skill. I just needed to endure the burn in my muscles and the pounding of a hardwood floor against my knuckles. During NYO practice, as everyone else leaped and jumped and pulled and tugged, I did as many pushups and sit-ups as possible before falling on my face. Then I'd do it again. Once or twice in practice, I'd give myself a trial hop down the gym floor — gut, chest and triceps burning, knuckles bleeding from scraped skin, earning my ticket to Anchorage.

At the 1999 State Tournament, we spent our nights at the Marriott. We spent the days at the campus of the University of Alaska in the gymnasium where the events opened with traditional ceremonies of drums and dancing and sealskin trampolines held by human hands. I was the only middleschooler from Bristol Bay, tagging along with highschoolers at Fifth Avenue and Dimond Center Mall where we watched *the Matrix* in the theater and killed aliens in the arcade. It was on this trip when I got my first phone number from a girl. She wrote the Valdez number on a torn scrap of pink paper, and I kept that piece of paper for a long time.

I went to the State Tournament every year, and every year I specialized in the Seal Hop. Every year, there was a controversial judgment to stop me for my elbows being too far apart or my butt being too high. I was convinced it was because I was white. Whether or not it was true or my own projection, I was never regretful. After all, competition was not my favorite part.

After the dance that always took place after the last day of the games, there were vans packed with Native Youth Olympians at almost every stoplight. One van would begin rocking side to side, the weight

of a dozen kids shifting weight. Another van would follow suit. Entire
fleets of vans rocked at intersecting roads across Anchorage. Some teams
had driven from places like Seward, Kenai, Homer, and Valdez —
towns on the road system. The rest of us, who had flown from places
like Togiak, Newhalen, Kokhanok, Bethel, Dillingham, and Naknek
rocked harder than the others. We were like waves in the channel, or
fish tails waving in the streets of the city where we were all born.

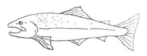

       The Alaska Department of Fish and Game has counted
nowhere near the expected numbers for the run to the Kvichak this
summer. It's early, but later isn't looking good either. No districts
are getting the numbers, but the Kvichak has the lowest of them
all. I'm 12, and it's my second season, but I can figure out how dim
it looks. Dad, Cameron, and I are at Graveyard when an emergency
order period opens the Naknek Section of the Naknek-Kvichak
District while the Kvichak Section will remain closed.
       By the Fourth of July, the entire district is closed and the
Kvichak run isn't looking any better. The entire Naknek-Kvichak
District will be shoved into the Naknek River Special Harvest Area
for the first time since 1982 — meaning fishing will happen in
Naknek River. In the Naknek River Special Harvest Area,
fishermen are allowed one half the normal gear, which means we
are allowed 50 fathoms with our two permits. Established sites are
non-existent and, according to law, anyone can set a net anywhere,
as long as it's the legal distance from the next site, but no site is
official until the opening is official. Friends, relatives, community
members, and strangers scramble to get a spot where they can catch
enough fish to feed their families.
       Dad is on the beach when the special announcement for
commercial fishermen in the Naknek-Kvichak District happens,
and he jams a sign close to where he thinks the border will be. He
doesn't know it's the first site in the Special Harvest Area. The next
site down, he claims for Lynn, a family friend who's staying at the
house right now, since she can't fish from her cabin. The positions

of the signs, however, are binding in no way except common understanding among people. They have no legal status. The legal status of a site belongs to the first net in the water.

The guy who wants our spot is lanky like a crane looking for clams in the beach. He squawks like Batman's adversary, the Penguin, and like the Penguin, he's committed some crimes worthy of jail time. To complete the image, a cigarette always dangles between his lips. The Penguin isn't about to let us have the first site without a fight, and Fish and Game has told Dad if this conflict isn't resolved, both of them will be fined, and neither of them will have the site.

There are only moments before the opening as Dad and Cameron prepare to set the nets. Skiffs line both sides of the river with nets ready to uncoil. Troopers are gathered on the beach around their white trucks. Choppers swoop from above and news reporters wait patiently with cameras. Driftboats in the channel wait as well. Crouched in an aluminum skiff behind one of them is our friend, ready to swoop. Dad stands in the stern with the motor idling, and Cameron stands knee-deep in the water, holding the bow on the beach. Mom won't let Dad let me in the skiff, so I'm on the beach with her as she paces back and forth, groaning.

Then watches beep, and we all know it's time. Dad twists the throttle, and the Purp forges toward the channel, one cork after another releasing into the water. Cameron jumps in and lifts Big Bertha, our biggest anchor of 60 pounds, ready to throw when the net stretches all the way out. The Penguin revs his motor, beginning his own set from the opposite direction. Fathom after fathom shoots out, and his aluminum bow smashes into the side of the purple skiff's wooden bow. Mom groans again. I clench my eyes shut, imagining it breaking apart.

When I open my eyes, our friend has wrapped his own net in his propeller. Dad's skiff has continued unharmed, successfully setting fifty fathoms into the water — 25 for Dad's permit, and 25 for mine. Cameron tosses Big Bertha and with a quick splash of water, its flukes are in the floor of the Naknek River.

300 feet down the beach, a local brother and sister are trying the same thing on Lynn, but they aren't quick enough, and they float away without a site.

"We shouldn't be fighting each other," yells the sister. "We should be fighting them!"

She points to the troopers on the beach, standing by their white trucks. Mom tells her she's wrong. Without the Alaska Department of Fish and Game, we don't have a sustainable fishery.

Drifters at the front line stop fish from collecting in any nets other than ours as they splash, charge, and barge each other to lay out a net in front of each other. Governor Tony Knowles calls 1997 a disaster. Of only nineteen million returning salmon of what should have been thirty million, thirteen million salmon are caught, half of them in Egegik. All districts suffer. On the Naknek River, I drive back and forth on the beach with my fourwheeler and see fishermen cooking their catch — two, maybe four, filets over a bonfire. Dad and Cameron catch more fish than anyone all summer, but that isn't saying much.

No one can prove why numbers are so low, but everyone knows why the imaginary current of the communities suffer. Dad says the low numbers are due to over-escapement of the parent year. He and the other veterans of fishing all say the same thing, and I hear them talk about it for years. The headwaters are only so large, and too many fish would break a delicate balance.

What they are saying is nature needs fishermen like fish need water, but I'm not so sure about that. This logic would assume there is too much crude oil under our planet's surface, and it needs to be extracted, refined, and pumped into the air by our motors so the climate can change. It would assume the garbage I see drifters toss from their vessels needed to be in the water and wash ashore or tangle into our nets.

On September 11th, 2001, Korean Air Flight 85 was about to land in Anchorage, and Dick Cheney and the Gang wanted the Air Force to blow it out of the sky. I was a junior in highschool. Mom and Dad were in Anchorage for appointments. Mom called the school office to tell me that the city was about to be evacuated. I headed back to

American Government to questions from my classmates that I didn't know how to answer.

The plane was diverted to Whitehorse, and one less load of passengers had an unfortunate end that day. Anchorage wasn't evacuated, but no one was allowed to fly for a couple of days either. Mom and Dad were stuck in Anchorage, my trip to science camp on Lake Bacharof was canceled, and the Air Force escorted private planes to the ground. Hunters and trappers who had flown away from the internet, TV, and radio had no idea the attacks on the World Trade Center had happened.

I wondered if I'd have preferred to be on the tundra, away from civilization, somewhere unaware of the devastation, panic, and confusing aftermath. I didn't need to leave Naknek to feel the awkward combination of patriotism and fear spreading across the country. Even in Naknek, flags flew from car antennas, and the talk of war was in the air. School was canceled for a day-and-a-half when an envelope arrived with a trace of white powder. Students gathered into the auditorium and cheered at the announcement.

Commercial air travel was never the same. TSA wanted shoes off, pockets empty, no knives, no sharp objects, and soon enough, there were no liquids, gels, or pastes either. They said to step through the x-ray machine and put your hands up. As they sent troops into Iraq, Dick Cheney and the Gang said to go shopping. Otherwise, the terrorists would win. They compiled a list of songs not to hear, shows not to watch, and movies not to see, including the upcoming *Spider-man*. They'd tell us who our heroes were, and it wasn't some teenager in tights, goddamnit.

I was in the midst of wrestling season, and I kept my own tights in an underwear drawer. In November, our regional wrestling tournament was Aniak, a village to the north of us, on the Kuskokwim River, and the Yup'ik word for "the place where it comes out."

Despite all the commotion, getting to Aniak required no security protocol whatsoever. We threw our bags into the back of the plane, and we were allowed onboard as long as we wore a coat, snowpants, boots, a hat, and a pair of gloves. My teammates and I boarded with no problems and no scrutiny. Most of us carried water bottles with much more than three ounces of fluid. I had a knife in the left pocket of my snowpants.

Tundra and sky soared through the windows. After an hour of music in my headphones drowning the engine noise, we landed on a gravel landing strip and stepped into a one-room terminal. A van picked us up and brought us to the school, where the parking lot was full of fourwheelers and snowmachines. Other than the van, there were no enclosed vehicles.

Food was waiting for us on a fold-out cafeteria table in the school's commons area. Bags of Oreos were torn open. Gatorade splashed into Dixie cups from plastic pitchers. Stacks of sandwiches were piled onto paper plates. Each sandwich was a slice of Velveeta cheese, two slices of bologna, and a half cup of mayonnaise oozing between the spongy white bread, soaking in the room temperature.

In Alaska, what was once a place of mass consumption of seal oil and whale blubber, this concoction in plastic jars had been assimilated as a condiment for Sailor Boy Pilot Bread, fries, fish, and fingers fresh for the licking. I scraped as much of it off the bread as I could. I dumped mounds of it onto my paper plate, passing it to anyone at the table eager to take it. It churned in my stomach the entire night, and I woke many times to roll over against the floor.

The first morning in Aniak, our team awoke on the vinyl tile of the Home Economics room in the satellite building across the parking lot. We scurried over to the gym for breakfast, frostbite chasing us. The chill factor outside was around 100 below zero, but the boxed milk in our Cheerios was as warm as the mayonnaise.

My tights were under my warmup outfit like everyone else. They were still clean before the sweat and the showerless days to follow. As always, Bob gave us a speech. Inspiration was his style. Like Henry V or Winston Churchill, his words motivated us to move mountains, and he told us that we could do as such. If we pushed to the best of our ability, gave it our all, and were willing to work 110 percent, we could do anything we set our minds to.

I felt what he said, but I didn't believe it. I figured there had to be limits to our physical potential, but I was sure I hadn't reached mine. I was sure almost no one ever did. I wasn't the best wrestler because I lacked the killer instinct, but there was still a thrill from fighting to get free, like a gilled fish, kicking and thrashing and fighting for my life.

Riel and I agreed that nothing could calm our nerves before a match. An amplified voice would announce who was in the hole, who was on deck, and who was now wrestling. Even when I was just in the hole, I was already jumping side to side, dropping to push-ups, jumping back up to run in place, and doing everything to get fired up and shake away the nerves. When I was on deck, nothing could hold back the shakiness, uneasiness, and dry mouth.

Then I heard it before my first match during that tournament. "And now wrestling…" shot surges of anxiety through my entire body as I walked onto the mat tense and jumpy.

I don't remember much of that match. Like the fastest races I've run as an adult, it was all a blur. I remember starting and pushing to finish as soon as I possibly could. All I remember is me and the kid from Togiak rolling, grabbing, and flipping each other around the mat. We went into the third round, taking turns in the dominant position. Then I pinned him. I looked up to see my entire team jumping and cheering at the edge of the mat. I wish I could remember it, as everyone, including kids I didn't know, told me how exciting it was to watch. I was even presented with a Match of the Year award.

On day two in Aniak, I woke up on the floor of the Home Economics room sore, smelly, and without much energy. I didn't win any matches that day either. It was evening when our team was gathered around the TV, watching the VHS tape I'd brought of *Saturday Night Live's Best of Adam Sandler*. Then the building started shaking. It was from footsteps. The Bethel Warriors raided our room. The Togiak Huskies followed them. Then it was the Kotzebue Huskies. Soon, all kinds of husky kids, skinny kids, muscular kids, and odd-shaped kids were in our room watching Adam Sandler.

Across the parking lot, smoke spiraled from the roof of the gym. A fire had started in an air vent, we were told, and everyone in the building had been shooed away. It seemed like the safety of our humble little abode across the parking lot was the place to go. Hundreds of teenage boys and a handful of teenage girls crammed between desks, into mini-kitchens, and against the walls. Shoulder to shoulder with the Bethel Warriors, I watched Adam Sandler sing "Lunch Lady Land" with Chris Farley.

I didn't win another match, and I welcomed the time to fly home. Once again dodging frostbite's jaws, with bags in hand, we boarded the van to the airport. Scrambling out, we regrouped inside the terminal to wait. A salty crust stuck my skin to my clothes, and I assumed all of us experienced the same feeling. We lay scattered over the pile of duffel bags in the room not much larger than a jail cell, and we waited for our plane. Then a pudgy woman from behind the counter waddled over to us. Her breath was a spew of bad news and cigarettes.

"Are you the boys from Bristol Bay?"

No one said anything. Bob nodded.

"Your plane is broke. You guys can leave tomorrow, uh?"

The Alaskan *uh*, like the Canadian *eh*, suggested that her statement was a question, but we had no choice. Everyone stayed silent as she waited for a response.

"Okay," said Bob. "I guess that's the way it goes."

She waddled her way back out into the wind and cold, a new cigarette already between her lips. The van once again brought us to the school, and we glumly found spots for our sleeping bags in a classroom down the hall from the commons area. Our coaches relayed what they had just been told by the principal. We weren't going anywhere tomorrow. Aniak was expecting a blizzard for the next two days.

The next day was Monday, and we were awoken early to move into the library, as much out of the way as possible. Outside was white wind and nothing else, but the library also had wall-sized windows into the commons area. Before school, students peered at us, tapping on the glass. None of us reacted. We just looked out at them, knowing that when class was in session, we had 50 minutes to roam the halls, living the secret lives of zoo animals.

In the afternoon, we shot hoops with local kids, and other teams stuck in Aniak. At night, we forced the latch of the kitchen door with a pocketknife to scavenge for food. We found Neapolitan ice cream, peanut butter, a jar of pickles, two loaves of Wonder Bread, and a big bowl of macaroni salad floating in mayonnaise. It was days old, and the sight and smell of it sent my stomach into a stir. That night in my sleeping bag, I held my stomach with my hands until I felt the need to fumble for my flashlight and stumble to the bathrooms. Nothing erupted but dry-heaves as I bent over the stains and streaks in the toilet bowl. I listened to the howling wind outside as I wandered back to the room.

We were on a plane on Tuesday, and I watched Aniak disappear beneath me, behind an oval of double-layered glass. I shoved in my earplugs, closed my eyes, and dreamed of a shower. I felt too hot wearing my snowpants in the fuselage, but I thought maybe new sweat would break away the old sweat, and I embraced it. Then a refreshing cool draft gently brushed the back of my neck. I turned around and the winter wind blasted me in the face.

Riel was in the backseat with his eyes wide open and his hands gripped tight around the door handle. Kyle was next to him, laughing the way Kyle laughed with that goofy grin he had. The wind was gushing in from the open door, and I could see the endless miles of snow-covered tundra soaring beneath us without a shield of glass in front of it.

The reality of being airborne, blazing through the sky, had never been as apparent as it was this moment. A window was just a barrier between one reality and another, but it was a thin one. It was like the fabric of a tent or the electronic screen between me and the towers crumbling in New York City.

The pilot said the door wouldn't open any more, but Riel didn't take his word for it. His grip on the handle didn't loosen for the rest of the flight, and the open space next to him exposed the open space all around us. Aniak was one small settlement in the middle of it all, and where we landed was just another one, but it was home.

I drove to the house, let the shower burn away the stick and salt of five days, and I plummeted face-down onto my bed. School was out in an hour and Riel had convinced me going was pointless, but when the phone rang, I groaned and got up to answer it. I knew who it was.

"You better get down here," Mom said. "It's called skipping if you don't."

I put on clothes, drove to school, and walked late into English, just in time to write another poem about September 11th.

It's not the wind or the waves but the sound of the motor that wakes me. It's slack tide, and the ebb is about to start. The fishing seasons are starting to run together. I could be thirteen or eighteen right now. Either way, the motor starting means it's time to check the nets. The skiff's wooden ribs are pressed against my own ribs while I lay on my side, but a raincoat, lifejacket, chest waders, sweatshirt, and long johns soften the pressure. My head is propped against the anchor, and my boots are pressed against the bulkhead in the bow. Both legs are asleep, so I reach the gunnel of the skiff and pull up my cold carcass.

Dreaming, I didn't notice the blood recruited away from fingers and toes to heart and lungs. Awake, I feel the numbness and the cold in my limbs. It's an involuntary function of my body to stay alive. I learned in school that if I can shut off the shivering, I'm fine. I can, but I don't want to, because it provides an illusion of warmth. I'm alive, and I can reach down to the buoy just fine.

We're at Johnston Hill. The Naknek section is open, but the Kvichak Section is closed, which means we can't fish our own sites. Between the Nushagak River to the north, and the Egegik River to the south, Bristol Bay narrows into the Kvichak Bay, and the Kvichak Bay narrows into the Kvichak River. The Naknek Section is maybe a third of it. It stretches from the once-was cannery of Libbyville, north of the Naknek River, to Johnston Hill, south of the Naknek River.

From Graveyard, Johnston Hill is a pimple on our planet's surface. North of the Naknek River, between the Y and Libbyville is a line of cabins along the bank, without a single open site. The stretch of beach by Johnston Hill has enough open spaces, where we are likely to find enough space to set nets the required 300 feet from the next ones. It's common practice to take a nap on the floor of the skiff when the fishing is slow, but at Johnston Hill, we don't have a camp. We lay out the nets and then stay all night.

Twenty-five fathoms into the pulling net, there have been six fish. I don't want to stop pulling to pick them. Pulling the net keeps me warm. The muscle contractions in my back and shoulders combined with the friction of the cork line against my gloves create a minor amount of heat, and I hope it spreads through the rest of me. My legs have full feeling by the time there are nine fish, but I'm still shivering by the time we are through the first net. I look forward to the Kvichak opening, or even the Special Harvest Area opening, because these Johnston Hill nights are brutal.

Late in the season, it's a different story except for the absence of other fishermen. Almost everyone has left Graveyard, and Dad and I have moved our nets to the available space on the beach at Graveyard Point. It means we get to sleep for another half hour every time we take a snooze.

Fish are hitting hard, but not too hard to handle. In a few hours, we've filled three brailers, which is well worth our time fishing into late July. Seeing these numbers wouldn't be a sobering feat if two thirds of them weren't pinks. Every time I pick a sockeye, I want to kiss it on the slimy nose before I throw it into the one brailer we've designated just for them. The other two brailers are full of pinks — small, spotted, easy-to-pick pinks. Smaller fish like pinks exit easier from the web, but when they are worth two cents, or five cents, or ten cents if we're lucky, the work is unrewarding. The thousand-pound bag of sockeye is what keeps us fishing the next opening, which of course, brings more pinks.

Pinks, at least in these kinds of numbers, return to the Kvichak every other year. Dad talks about the days he used to use pink gear, nets designed to catch them on purpose, when pinks were more valuable in the invisible current. I've never seen this many of them, because they are running early, and we are fishing late. Over the next two tides, there are more pinks and less sockeye. It's time for our season to come to a close.

Soon we're in Naknek, and Dad turns onto a dirt road to Red Salmon Cannery and parks at the end of a platform on the dock I'm not sure will sustain the weight of the truck. Boards are falling apart almost as bad as they fall apart at Graveyard. When we get out, it's not rain but heavy mist permeating my sweatshirt, and the smell of mud does the same. Forklifts ramble along the boardwalks where I follow Dad down to the dock where I can hear a captain on the deck of a drift boat hollering at his crewman below him for not understanding the tide is going out and they need to get this boat out of the water, goddamnit.

We're here to put our gear in the netlocker. Beneath us, the Naknek River rises against pilings. Sticks and grass float toward the mouth. Sterns are faced that way with bows upriver. There is a wake behind every boat in the water, but they aren't moving. Above a flimsy wooden staircase is what looks like a dark, wooden prison with nets, buoys, and anchors hanging in the cells shut with padlocks. Fishermen sit on spools, hanging net by weaving twin around corks, lines, and web. Dad asks almost every one of them how their winter was as our sneakers echo against the floor. Our net locker is the final one on the left. I haul Big Bertha, Little Bertie, and the other two anchors without names because they are less than forty pounds, and I carry them, step by step, up the stairs.

I'm not sure what's more exhausting — hauling a forty-pound anchor and the chain attached to it up the rickety, wooden staircase or taking dozens of trips with light items like buoy lights, lines, and little toolboxes. I know that although we don't get paid more for them per pound, catching a forty-pound king has more satisfaction to it than catching five six-pound sockeye. I know I don't like catching a thousand pounds of two-or-three-pound pinks. I can ask myself these questions later. For now, each step carrying an object to the net locker is one more step toward being done with fishing for the summer. It's also another step toward the next season.

My senior year was about to start, and Dad was spending weekdays in the village of Iliamna, where he'd been hired on the crew to build a new clinic. At the same time, he was finishing a spec house on Wolverine Drive, a gravel loop closer to King Salmon. The spec house, however, turned into what would be our new house, because the people who were interested dictated new changes, increasing the price, and they abandoned the idea to move to Anchorage.

I was less than excited to move to a new house before I moved out of Naknek. In my basement bedroom, my mattress absorbed my body as I watched the world through the TV in front of me. Corn Nuts crunched between my teeth until I swished Barq's Root Beer to wash them down. Wrestling season was on its way, and I wanted to enjoy junk while I still could, but I'd overdone it. I wasn't obese, but I was heavier than normal, and my gut jiggled when I poked it with my finger. After the fishing season, I'd spent the remainder of the summer embracing my introverted nature, not by biking or trying to run to the top of the hill, but by reading comic books and eating junk food. Any time I bent forward or to the side, it folded and creased, pestering me with its existence. I wasn't part of me. It was a symbiotic parasite.

I'd been thinking about running off the weight, and now was a good enough of a time as any. There was no wind, there were no mosquitoes, and the sky was clear and blue. With basketball shoes, sweatpants, and a hoodie, I left my bedroom and walked out the basement door, up the stairs onto the wooden plank walkway next to the lawn. I stared down the gravel driveway, already breathing hard from the stairs. In each fist, I clutched the mass attached to my waist. I wanted to tear it off and throw it to the side, but it wouldn't happen as much as I tried. I'd have to outrun it. To the highway and back was one mile — down the hill a quarter mile, up the other hill another quarter mile, turn around, run downhill, and run uphill again. I did it when I was in third grade, so hell, I could still do it.

One small stride at a time, the gravel crunched beneath the rubber of my long-dormant basketball shoes. By the time I reached the end of the driveway, I was panting and swearing. The left side of my digestive tract burned, the nerves in my legs shocked my brain, and my lungs stretched inside my chest, but I didn't stop. My shoes shuffled in the gravel toward the bottom of the hill. I didn't stop there either. No stopping was allowed until I got to the stop sign, where the gravel met the road. Then I could catch my breath, let my legs cool, extinguish the burning in my side, and see if any fat was burned away.

When I turned toward the highway, my lungs sucked wind like turbines. The stop sign didn't seem to get any closer, but I wouldn't stop to rest until it did. Then four gasps per shuffle forward, I struggled my way up the hill. My strides were short, and my chest stung as my lungs pushed to capacity. Then, in big white letters on a red octagon, I read my message, and I was happy to comply. I planted my shoes, put my hands on my knees, and wheezed in and out.

When I moved my hands to my midsection, no blubbery baggage had budged. I don't know what I was expecting other than having to carry the package of sludge back to the house with me, back to the basement, back to my bedroom, back to probably gobble down another candy bar and forget this dumb idea. Wrestling in the next weight class wouldn't be so bad.

On the first day of school, my class sat in the back of the auditorium while Miss Dahl, our current principal, introduced my class as the new seniors. Then our traveling superintendent from California spoke in a monotone voice about a school he cared less about than we did. The clock was ticking toward college and career choices, but first, we had to go through the motions — homework, sports, teenage drama, pop quizzes, and unit tests.

Then Mr. Krepel, our science teacher and longtime friend of my family, announced he was sponsoring a running club. Anyone interested could show up after school Monday, Wednesday, and Friday. The students were silent, more silent than during Superintendent Hephardt's speech, but my interest was held. Thrice-weekly outings would start right after Mr. Krepel got back from the Spirit of Becharof Science Camp, and I'd get down to the 152-pound weight class.

I was at Becharof with him. The previous September's flight ban had snuffed science camp, but this year I was there, my first get-out-of-school-and-get-out-of-Naknek ploy of the year. I answered a questionnaire explaining how much I loved math and science classes with my real reasons for hating them. There was one absolute answer to seek rather than using creativity. Me, Shoosh, one other senior, and some of the more scholarly juniors splashed onto Lake Becharof in a floatplane with Mr. Krepel. Kids from other schools met us there to learn about weather, birds, bears, fish, and the pH balance of ponds red with iron.

After almost 18 years in Alaska, I learned bears were attracted to insect repellent. I thought this group of environmental conservation-minded adults was trying to scare us from using harmful chemicals. Then one of our scientist-chaperones sprayed it on a stick and threw it to a bear sauntering by the main quarters. He rolled back and forth over it the way a dog would roll over a rotting squirrel. Dad had told me a million times that you didn't need to run faster than a bear. You just needed to run faster than someone else.

I thought about whatever bears were still wandering around Naknek when Mr. Krepel and Mo started a small group of kids on our first run where I learned a mile was not the pinnacle of human endurance. We would run from the school, up the Highway two miles, turn around, and run back to the school.

"Can people really run that far?" I asked. A chuckle was the only response I got.

Single file, we ran on the left gravel shoulder, turned around after two miles, and ran back on the shoulder on the other side. At a relaxed pace, my basketball shoes covered more distance than they had ever covered collectively, and I couldn't believe how easy and manageable it was. I would lose the weight in no time. Then I came home to the smell of chocolate chip cookies baking in the oven.

"Who wants a cookie?" Mom called as I opened the door.

I didn't respond but she repeated.

"I said who wants a cookie?"

"No thanks," I said.

She was confused.

"I guess I should get started on dinner. How about BLTs?"

As she started frying bacon, I asked if I could put turkey on my sandwich instead. My diet wouldn't be perfect, and I had much to learn, but I wanted to make the best decisions I could with the options I had. I always ate what Mom made for dinner, but I took small portions of pasta and cheesy casseroles, and I pulled the skin off of deep-fried fish. I took second helpings of Brussels sprouts, salads, and steamed broccoli. I stopped eating dessert entirely. I already had no problem leaving mayonnaise off a sandwich.

In three weeks, I ran nine times. I didn't touch a candy bar, soda, a chip, or a Corn Nut. At first, it was hard. I would find a Milky Way, Snickers, or a Butterfinger, stick it in my mouth, chew, and then spit it out in the toilet. Then I vowed to put an end to it. My mouth and my gut and my brain screamed for the sweet, salty blend of milk chocolate and high-fructose corn syrup, but all I had to do was not go to the pantry, not open a wrapper, not put it in my mouth, not chew, not swallow, and not feed the blubbery parasite controlling my desires. In the meantime, I kept running. I lost ten pounds. I knew it because I walked upstairs every day to Mom and Dad's bathroom and checked with the scale.

"Just take the damn scale to your room," Mom said, and I began checking several times a day — after peeing, pooping, eating, drinking, or running.

I was always two or three pounds lighter in the morning than I was at night. Being a wrestler had made me well aware of the loss and gain of weight through sweat and breathing, even in our sleep, so nighttime was when I counted it.

By the time the wrestling season started, I still had three more pounds to lose. During practice, I wore a layer of cotton on top of a layer of cotton. Sometimes I wore three or four layers — long johns, long-sleeved t-shirts, hooded sweatshirts. Riel said I looked like a ninja with my hood synched around my face, but I felt more like a marshmallow. Maybe it was because I would have loved to eat one.

Bob had me, Riel, and Shoosh lead calisthenics after laps. Then Bob dictated our drills, sprawls, and sprints as sweat soaked my cotton until the taste of salt leaked into the top layer. After the first practice, I was four pounds lighter, and when I was finished drinking water, I was four pounds heavier again. I kept at it, because the number on the scale moved a fraction of a notch every day until I made it to 152 pounds.

Our first tournament of the year was in Seward, a town on the Kenai Peninsula, but there was room for just one person from each weight class. Zach and I had to wrestle for the spot. The team was instructed to stay silent during our match — no cheering, no encouraging, and no advising, but I could hear them breathing. Zach was two years younger, and I was in the best shape of my life, but I was still not a great wrestler, whether or not I would have admitted it. We went for three rounds and I lost by points.

Losing to an underclassman didn't bother me. Having to wrestle at the 160-pound weight class bothered me. I didn't even hesitate to tell Bob I could go to 145, and it wasn't hard to convince him. After all those speeches about how anything is possible if you set your mind to it, if you give it your all, you could achieve anything, there was no way he could tell me no.

I believed in limits but getting to 145 wasn't beyond them. I'd already signed a waiver about my lowest possible weight, but all it took was another physical examination at Camai Clinic to sign another one. I got the physical, signed the waiver, and started running on weekends. I ran over the driveway, down the hill, up the other hill, and beyond the stop sign. I ran toward King Salmon, because on a clear day, I could see the mountains in the distance beyond the airport and beyond the spawning grounds. On most days, it was overcast. On plenty of days, it rained, or the wind nearly knocked me over, but it was those clear days I loved, running toward the mountains.

Three days after my 18th birthday, we moved into the house on Wolverine Drive, and five miles closer to King Salmon. Sometimes I ran to the end of the Alaska Peninsula Highway, but no matter how far I went, I always had to turn around and go home. It was a different house though, and where I was returning didn't feel like home anymore.

I wrestled in the 145-pound weight class in Seward, Dillingham, Bethel, New Halen, and even Anchorage, all before the 2003 Regional Tournament on the floor of the Bristol Bay School's gym, at home in Naknek. On Friday, I won my first match and lost my second. There was nothing to worry about yet. Anything was possible and my dreams would come true if I set my mind to it and gave it my all. I almost believed it. Then on Saturday, I lost two matches, didn't qualify for State, and I retreated to the locker room to hide in a stall and cry.

When I emerged to watch the rest of the matches, Mom sat next to me in the bleachers.

"This is the best shape you'll be in your life," she said. "It's all downhill from here."

I thought about what she said for a long time. I thought about it the rest of the tournament and all the way home. I never stopped thinking about it.

"Maybe this will make you feel better," she said at the house. She had made some kind of chocolate-covered cookie bars. I picked one from the tray and glared at it. It had been four months since I'd eaten anything like it. Anything like it had been burned away in the laps and miles and sweat and struggle. I shrugged and ate the whole thing.

The sweetness wasn't unpleasant, but I felt my inner blob of sludge awakening, demanding more. The sugar and lard were feeding a dormant parasite waiting to grow again, to hold me down with extra weight, keeping me from hard work one day at a time for my dreams to come true, which were possible if I gave it my all and put my mind to it, and all of that stuff I didn't know what to make sense of anymore.

In the morning, facedown on my pillow, my body was absorbed into the mattress, now in a different room in a different house, eight miles from Fisherman's Bar and eight miles from King Salmon Airport. It was a beautiful day, but there was no reason to run, so I just imagined it. Then something in my head clicked. The thought of striding forward one leg at a time, the rhythm of my feet, the perspiration, the accelerated breathing, and the drive forward, uplifted me. It brought me out of bed.

I didn't need to run. I *wanted* to run. I ate some cereal, put on my torn and tattered sweatshirt and sweatpants, washed and intended only for fishing from then on, and stepped outside onto the gravel with the same pair of basketball shoes. Each shoe fell into the grasp of gravity for just an instant before propelling up in the sky one more time and falling into the grasp of gravity again. As my shoes traveled the miles alongside the Alaska Peninsula Highway, my consciousness surged thousands of miles through synapses. Time between instants disappeared as thoughts branched outside my vessel of bone and muscle. It expanded outside instants of force from the ground in Naknek.

For the first time, I rethought what I believed about limits. From the shoulder of the Alaska Peninsula Highway, I looked to the mountains reaching to the ocean, scraping the sky. My body could collapse, but my thoughts were out there. The time between footstrikes, the time between heartbeats, and the time between breaths merged. The rhythm of my shoes was part of the harmonic chaos of the cosmos. It was stillness within movement. The distance didn't matter, because distance was infinite, and Naknek disappeared. I had arrived at the airport in King Salmon. I was at the end of the road. The mountains and ocean remained in the distance. I turned around and headed back toward Naknek.

Every day after school, I fueled up with a snack and hit the road one foot at a time. On the weekends, I'd run after digesting breakfast. I wasn't burning away a parasitic fat-monster anymore. I was burning away stress, teenage hormones, frustrations, and the gravity holding me down. I was looking forward to graduating from high school and attending Northern Michigan University. After the upcoming fishing season, I'd arrive at the King Salmon Airport, board a plane, and fly up in the sky to land in a new chapter of my life.

Every time I ran, I picked up another piece of myself along the way. It wasn't a search. The pieces happened to be there, and they fit together as I gathered them, like Dad building a house or Mom teaching a child with special needs. Running is how I found myself. It's where I had been all along. I'm still out there, moving in one direction or another, like the rhythm of the tide, or the lifecycle of salmon, moving forward on a road out of Naknek — but I would always turn around somewhere up the road to head right back.

It's the last summer before my first year of college, and I imagine a light at the end of a tunnel, but I don't see a tunnel. We're in the midst of a six-hour opening in the Naknek River Special Harvest Area, and I see a beam from a headlamp strapped to my forehead, illuminating drops in the air and the waves splashing against the bow. The rain stings my face like shards of glass. We just finished delivering a boatload of fish to the tender, and we're coming back to the nets for more. Water splashes against the part of Dad's face not concealed by the cinched hood of his raincoat.

Stumbling to the bow with my boat hook, the pounding from the waves shoots through my legs. The humming of the motor quiets as we approach the wobbling, blinking white light attached to the buoy. Something is wrong. I can't see the cork line.

"Holy shit," I whisper, and I scoop for it once, twice, and again before hooking it. The tide is moving fast, and it yanks my chest into the bow.

So far, this season, we have been catching maybe twenty fish in an entire net. There are about twenty fish right here in the first half fathom, splashing my face. The run is here.

Dad runs up to join me.

"Holy shit," he says.

He holds the corks, and I work my hands down to the lead line. His grip slips, and he swears. I pull harder. He pulls harder. The square hooks dig into my calluses. After a one-two-three-oomph and another one-two-three-oomph, we manage to get the net over the PVC pipes we have as slides on the sides of the bow.

With our feet against the side of the skiff for leverage, we pull along the lines. Fish pour into the bow and bury our ankles. They slide down our legs, thumping against the bottom of the skiff. We squeeze our fingers into square hooks, pull away the gills, and toss them into brailers. So far, we've needed one, or maybe two of them. Now fish overflow all four of the brailers, and we've only picked one net.

The two of us lean against the sides of the skiff and look at the fish flooding it, sinking the bow. We throw some of them into the stern for balance. Dad starts the motor again. No more than two inches of purple rock above the surface as we putter to the tender. The crane lifts the bags, dumps the fish into the tank, Dad collects the ticket, and they throw the bags back to me. I hook them over a pipe to rinse them, and the tide moves so fast that it takes a matter of seconds in the waves and current to rinse the blood and gurry out of them. I don't fold them. I tie them up again right away.

Dad hops back into the skiff, and I look at him waiting for the poundage. It's over four thousand, as I guessed. He pulls back the sleeve of his raincoat and his sweatshirt underneath to look at his watch. He's worried about the closure.

"Untie us! Let's go!"

He starts the motor, and we race back to the nets. There is still net we haven't picked yet, and the net we have picked has duplicated. Dad stops the motor as I grab the net. It's plugged. Fins, tails, and heads protrude from the water, splashing, the net still catching more. I've never seen so many fish in one net. Each of their wide, unblinking eyes taunt me. It was not a time for celebration.

Dad turns to me with fear in his eyes and fish slime dripping from his mustache.

"We're fucked."

He's right. We have one hour left until closing time with these two loaded nets still in the water, and they keep splashing. We begin picking the net. Each pull into the skiff takes all our strength, and each pull takes more than one try. The skiff leans to the side as we resort to picking them from the nets before pulling. We do not pull by the fathom. We pull by the inch. Dad looks at his watch again. He then looks out to the net in the water, pauses, and looks at his watch one more time. He sighs.

"Roundhaul."

It isn't real roundhauling. Roundhauling is when we pull the net into the skiff, fish and all. Now we can't pull without picking some of the fish out of the net first. It's too heavy. Then we can continue roundhauling, piling net on top of net with fish still in it. I stand to my hips in sockeye salmon and the web in their gills. Most of these fish are dead, but still limp, cold against my legs — even through my chest waders. Dad looks at his watch again.

"How much time do we have?"

At first, he says nothing.

"We were supposed to be out five minutes ago."

We keep pulling. It's all we can do. Then Dad stops.

"Let's at least turn the lights off."

Then it is dark and only dark. Fish and Game isn't going to come out at this hour, but Dad hates being late out of the water. It's more of a self-punishment than a precaution. It is black and only black other than mere outlines of the objects surrounding us. Fish by fish, and fathom by fathom, we finish without the aid of light. Sweating, grunting, and looking over our shoulders, even into the darkness, we get every fish and every inch of net into the skiff. We aren't caught or fined or getting our nets confiscated, but I think it's the least of our worries. We sit dangerously low in the water. It's just an unpainted wooden gunnel above the surface, and any of these waves, however small, can pour into the skiff and swamp us.

We tie to the tender, and we pick fish and organize the net until dawn. Under an orange glow of morning and the cool sweat saturating our clothes, we deliver over 6,000 more pounds of fish, bringing the total for the day over 11,000 pounds. It's the most fish we've ever caught in the least amount of time. We cheated, but it was unintentional. Wanton waste, to dump the catch back into the water, would be a far greater evil.

Contemplating greater and lesser evils, looking at the gray area, reminds me of a story. It's about a villager, who in the dark of night, whispered magic words into the water to conjure salmon. He caught more salmon than he had ever seen, but he wanted them all for himself. While his family slept, he cooked them and ate them one by one as the daylight approached. His son, however, awoke early and caught his father shoveling salmon flesh between his teeth, chomping down on the meat.

The man's son ran to tell his mother, and his mother told the village shaman. The shaman, who believed no kind of animal was more despicable than the fowl, transformed the man into Raven. Raven, of course, loved his new form, as he could fly anywhere, swooping down at will to scoop up whatever appealed to him. Then, with his newfound freedom, he realized he could create an entirely new planet, our planet, a place that meant the world to him, where limits were endless. I couldn't wait to start my new life outside of Naknek.

After its voyage on a barge down the Pacific, my truck awaited me at the Port of Seattle, where I climbed into the cab with the ocean in my rearview mirror. In my windshield was a vast network of roads accessible by the engine under the hood, the pedals beneath my feet, and the wheel in my hands.

Of course, my family was there, too. We were all heading across the country together, stopping along the way at cheap motels, homes of old friends, and a dude ranch in South Dakota where the horse I rode wouldn't follow my directions.

Dad had bought a new Dodge Ram, and Luke and Erica rode with him. Mom rode with me, instructing when it was time to pass, when I could turn, when I was speeding, and when I was going too slowly. Along our route of honking horns, slamming brakes, tense muscles, and sudden screams, I wasn't sure if it was the alien idea of traffic laws, or the parental supervision that made me nervous.

I was bored by the farmland but relieved by lakes and woods, but the descent downhill into Duluth, Minnesota is when I was first overcome with awe of Lake Superior, because it meant that Marquette was getting close. It was somewhere along that same lake. It was just a quick drive across the northern part of Wisconsin into Michigan's Upper Peninsula.

The UP was populated by a culture of Yoopers with ear flaps, deer camps, private property, and the Green Bay Packers who they'd adopted from across the Wisconsin border. Northern Michigan University, however, kept Marquette young and exciting, with concerts, festivals, and bike trails, along with all the amenities I looked forward to like movie theaters and grocery stores.

I arrived at Van Antwerp Hall with a slip of scratch paper with my roommate's name and phone number someone had scribbled at the housing department. He hadn't answered his phone, so I'd talk to him for the first time in person.

Humidity from Superior summoned beads of sweat that rolled down my forehead. A group of girls surrounded me in the hallway and let loose shrieks about the school spirit rally, all the upcoming activities, and how much fun I would have in this fun hall because of all the fun with all the fun people.

"It sounds fun," I told them. Then they wanted to know where I was from, and I instantly regretted telling them.

"Oh my gosh! Aleeaska? Is it, like, always cold there?"

"Have you ever seen a polar bear?"

"Did you live in an igloo?"

"Don't they have colleges in Alaska?"

"Yeah. Why don't you go to college in Aleeaska?"

I asked about Alan, my roommate, and it was like someone had hit them with a pop quiz over a book they hadn't read. The school spirit flew right out of them and faded into the outer reaches. One of them said Alan's face was messed up. Another one of them said he was always with his sister.

Then they slowly backed away, speeding up again as they disappeared down the stairs, screaming about lattes and frappuccinos from the new Starbucks on campus. The founder, I had been told, was a Northern alumnus and this was so, so, very exciting. Could I believe, I was asked, that this was the last place in the world without a Starbucks?

No. No, I could not.

Kasey Swanson, who had pushed me out of my highchair when I was a baby, was living at the end of the hall. I knew she was at NMU. Her parents were Michiganders, and our families had kept in touch since the Swansons left Naknek. We had even visited them in their cottage in the southern Upper Peninsula, along Lake Michigan. It was comforting to have her there. Even if Kasey had no memory of Naknek herself, to have her right down the hall was a reminder that I hadn't imagined the first eighteen years of my life.

I was on my own when I turned to my plain, blue, metal door for the first time and knocked three slow times. There was no answer, so I used my key and walked by a closet on the left and a bathroom on the right to a space of whitewashed cinder blocks, inside of which there were twin beds, two dressers, and two desks — all counterparts parallel to each other. Alan had left me the side nearest the window, which I appreciated.

A fan was spinning on his desk, and I stood in front of it to dry the sweat pouring down my face. I wondered what Alan was like, and looking around at his stuff made me wonder even more. A giant poster of the Periodic Table of the Elements was displayed above his desk, and in the middle of his flowery, pink-and-purple quilt was a copy of the King James Version of *the Holy Bible*.

As I stood there, the doorknob twisted, unlatched, and the door squeaked as it opened. A pair of sneakers dragged across the laminate floor, toes pointed inward. Hunched forward, a misshapen figure with arms bent to the side shuffled into the cinder block square.

He wore blue jeans that were too big and a green-and-white striped polo that was too small. I'd describe his hair as a matted-down red afro on top of a large, bulging forehead. There were patches of thin hair growing on his cheeks. Saying nothing, he tilted his head and stared.

"Hmph," he grunted, and he shuffled closer.

"Hi. I'm Alan, your roommate," he said. His voice a cross between Yoda and Kermit the Frog. His smile might have been friendly, but I wasn't sure.

"Hi," I reached out my hand. "I'm Keith."

His palm was greasy, and the back of his hand had the same red curls as his head. It was like the hand of a red-headed hobbit.

"I have one request," he said.

"Sure."

"No sex in the room."

"Nice to meet you too," I said, faking a laugh.

His face was as still as a stone gargoyle.

"Well, Alan," I said. "You have two fans, because I am your fan for bringing one."

I regretted the joke right away. There was no laugh. Instead, he glared into my soul — maybe searching for memories of former sex partners. He must have seen the lack thereof, because he abruptly relaxed and smiled, his arms straight with his shoulders loose.

Then my lame joke registered, and I heard his laugh for the first time. I would have been relieved, but it wasn't a pleasant sound. There was no separation between laughs. It was loud, and it was a single stream of sound, like the honk of a horn at an 18-year-old driver from Naknek cruising on the I-95 in a red Ford Ranger.

"I have something I have to do right now," he said. "But I'll be back in a bit."

I stood without reaction as the sound of feet dragging against carpet faded down the hallway. I sighed and started hauling things up the stairs from my truck. I was making my bed when Alan returned, this time with a short, penguin-shaped lady.

"You must be Keith," she said in a high-pitched voice and a strong Yooper accent, which can be described as a form of what people think of as an accent from Minnesota or Canada. Her shirt had thick purple horizontal stripes, accentuating her egg shape.

"Yeah," I said. "Nice to meet you."

"I'm his sister," she said, her voice a penguin's squawk. I was relieved that she spoke first, because I had assumed that she was Alan's mom, and I was about to say so.

"Keith was enjoying my fan," Alan said, looking at me with anticipation. As he had hoped, I repeated the joke, and Alan repeated the laugh, this time alongside Cecile's. Hers was similar, but high-pitched — a screech, like the squawk of a seagull.

My first pleasant surprise was the cafeteria. It was called the Marketplace, located in the resident hall next-door. There was always plenty of junk, but there was always a salad bar, there were always grilled chicken breasts, and the morning offered delicious egg white omelets. Nothing was gourmet, but with every meal, I was able to load plates and bowls with heaps of vegetables.

Other 18-to-20-year-olds made fun of me, but I didn't care. For the first time, I was choosing my own food all the time, and I had an unlimited meal plan. Every time I went for a run, I knew I was running on above-average octane, and I could have as much of it as I wanted.

The cafeteria, however, didn't serve lobster, as Alan complained, so he munched on dry ramen noodles from the boxes underneath his bed. I could appreciate and get along with a seafood man, but this attitude seemed like pure snobbery.

Our dorms were separated and named as different houses, two of them on each of three floors. I lived in American Graffiti house where the cinder block walls were decorated in murals of musicians, portraits of cartoon characters, and slogans like *Yooper Power* and *Go Wildcats!* — none of which resembled real graffiti.

AG was the Honors House, and Van Antwerp was the wellness hall, which meant none of us were the type of kid to spray-paint gang signs in subway tunnels or onto brick walls in alleys. I was happy about that, but no one I'd met seemed to be too much into wellness either.

Wellness, to me, was exercising and eating wholesome foods, which is why I choose Van Antwerp. Instead, what I got was Campus Crusade for Christ and their posters about how terrible alcohol and drugs were. I didn't do drugs, and I didn't drink alcohol — at least not until I lived in the wellness hall — but I never felt the need to focus so hard on the things that I didn't do.

Alan was Catholic, so he wasn't welcome as a Crusader. At least that's how he explained it to me, which I found ironic. I was sure it was because they thought he was weird, too. Alan was a geology major, of all things, but the rocks he found most interesting were the tablets containing the Ten Commandments.

Alan and I had some things in common, like getting teased as a kid and feeling like a misfit, and I preferred to keep the subject about those things for the sake of getting along with him. Because of his looks, I was sure he had it worse than me, and had coped with it differently. I got this impression when he told me how his highschool PE teacher didn't allow bathroom breaks, so he intentionally peed his pants to spite him. Still, I told him congratulations on his rebellion. I didn't want to discuss religion, and for a while, he didn't bring it up.

It wasn't Alan but Cecile who asked the first question. "Do you think the Ten Commandments should be in the courtroom?"

"Um," I said, shrugging. "No. Not really."

I diverted back to struggling through a stack of math problems, but in my peripheral vision, they were staring at me.

"Why?" Cecile asked.

"Separation of church and state," I said, shrugging again.

They glanced at each other before turning back at me. Then I heard the first of Alan's sermons about eternal fire and suffering as a consequence of not living by the Commandments.

"Oh," is all I said.

There were other times where he went on rampages, too. He talked about Noah on his Arc, Moses on Mount Sinai, Jesus feeding the multitudes, and the firmament separating the waters. I didn't tell Alan that I was raised with the occasional visit to Catholic church, and I'd heard this stuff before, but I figured that would make it worse. Telling

Campus Crusade that I was Catholic kept them away. It would do the opposite with Alan.

The way I scared him wasn't on purpose. I was hunched over my desk one night, drawing another macabre, spooky, or what-have-you character. The volume of my headphones was low enough for me to hear Alan's feet slowly sliding across the tile floor.

"I have a question," he said.

I turned around to see him behind me, fear across his face.

"About the obsession with drawing demonesque characters."

Shrugging had become my default response, and I responded this way one more time.

"Where does the influence come from?"

Another shrug was needed.

"You don't worship the devil, do you?"

"Yeah," I said, making a face. "I worship the devil."

My sarcasm was lost on him. Gasping, he stepped backward, stumbled over his own feet, and scurried down the hallway. He didn't sleep there that night. He spent the night in Cecile's room. The next time I arrived from class, an elaborate, Catholic crucifix was hanging over his bed, next to his rock pick.

I supposed it was there to protect him from my demonic presence, but I couldn't help but wonder who would protect me. Every time I looked at that cross, mini-Jesus stared back at me, nails in his hands and feet, no escape from Alan. Each of us thought the other was a roommate from hell, but Jesus was stuck there, crucified forever — and he wasn't even crucified accurately.

One time, I walked into the room, put my backpack onto my bed, and flipped the lightswitch. In the fluorescent illumination, Cecile appeared on Alan's bed, not doing anything in particular, blank eyes out the window — a faint grin over her face, like she had just done something devious.

"Oh," I said. "I didn't know someone was here."

Cecile said nothing. I retreated to the bathroom, changed into running clothes, and escaped the way I knew best how to escape.

Pat and Nick were our suitemates, meaning that their room was attached to our room through the bathroom. I biked and hiked on occasion with Pat, and we had an understanding that sometimes, I would walk into their room to leave from their door. Then I'd walk down the hallway, down the steps, onto the sidewalk, to the bike path taking me along the shoreline.

Sometimes I headed into Presque Isle Park— a small peninsula reaching out onto Superior. Sometimes I ran along the bike path along the lake toward town. Sometimes I ran onto the Noquemanon Trail Network and got lost in the woods on purpose.

I had been running again when I returned to the room to an egg-shaped pink-and-purple mummy in Alan's bed. I thought it odd that a sister would curl into a brother's bed.

"What's going on?" I said to Cecile.

There was almost a minute of silence before she told me she was just waiting for Alan, and his bed was much, much more comfortable. Her room was on the same floor, in the same house, right around the corner, but she chose instead to be in our room, doing nothing in particular until Alan returned.

As much as Alan acted afraid of me, he still liked to follow me around campus, and I think he genuinely wanted to be friends. He wasn't mean. His warnings of eternal perdition were out of genuine concern. It didn't mean he wasn't annoying as hell.

For instance, no matter what time I left for the cafeteria in the morning, he got up and followed. There, preached just like he preached in the room.

"If you want to get into heaven, you have to have full devotion to God," he said over a bowl of Lucky Charms.

"Don't be a glutton. It's one of the seven deadly sins," he said over a bowl of oatmeal smaller than mine. His bowl did have, of course, a mound of sugar.

"If you have impure thoughts, you'll go to hell," he said over Cocoa Puffs as an attractive girl walked by. I hadn't even noticed her until he said something.

On my 19th birthday, I made it to breakfast without him, and I ate a bit faster than normal. I had decided to binge on a treat of white-flour waffles, strawberries, frozen yogurt, and syrup, a rare treat in my fairly clean diet. I was halfway finished when the darkness of shadow suddenly moved over my plate. I looked up to see a menacing, protruding forehead and curly locks of red hair.

"What is that?" Alan asked. He was pointing at my waffles.

"Waffles," I mumbled, crouching over them.

"Is that yogurt?" he asked.

"Yeah," I said, taking another mouthful.

"Waffles with yogurt?" he asked.

"Yeah," I said.

He stared at them, his neck flexed, his mouth open, his nose wrinkled, and his eyes wide. Every detail was amplified, from his nose hairs to the red cracks in the whites of his eyes.

"That looks absolutely disgusting," he said. Yogurt, Alan explained, was an atrocious product as it was nothing but milk tainted with bacteria. Besides, he told me, he could smell it from a mile away. It was probably against the Ten Commandments, too.

I sat across from him and his bulging forehead, his red afro, and the thin patches of hair scattered over his cheeks. This moment was the first time his looks alone bothered me. This demonesque character was crawling under my skin with a torch, poking at every nerve he could find. Then he made the sign of the cross, took a gulp of his Fruity Pebbles, and instantly spit them into rainbow spray.

"This food has such poor quality," he said.

Over the course of the semester, other people in American Graffiti had asked me about living with Alan. They made fun of him and Cecile and accused them of incest. Sure, they slept in each other's beds, and sure, they had pictures of each other in heart-shaped frames, but I attributed their closeness to their being so weird and having no one but each other with whom to be that weird. There was plenty of uneasiness to living with them, but Kasey put it best.

"I don't know how you live with him," she had said. "He just annoys the hell out of me."

Annoying, he was. How I lived with him, I didn't know. I enjoyed reprieve one weekend while Alan was at a Christian camp. All was quiet until Cecile waddled into the room and sat in the chair at Alan's desk.

"Did you get my email?" she asked.

"No," I said.

"I sent you an email," she said.

"Oh," I said. "I haven't checked it yet today."

"I can just tell you what it said," she said.

"Okay," I said.

"I was wondering," she said shyly, looking to the ground.

My stomach churned.

"Do you like me?" she asked.

"I'm sorry," I said. "I don't feel about you that way."

"Okay," she said. "But we can still be friends, right?"

"Yeah, of course," I said.

I went for a long run after that. As I ran, I wondered what I could have done to give Cecile the wrong impression — but mostly, I wondered how I would maintain my patience.

Lake Superior's waves crashed against the boulders across Lakeshore Boulevard. Gray clouds drifted above me. I had watched the weather over Superior shift and change hundreds of times, not as spasmodically as Bristol Bay, but almost. Gray clouds swirled and winds churned waves onto the shore. Running, appreciating the world beyond the shoreline, I hoped for a miracle. I hoped that Alan and Cecile would be taken out of my life. As I looked out at the water, imagining that it would somehow answer me, I couldn't help but wonder if these thoughts were my version of praying.

There was one thing that Alan had preached that made some kind of sense to me. There were no harps and or halos or giant dove wings in heaven, he had told me. Heaven was a place without memory or awareness of self. It wasn't even a place, he said. It was just something out there that we couldn't explain or understand. After all, memory was stored in our bodies — and our bodies wouldn't ascend into heaven.

For a moment, one of his sermons began to make sense. For such an idea to make sense, the explanation didn't have to be supernatural. Maybe this whole "self" thing wasn't real, and that our consciousness came from some kind of universal storage facility. Then I remembered he had also told me the best thing about heaven was looking down into hell and laughing as the wicked burned.

Maybe I was wicked. I started to wonder what would happen if he got into some bad ramen, or if he happened to fall in the shower or onto his rock pick.

Then, during the weeks before Christmas break, I walked into the room after class. Alan was sitting at his computer, reading about the Bible Code.

"Hey, guess what?" he said.

Anticipating a sermon, I shrugged.

"Cecile and I got an apartment for next semester."

"Really?" I said.

"Yeah."

A weight on my spine lifted. The next time I ran, there was more spring in my step and more length in my stride. I could hardly believe it as I helped carry their possessions to their car. I hauled out the quilt, the Bible, the rock pick, the heart-shaped frames, and Jesus nailed to the cross. Then I watched them from the window as they disappeared around the corner of our red brick building. The clouds opened, and the sun shone down. I couldn't help but think that my prayers had been answered.

The Naknek Beach, the space between Libbyville and the mouth of the Naknek River, is a sandy, rocky beach expanding into a mudflat at low tide. Out farther is Hungary's Flat, an expanse of mud sealing the mouth of the Naknek River from the Kvichak. Hungary's Flat is exposed as Dad and I roll down the beach in the Dodge Ram with metal, red-painted barrels in the back of it. Bursts of water from clams underground spurt like fountains all around us. There are screw anchors already augured in place, and running lines are ready for nets, but no one is on the beach but Dad and me. Rocks fling into the undercarriage as we roll along the mud.

Chances are the Naknek section will open, but the Kvichak will be closed for the start of the season, so we're borrowing someone's sites on the Naknek Beach. What it means is we won't have to go to Johnston Hill and spend the night freezing. The barrels will make good buoys here. It's an area where drifters tend to get too close and wrap nets, lines, and buoys in their propellers. Then we drag the barrels out onto the mudflat and tie them between two screw anchors. The muffler growls as we roll back up the Beach Access Road.

On the way back to Wolverine Drive, Dad reaches for the cell phone on the dashboard. It's a big, black rectangle — a brick of a phone, and nothing like what I've seen around campus, held by students that I assume are rich.

"Hey, Kitty," Dad says and turns to me with a mischievous grin. "Keith and I are stuck on the beach."

"She's not going to believe you with that muffler in the background," I say.

"Yeah," he says to Mom. "We need you to come get us. Bring the tow rope."

I can't hear what she says, but I can hear the intonation of her voice go from high to higher in a flamboyant panic.

"Oh, and your chest waders, too," he says. "We're in deep, up to the axle."

I snicker. "Tell her the tide's starting to come in, too."

"And hurry, because the tide is coming in," he says. "Oh, and, hey. Hello?"

The phone cuts before he can say he's just kidding. Then he tries to call back to no avail. There is just static and the sound of the muffler beneath our feet. Neither of us say another word. We both know the ramifications of what we've done.

When we get to the house, Mom and Erica are outside in their waders, tossing a rope into the back of the Jeep idling in the driveway with the back hatch open. Dad and I stay in the truck, but the longer we sit here, the worse it will be. Dad's face is toward the gravel when he steps onto it.

"Asshole!"

Mom is furious. Arms fling. Feet stomp. A door slams.

Mom's already stressed, trying to pack to move to Washburn, Wisconsin. There are a few factors that led to this decision. After the seasons of low returning numbers of sockeye, the State of Alaska offered to fund retraining for fishermen to mitigate years of lower prices and small harvests. Dad is taking them up on it to get an HVAC associate's degree, which he can use to add refrigeration units to drift boats, increasing the quality of their fish, increasing the value of all our fish. The school has also gone downhill, and Erica is too ambitious for what the Bristol Bay Borough School has to offer. We're still sleeping, eating, living in the house on Wolverine Drive, but more of its inside contents are packed into boxes every day.

The plan is to construct a pole building, a metal-sided garage with a three-bedroom apartment. It's a downsized location closer to the fishing operation. The property is one mile from

Fisherman's Bar, across the street from the Alaska General Seafoods cannery, and less than a mile from City Dock. It's in the gravel lot where Napa Auto Parts burned to the ground.

Dad and I jump into the truck and drive there, holes in the muffler roaring the entire way. Layers of aluminum foil are wrapped around it, but they keep melting. When we get to the lot, Dad uses orange spray paint to mark where the corners of the building will go. A guy Dad hired pulls levers from an auger truck drilling holes into the gravel. Dad and shovel excess sand and gravel around invisible walls.

Every day, at the house on Wolverine Drive, more familiar objects go into boxes. Our family has had plenty of garage sales over the years. Forgotten family possessions are remembered again as they sit on sawhorse tables in the open garage, like clothes that don't fit, books we'll never read again, and a lamp with a plastic horse that used to be next to my crib.

As friends, neighbors, and strangers from out of town pick them up in exchange for 25 cents, 50 cents, a dollar, they are forgotten once more. This time it's a different garage at a different house — a house where I lived less than a year. Inside, there are other possessions, unforgotten, stuffed into boxes and totes piled in the living room. A guy I don't know wants to buy Murphy, and we tell Mom, that no, we aren't selling him. Yes, he digs in the garden. Yes, he's peed on the floor in the windbreak, and no, he never follows a command unless a scrap from the table is involved, but come on!

Soon, there's an opening in the Naknek Section, as anticipated. On the Naknek Beach, the tide runs hard against the hard surface. On the Naknek Beach, there is no choice but to use a running line. Instead of powering toward the channel and throwing an anchor, we pull along a line in place between the anchors and tie our corkline to it every four feet to a fathom. The lead line is left alone since it sinks on its own.

"Is this how we're going to do it every time?" I say.

"Yeah," Dad says. His frustration speaks through the roll of twine clenched between his teeth. The spool is in his mouth. "That's how they do it here."

I don't say anything else. We don't catch many fish.

When we're closed again, back at the gravel lot, Dad takes measurements and cuts wood while I shovel more gravel and throw it along the invisible walls. I pound in stakes with a sledgehammer. It rains, it shines, and it rains again. Dad takes measurements, carries numbers over other numbers with a pencil, and constructs tresses from lumber. He shows me how to attach the braces, and we attach them together. He says nothing but instruction. At Wolverine Drive, Mom says we can make sandwiches for dinner. Everyone else ate already. When I go to my room, the TV is gone. The chair is gone, too.

In the morning, there is still no opening. Dad and I fill holes and put tresses in place for the crane. Then he tells me we've put in the braces wrong, so I pull them all out and put them back the right way. Dad's motions are hurried. A Kvichak opening will likely happen soon, and we still don't have our buoys out there.

It's still the same day when we take the Lund out there and then check on fish camp. Graveyard Creek has shifted. The boards that used to be nailed to the old dock for unloading have crumbled away. Grass has taken over much of the boardwalk. The bushes have grown taller than the hospital. When we finish checking the camp, we go to wait for low tide, and we tie the buoys to the screw anchors that are marked with old corks.

On another day without an opening, we pound nails into tresses. The crane operator raises them for us to bolt them. When we get home, the shelves in the living room are empty. Fish is in the refrigerator. After I eat, I'm supposed to put my belongings into two piles. Most of my own things are the back of my truck in Marquette, but there is more of it here, too. One pile of it will stay in Naknek. The other pile will go into the truck and onto the barge and to Wisconsin. I can take it to Marquette from there. After dinner, Dad goes back to work. He does it without saying a word.

In the morning, Mom wakes me. "Dad left a note. The tresses may be too high. He's going to come back later to get you."

It's not even 7:00 AM, which means he was awake hours ago with the thought haunting him. He comes home and confirms the tresses are too high. I spend the day pulling out the bolts that I put in the day before moving them eight inches lower. This time, dinner is reheated pork chops that have to stay in the microwave a little longer than last night's fish. Someone mentions that it's Mom and Dad's 25th anniversary.

Dad and I spend another day working on the building, and on the way home, cop cars are gathered at Mile Five. We find out later that an Iliamna man was murdered, and the body was found by the police officer buying our house. Tonight, I heat the spaghetti in the microwave. It's still too cold when I eat it.

I spend the next day handing Dad two-by-sixes, and he nails them into the tresses. The wind is blowing hard. When we get home, I learn that a guy my age fell out of his skiff today. His brother jumped in and saved him, but then that brother drowned. There is more leftover spaghetti, but Mom says we need to save it for tomorrow's casserole. I open the pantry and make a peanut-butter-and-jelly sandwich.

On Father's Day, I give Dad some lures. All he needs now is the time to use them. We spend the day hauling the rest of the gear from the netlocker and launching the skiff. At the dock, I look down at the flocks of seagulls and the skiff and driftboats leaving wakes behind them. The price is rumored to be 35 cents a pound, the lowest I've seen it.

After one more low catch in the Naknek Section, there is a new announcement. The Kvichak Section is opening, so Dad and I head out right away. We take a full tote and full cooler of food and haul it to Graveyard. On our way, beluga whales are surfacing, which means there are some fish. We set up camp, lay out the nets, and the first delivery is 3,000 pounds. The next tide gives us a little less poundage, but I'm still tired, and I crawl into my bunk and fall asleep right away. The next tide brings us even less poundage, and too many of them we find chomped in half. Seals have been in our nets, and it seems like there are more of them than fish.

The next tide is when the fish hit, and after two big deliveries, the fish keep hitting. There are fish, fish, and more fish, and they don't stop. The second we finish picking one fathom of net, it starts splashing and wiggling again. We start pulling the nets out of the water when we have six hours before the closure. We try to pick the fish as we pull in the net.

It's not enough time. We roundhaul three of the nets, and all three of them are still full of fish. There is still one of them in the water, and here are twenty minutes left.

"There's only one way out of this," Dad says.

He drives us to the outside end of the net, and I untie it from the buoy. I wrap the line around the rail, and we drag everything into the beach, fish still splashing, kicking in the mud. The net lays horizontal against the shoreline for just a few moments before it goes completely high and dry. We anchor, wade into the beach, and start picking fish and placing them in piles. Fish and Game's chopper swoops over us, but all of our nets are out.

Dad is a faster picker, but I'm quicker at moving up and down the beach. Mud sticks to my boots, and my boots sink into the soft spots. Sometimes I'm not quick enough, and I lose my boots. The more I follow my own footprints back and forth, the softer the spot gets, and I have to choose a new route down. Dad keeps picking, down on his hands and knees, mud splattering all over him, and I start carrying them down, rinsing the mud from each fish before throwing it in a brailer.

I slog down to the skiff, as many fish in my hand as possible. At first, I can carry five. My index finger, my middle finger, and my ring finger of my left hand, each holds a fish by the gills, the tip of the finger spitting out the mouth. My right hand carries two fish since I don't have a free hand to place them there. Sometimes the gills break, and I don't bother to pick them up. I keep slogging as my fingers fatigue. I bring fish down to the shoreline, and I splash their scales clean before tossing them into the brailers.

This night is never-ending. Dad picks. I carry. The tide starts coming in. We both try to move faster. The tide waits for no one, and it's about to carry away our catch.

Then there is another set of boots squishing in the mud. It's Pat, our neighbor fisherman's crewman. He walks down the beach and starts helping haul fish down the beach. All three of us carry them, making dozens more trips.

Dad picks the last fish, and the three of us carry as many of them on our fingers as we can, down to the skiff. Dad and I organize our roundhauled nets as we pick the fish out them. As the tide floods, we pull our beached net into the skiff, Dad starts the motor, we head to the tender, and deliver brailer after brailer to make it more than a 20,000-pound day, about 6,000 of which came from the beach — about 6,000 pounds carried by hand.

We get back to camp at breakfast time.

"So, peanut-butter-and-jelly sandwiches?"

"No," he says. "Jesus, no! We have cereal."

"I don't see it."

"Right here," he says, picking up what he realizes is a box of crackers. We sit down for peanut-butter-and-fucking-jelly, as Dad calls it, and we go to bed. The next opening starts in five hours, and so begins our season routine of short shots of sleep and hard days and nights of setting nets, picking nets, pulling nets, and eating peanut-butter-and-fucking-jelly.

After the season is over, we vacate Graveyard. The skiffs are unloaded and pulled, and nets are stripped. The first day back at the pole building, Dad tells me to get the door frames out of the container van. I carry them out one by one and lean them against the van.

"Goddamnit," Dad shouts. "That looks like shit!"

If he took a ruler to them, they wouldn't align, he explains.

"Aren't we just moving them inside in a second?"

He throws his hands up.

"If a guy gives you a task, you have to go above and beyond the expectations. When people give me compliments on how nice the house is looking, do you think it's just because?"

I don't say anything. I know better.

"I don't know what kind of worker you're growing up to be," he says as he shakes his head. "You have to do your best. I thought we taught you that."

I still don't say anything. I don't know what I'm best at doing. I don't know if I've ever given my best toward anything.

Dad stays in the same mood for the next three weeks. He yells when I don't know where he put the nails. He yells when I ask him where to put the hammer when I'm done with it. He yells whenever we have another visitor, and he struggles to stay pleasant when they get out of their cars to talk.

While we work on the house, and Dad remains in a constant state of anger, the buoys are still out on the Kvichak, floating with the ebb and flood. The only salmon still swimming through it the coho and some chums. Mom spends every day packing, and dinner is often peanut-butter-and-jelly sandwiches.

We have already pulled the skiffs, so we load the Lund into the water to get our buoys. We wait for the tide to ebb enough to expose the eyes of the anchors. Then we untie the buoys and tie a rope with some old corks to mark them from next year. I exchange as few words as possible, because I don't want Dad to explode.

On our way back, Hungary's Flat is fully exposed, sealing the Naknek River from the Kvichak. The bow of the Lund plows into the mud, Dad stops and raises the motor. I stand up to get out and push, but he tells me not to bother. The flood will come in soon enough. For now, the Naknek and Kvichak drain into Bristol Bay, and the Lund is high and dry, surrounded in mud. Dad isn't upset. He's leaning back with his feet up on the splashwell. The water is still, and the tide is as low as low tide gets.

Slack tide is broken with a gust of wind brushing against the surface. Bubbles and ripples drift slowly along the mudflats toward Naknek. The water is pushing into Naknek again. Soon white water gushes over the mud, pushing the Lund spinning circles in shallow water, drifting with the bubbles. I stand to get out and push, but Dad shakes his head. He remains leaned back in his seat, feet still on the splashwell, relaxed in a complete state of calm as the tide does with us what it will. As the current rushes, now is the most still that Dad has been since we started building the new fish camp. Now is the first time I've seen him smile all summer.

When I was growing up in Naknek, sometimes our family went cross-country skiing, but I often went skiing alone. I clipped the three holes in my boots into the three prongs in my bindings, slid across the tundra to the Alaska Peninsula Highway, detached the skis, walked across the pavement, and then slid back onto the tundra. It was after the pavement when the journey became limitless.

One glide after another, over hills, across frozen ponds, and out to herds of caribou, I trod through snow, sinking with each stride unless there was a snowmachine trail to follow. With TV, internet, and my imagination, sometimes I could lose sight of Naknek's isolation, but being on the tundra was a reminder, especially in the wintertime, that I was a tiny spot, floating on a white ocean. I wasn't skiing on snow. Friction melted the snow. I was skiing on water.

Make no mistake. It wasn't always a winter wonderland in the dark months. Most often, it wasn't. Arctic and Pacific fronts collided over Bristol Bay, bringing rain one day and subzero temperatures the next day. School was canceled more often for ice days than snow days. The principal once slid his truck off the road and crawled home on his hands and knees to make the call.

Before Alaska's neighbors across the Bering Sea began rushing over to invade, people got around on foot, on snowshoes, or by mushing dogsleds. These modes of transportation went as far east as Nunavut, on the Hudson Bay, and the archipelago into the Arctic. It was in a place beyond Nunavut, across the Atlantic, where skiing was the invention of blonder, paler Norsefolk. They strapped slivers to birch bindings.

The skiers sailed across the Atlantic, first colonizing Iceland and Greenland before navigating tributaries into the Great Lakes to settle Minnesota, Wisconsin, and Michigan's Upper Peninsula. They fermented milk into cheese, turned cattle into bratwursts, brewed Leinenkugel's Beer and assembled the Green Bay Packers. There must have been a time, however, after they landed on the shores of Nunavut, that they encountered the walkers, snowshoers, and mushers.

Brian lived two doors down from me in the dorms, and he introduced himself as a one-hundred-percent Norwegian, Lutheran Democrat from the quaint town of Darlington, Wisconsin. I went to my first party with him where we handed some kid at the door a five-dollar bill for a red Dixie cup. Brian's plan was to share the cup, but I kept guzzling more suds than liquid and handing it back to him. Then he'd call me a son-of-a-bitch and refill the cup like a sucker, and I laughed deviously. I had always told myself that I'd never drink, but I had fun with the first beer buzz that I ever had.

Brian was the only person I'd met in the Wellness Hall who seemed to be at all interested in wellness, even though he touted a deep devotion and love for beer, brats, and cheese. When he found out that I had skis, he said we had to hit the trails as soon as there was enough snow. Then he told me about the American Birkebeiner, the largest cross-country ski marathon in North America, taking place on a trail from Cable to Hayward, Wisconsin. Brian's family had a cabin in

Hayward, and he'd been skiing the Kortelopet, the half-distance of the race, since highschool.

The Birkebeiner tradition originated in the 13th century. When the tyrant king of Norway, known as the Pretender, was threatened by a true infant heir to the throne, orders were to find him and kill him. The Birkebeiners were a political party, named for their birch bindings, who came to the rescue of little Haakon. Two of them carried him into the woods and across the mountains, 50 kilometers to safety. Every year, a course from Rena to Lillehammer invited skiers to commemorate the rescue.

The Birkie was the American version. Its website had pictures of bright, color-schemed spandex, sponsorship labels, and fabric number bibs strapped around athletic torsos like vests. Athletes trained year-round, across the endless snow in the winter, and on roller skis in the summer. They flew from around the world for this race, taking with them professional wax technicians to customize for the temperature, humidity, and texture of the snow. I was a teenager with a pair of low-key touring skis.

I was no longer just skiing, I had decided. From then on, I was training. Blueberry Ridge, the Fit Strip, and the Noquemanon Trail Network routes in Marquette were groomed with machines that left clean stripes of corduroy and perfect grooves for skis to slide forward. Instead of watching my step, sinking into snow as I'd done on the tundra, I glided through the woods faster than I could run, and it was more of a thrill ride than exercise when I tucked my knees to zip down hills, gathering enough momentum to fly as far as I could up the next hill. I registered for both the Kortelopet and half Noquemanon, which was a month sooner, right in these trails.

On race morning at the Noque, I stood in a sea of skinny Caucasians in spandex and Swix hats. Skiers slid and scrambled across snow, testing the stickiness of kick wax applied to the middle section of their ride.

"What do you have today? Blue?"

"Oh, I went with purple. It's supposed to warm four degrees by 10:30."

"I heard the snow gets a little softer by Forestville, but most of the course will have hard-packed snow. I'm carrying a tube of klister just in case."

Brian told me I didn't need to worry about kick. My skis were waxless skis, with ridges in the kick zone beneath my boots instead of a place to apply sticker wax. He had helped me apply layers of glide wax over the rest of my skis with an iron, a scraper, and a brush. I was more concerned about my skiing ability.

I liked skiing, but I thought if I were participating in a race of any kind, it should have been a run. Brian reminded me I was a quarter Norwegian, so I'd be fine. Sure, I told him, but I'd spent much more time running than skiing. Even though I'd descended from the blonder, paler, people across the Atlantic, I had more in common with the people who got around on foot.

At the start line of the Half Noquemanon Ski Marathon, bright colors and intricate, aerodynamic designs decorated the spandex outfits surrounded me. My tights were black, and my REI jacket was dark gray. I stood and waited for someone to point me out as a fraud. I knew I'd been discovered when the skier next to me started asking questions.

"How many Noques have you done?"

"None," I said, looking straight down. "This is my first one."

"Are you from around here?"

"No," I said. I stuck the tips of my poles into the snow and slid my skis back and forth like others were doing all around me.

"Well, where are you from?"

"Alaska," I said, bracing for questions about igloos.

"Oh yeah?" he said. "Where in Alaska?"

"You'll never know it, but it's a small town called Naknek."

"Oh," he said. "My daughter went to Naknek for a summer. She worked at some kind of sandwich stand."

"Tundra Sub?"

"Yeah, that's it!" he said.

Then the race started, and I was caught in a current of spandex, Swix hats, and skis. I propelled forward with my knees bent, pushing with both poles like everyone else around me was doing. As we arrived onto the trail, we put one ski in front of the other, striding over the flat sections, herringbone stepping the uphills, and gliding on the downhills. We were not wandering an ocean. We were headed up the same river in the same direction, toward the same finish line.

Every so often, a crowd of Yoopers cheered from a bonfire, beer cans in hand. I knew the waves of skate skiers, employing a faster style of skiing, would catch up to me soon. Brian was one of them, and he taunted me in 19-year-old-guy fashion as he blazed by me and kept soaring over the snow through the trees.

I never saw the guy who'd heard of Naknek, but I began to think that I wasn't so far from home after all. This style of cross-country skiing, soaring up and down hills over a trail through the trees, was different than the style of my upbringing, but it was somehow more fitting. I wasn't a single speck on an ocean, but one of many, charging ahead toward an ultimatum. I finished third place in my age group.

It was a month later, at the Telemark Resort in Hayward when Brian and I were admiring the portraits on the wall of all the previous Birkie champions. Both of us had won our age categories in our divisions at the Noquemanon, and I was going into the Birkie a little more confidently than I'd gone into the Noque, even though I attributed it to most people our age being hungover on Saturday morning.

"Hey, do you fish in Bristol Bay?"

I turned around. It wasn't the guy from the Noque. It was someone else this time.

"Your shirt," he said. "It looks like you've been there."

He was talking about my cotton Fisherman's Bar sweatshirt.

"Have you been to Naknek?" he asked.

"Yeah," I said. "That's where I'm from."

"I fish mostly in Egegek," he said. "But I keep my boat stored in Naknek."

These encounters weren't that strange, I guess. Naknek, a town of about 500, known for nothing, grew to about 6,000 because it was known for its world-class commercial fishing. Hayward, a town of about 2,000 known for its world-class musky fishing in a pond of a lake, grew to about 11,000 for Birkie weekend. That summer, that guy stopped by the house while I was adding another purple layer of paint to the skiff, like he was there to prove to me that these different worlds in which I lived were on the same planet.

The lavender shade of the skiff could have been the color of any of the spandex suits surrounding me at the start of the Kortelopet. Brian and I watched the elite skiers and the waves to follow. Each time, the oversized ribbon, comprised of banners of sponsors, lifted — and a surge of bright colors propelled forward onto the trail.

Brian began in wave three. I started in the tenth and final wave. I wouldn't begin in wave one for several years, after several times skiing the full Birkie. In the meantime, I stripped my top layer of clothes, shot through the gate with the others, and sprung onto the trail, like a salmon swimming upstream.

Upriver from Graveyard, downriver from Levelock, is a tributary to the Kvichak called the Alagnak River, also known as the Branch. It is a thin, shallow waterway that forks into two lakes — the Nonvianuk and the Kukaklek. Alagnak is a word for making a mistake, like taking a turn into the wrong lake. Like Graveyard, the canneries on the Alagnak, and even the original villages, have long since been abandoned. There is almost nothing left of it since most of the lumber was gathered and salvaged to build new homes in Levelock, Igiugig, and Naknek.

There are two sportfishing lodges on the Alagnak. The Royal Wolf Lodge is at the mouth of the Nonvianuk. Our family, as well as two other families, stayed there for a weekend one winter. We slept in cabins with no lights or heat, sat in a dark lodge, and spent the days cross-country skiing and playing in the snow. The other lodge, the Big Ku is at the mouth of the Kukaklek. It touts its trophy trout fishing, but plenty of salmon are caught there, too. Understandably, sport fishermen are not happy when the Alagnak is open to commercial fishing, just like lodges in King Salmon on the Naknek River are never happy about the Naknek River Special Harvest Area.

Dad and I have flown north together to finish the house before Mom, Erica, and Luke arrive. Somewhere between Minneapolis and Chicago and Seattle and Anchorage, the airline has lost our bags. The hotel has given away our reservations, because we arrive after midnight after trying to get our bags back. We stay, instead, at the motel where there is a mirror in front of the toilet, where Norm once observed on an NYO trip how he could watch himself take a shit. Dad stays calm and collected. He hasn't yet gone into what Mom calls fishing mode. He hasn't gone into that other mode, either.

Dad stays in Anchorage to shop for groceries and supplies. I fly into King Salmon and stay the first few nights at Joey's where we work with his dad, painting porches and railings at their lodge, and installing the dock. Joey has worked with his dad as a guide sportfishing longer than I've worked with mine in the commercial world. They grumbled only a little about the anticipated in-river fishery again. Although I've caught a fair share of trout and salmon on a rod and reel, including a massive king with Dad, it's the most I've ever seen of this side of fishing as we scrub skiffs, paint buildings at their lodge, and float a dock onto the water.

Their operation is a low-key operation compared to the Bear Trail Lodge in King Salmon or even the Royal Wolf or the Big Ku on the Alagnak, but aesthetics are all-the-more important than a commercial fishing operation.

When Dad arrives in King Salmon, the plane is five hours late because it's Penn Air, and Penn Air is always late. We stay with Mo and Smiley as we resume our own project, finishing the house we started last summer. He stays calm the whole time, even though I am slow and unskilled. I shove insulation into the walls and screw sheetrock to studs. I know about as much about this kind of work as I did last summer, but Dad is patient, and by the middle of June, Dad and I have made the house inhabitable. The walls are exposed sheetrock and the floor is white paint over the plywood, but the electricity works, and the appliances are connected. It's more comfortable than Graveyard.

When Mom, Erica, and Luke arrive, we are a family living in Naknek again. The difference is that we are in a house in a gravel lot across the Alaska Peninsula Highway from Alaska General Seafoods. The view of this town is much different right in the heart of it. Instead of looking over the tundra or the Naknek River, a yellow, metal gate is open all summer for trucks to haul driftboats in and out of their boatyard. The Alaska Lou is a massive aluminum driftboat with high antennas, and we can see the crew through their windows across the road, and they can see us through ours even more easily.

In the ditch alongside the road, there are rocks and dirt packed from decades of threewheeler and fourwheeler traffic. The dust is thick, and it swirls in the wind from fourwheelers blasting along in the trail swooping over driveways. Fourwheelers blaze by the house, and the dust they raise shrouds the brush and the skiffs parked in the corner of the lot. The gravel is without vegetation except patches of grass that we pull with our hands from time to time. Dad moves boulders onto our driveway to force fourwheelers to slow when they pass our house.

Cannery workers can't help but stare into the property as they walk back and forth on the shoulder. Dad has built a circular brick floor around a stone fire pit, like the one at the old house. The bricks are from crumbled buildings at Libbyville. Before fishing begins, there are parties around the fire, some intended, but others by happenstance when friends drive by and see us. Sometimes they aren't friends at all.

As the solstice approaches, the days drift into nights without notice until a glance at a clock. There aren't many mosquitoes in the gravel, even in calm, warm weather. There is almost no feeling of an upcoming fishing season when the wind seems to blow harder, rain pours heavier, and temperatures drop to near-freezing.

One afternoon, when it's still warm, Dad, Mom, Luke, Erica, and I sit in chairs, watching traffic, beer cans in our hands. People have moved the boulders, so Dad has dug a divot in the ditch. We're waiting to see a fourwheeler thud into it and think twice about moving so fast. A kid on a bike, the only kid on a bike we've ever seen ride by the house, is the victim of the trap. He pedals through it like a champion, and we can't help but laugh at the ironic injustice.

Schoolbuses haul workers from the King Salmon airport. Another group of tattooed, bearded, pierced bad dudes passes. Living downtown has made us all take notice of the workers more than ever, and we all hope for the season to start. Waiting, as the Tom Petty song on the radio says, is the hardest part, but now, along with TV, internet, and board games, we have the traffic to entertain us, frighten us, or concern us. As we wait for an opener, more workers stroll by as fourwheelers roll slowly over the logs and boulders.

Before the regulatory season begins, fishing is open from Monday at 9:00 AM to Friday at 9:00 AM. We fish this schedule for a week. Free Week, we call it. It is usually a time to catch water flowing through the web, but it's a time to get out on the water, work out kinks, and get back into the rhythm of things. Afterward, there is more waiting for the first official announcement.

With poor escapement, the Alagnak is open to commercial fishermen in the Naknek-Kvichak District. Erica comes with me and Dad, and we take the skiff beyond Graveyard, beyond Nakeen, and up into the Branch. It is so shallow and clear that I can see the fish swimming along the gravel and against the weeds.

Because of the difference the tide makes in a river this small, the period is for a mere two-and-a-half hours. Although what we are doing is legal for today, everything about it feels wrong. The familiar fishermen in grungy Grundens rain gear and scale-swathed skiffs are not in a muddy place, but in a clear, clean one. Our nets don't block the width of the river, but almost half of it. I can see the fish through the water, hitting the net, attempting to back away, and then starting what is almost always a futile fight.

Past generations of these fish heading into the Kukaklek and Nonvianuk have not had this kind of interference. Now here we are, and there they are, and they don't stop either. In less than an hour, we have filled three brailers, and when the first hour does pass, all of them are full. We start pulling the nets, but the fish keep hitting, and soon there is only a half-hour left of the opening.

Our neighboring fishermen have their gear out of the water, so Dad buzzes over to them to ask for help. In our two-and-a-half-hour opening, we catch about 5,000 pounds. We keep about 3,500. By the end, the day is no longer calm and sunny. First, it starts raining. Then it thunders, a rarity in Bristol Bay. It's a long, bumpy ride back to Naknek.

The Alagnak opens again, and because of the situation last time, we're taking two skiffs. This time, Dad recruits Mom to come with us, which means Luke comes, too. The whole family heads to the Alagnak together. Go figure this time we only catch about 1,400 pounds, half of it in the green skiff I drive.

Mom and Luke ride with me back to Naknek, and it's wavy and water splashes my face. Luke and Mom sit on the bench, facing me with their hands tight around it. Just upriver from Graveyard Creek, the motor fails. Onshore wind pushes waves curling and crashing against the beach. In seconds, we'll crash with them.

I know that there are boulders beneath the surface, and the beach there is hard as rock. Colliding with it at the wrong angle could send me, Luke, Mom, and the nets underneath the weight of the skiff. Luke is young, but I'm sure he can lift the bow anchor. It needs to grapple the bottom to keep us from shore. Dad will be angry, but he'll be able to help us get the motor going again.

"Luke, throw the anchor!"

He lifts the anchor still tied to the end of the net, still laying on top of it.

"Not that anchor!" Then I point to the one on top of the coil of line in the bow.

"What anchor?"

There's not enough time, so I run up and throw it myself. I hold the line as the skiff jerks and holds in place.

Dad tows us into Graveyard Creek and works his magic there. He drives away, and it fails again before we even move. He fixes it again and takes over, telling me to drive the Yamaha back to Naknek. It operates smoothly, and Dad pulls ahead of us. He keeps the other motor going with his magic as waves hit.

I think his throttle must be failing again because he stops. "Go faster!" He's waving his arm toward Naknek.

I already have the throttle on full blast. I look at Mom and Luke and tell them.

It isn't long before he does it again. "That skiff goes faster than this skiff!"

I look at Mom and Luke, but I don't need to tell them what they already know. Nothing I say or do is going to matter. Dad is in full-fledged fishing mode.

Days go by. Drifters don't have their 80 percent allocation. After a long closure, the Naknek River still won't be open to setnetters, but they are opening the Alagnak again, so another adventure awaits. This time only Erica comes with Dad and me. The Alagnak run has slowed, and the fishing settles. It doesn't seem worth the trip anymore.

By July 12th, the Kvichak opens, but we stay in the Naknek River because there are more fish here, and there is only a week or so at most left of the season. For each opening, we leave in the truck, hop into the Purp on the beach below City Dock. Then we drive to our in-river site just below the bank by the old neighborhood. It's a spot before it bends, forcing fish into an eddy. With the gravel roads and the cedar home where we once lived above us, we are down on the Naknek River with the salmon.

Darwin was a white rabbit in a cage across a dusty, laminate floor. His nose, his tail, and his ears twitched the way I twitched at four-way intersections, traffic lights, semi-trucks, and honking horns. He twitched the way I twitched at the thought of getting lost on a road I didn't know, turning the wrong way and turning the wrong way again until I'd turned in every combination of wrong ways, still unable to find my way home.

I had been among the Lower 48's endless, interconnecting system of pavement almost four years, but it hadn't helped my sense of direction. I'd gone downstate with a roommate, I'd gone to Hayward with Brian, I'd driven over to Washburn, and I'd been to Big Bay — a half-hour up a road along the shore — with a girl I dated, but I hadn't driven anywhere five hours outside of Marquette. I was fascinated by the idea of travel without a plane ticket, without a boat, without even making a plan, but in a time before smartphones or affordable GPS units, venturing out on my own was terrifying.

As Darwin twitched, I was lying on a mattress without a bed frame, and the mattress belonged to a girl next to me. It hadn't gone the way you might think. I was too careful and cautious for that kind of thing. Sure, I'd left the bar with her. Sure, we'd gone to her place. Sure, I woke up with her next to me. Maybe it was the alcohol, maybe it was the lack of sleep, or maybe it was an immature desire of a 20-something to be seen friends leaving the bar with a cute girl.

We had been introduced by mutual friends, and our friends had no doubt watched the verbal exchange of subjects that I don't remember until arose the age-old question over her place or mine. Her place was closer, and now here we were.

When we'd left the bar, my truck remained parked downtown, accumulating snow in the Upper Peninsula winter night, and the two of us walked a straight line up the street — no turns, no intersections, nothing complicated. Under a streetlight, in the snowfall, my feet were cold, and I thought about how to back out of this rabbit hole. High school health class was coming back to haunt me with the video of a live birth. Although symptoms may not appear, the more recent TV commercial had said, it still may be possible to spread herpes to others.

I had seen Clint Eastwood, James Bond, and even Bruce Wayne leave social functions with women, but these were fictional characters — and I'd never actually seen anything explicit happen. Bruce Wayne was always interrupted by the bat signal flashing against the clouds. He'd always excuse himself before leaping into the night, cape flowing behind him, to stop Penguin, the Joker, Two-Face, or whoever was terrorizing Gotham City. In any given Bond movie, the screen transitioned to the next shot of a Bentley, BMW, or Rolls-Royce with machine guns and an ejector seat blazing down the road to finish the real mission. Tonight, there was no bat signal. Tonight, there was no mission, now I was sure that I was making a mistake.

The girl told me that she shared a house with roommates, so I should be quiet if I came inside. Instead of taking the opportunity to say goodbye at the door and wish her a good night, I walked into the door with her and discovered the living room was a zoo.

She introduced me to every one of the animals. There were dogs, cats, fish, and even a parrot. I gave every one of them a pat on the head, a stroke of the back, or a polly-wanna-cracker, until I saw she was standing at the foot of the staircase waiting for me. It was another chance to part ways, bid her adieu, say something's come up, and pretend I had something important to attend to, but I went up the stairs with her.

Some of the steps creaked. Others didn't. She whispered as we climbed up, reminding me again of her human roommates. Outside her bedroom door was a cage of rabbits, brown and gray and spotted, to whom we also said hello. Then she opened the door of her bedroom, where the mattress was on the floor, and where Darwin had a cage to himself. She unlatched the cage, opened it, and handed him to me. His nose twitched back and forth, and he stared at me with blank eyes.

"Give him a kiss goodnight," she said.

Here was another opportunity to say goodnight, but instead of walking down the stairs, or taking it the other direction and making some quip about wasting a good kiss on a rabbit, I bent my neck and gave Darwin a quick peck on the forehead. I waited for approval.

"That's not a real kiss," she told me.

Instead of an I-don't-think-so and an I-gotta-go or taking it the other way and going for the human kiss, I held my lips against the fur just above Darwin's nose, exaggerated a smooching sound, and waited for a count of two seconds before looking again to the girl. She was grinning this time, satisfied. I was finally satisfied, too. At last, I had mustered the courage to suggest that it was a good idea to go home.

Before I could speak, she interrupted.

"Now we can snuggle," she said.

I was okay with just snuggling. We stripped down just to underwear, and I lay down, sighed, closed my eyes, faded to black, and blurred into the next scene.

In my dreams, I drove through intersections and highways, speeding to important locations, finding important clues, saving the day, disappearing mysteriously into the night, or day, or sunrise, looking up for the bat signal for some point of reference.

The preceding day's events, however, were no dream. Alice, not the girl next to me, and not her real name, was a girl I'd met in class. We often conversed after we were dismissed, agreeing on politics and talking about running.

I'd walked into Subway on Washington Street to order a sandwich between errands. Alice was there on her phone, so I nodded hello and proceeded to make my order. When I sat down, she sat down across from me and said she was looking for a favor. She was attending a conference in Orlando, and she needed to be at the airport in Milwaukee that night.

I asked if there was anyone else who could lend a hand. I barely knew Alice, and I was supposed to go see *Sin City* with the guys that night. She excused herself to make a phone call and stood with her phone to her ear, nodding, glancing over to me as though making sure I was still there. When she came back, she told me if I drove her to Escanaba, less than an hour away, she could catch a bus from there. It seemed like a fair compromise.

I didn't know she had to go home and pack first. Alice lived with her parents, in her childhood home, where an entire family greeted me, and I wondered why none of them were driving her. I learned that her Mom had to work at the courthouse, her dad had an appointment, and her sister had to get to work at the Marquette Co-op. Fair enough,

I figured, and I asked Alice what time the bus left from Escanaba. She changed the subject, and I answered questions about fishing. It seemed every time I expressed concern about the time, she should promptly ask me something about fishing.

We went upstairs, where she packed her suitcase. Shuffling around the bedroom, Alice picked up items near and dear to her, explaining to me their history — papers she'd written in highschool, a jewelry box of polished rocks, dolls, a hairbrush, and clothing that she never wore. She held up a dress and asked if I could believe she had ever worn it. I kept glancing at my watch. Almost three hours passed, and I asked again when the bus left. Fishing in Bristol Bay is nothing like *Deadliest Catch*, I told her.

When we left the house with her suitcase and a cardboard box in the back of my truck, she said we had to stop at the Co-op to say goodbye to her sister. When I reminded her that we had said goodbye to her already, she said we needed snacks.

We stopped, and as Alice began chatting with her sister, I gathered almond butter, bread, cans of sardines, and asked again when the bus left. No, I told Alice, sardines aren't as quite as wholesome and sustainable as wild Alaskan salmon, but they were a close second place.

I made my purchase, and we were back in my truck. We were almost on the way, but first, she had to stop and say goodbye to her mom at the courthouse. Again, I asked when the bus left. No, there is no significant bycatch in our nets other than flounders we throw back into the water, usually still alive.

We took a tour of the building and chatted with her mom before we were on the road, tiny Upper Peninsula towns flying by us — log piles, fishing holes, woods, cheap motels, and on the other side, the massiveness of Lake Superior.

"One time I ran out to this spot," I told her for some reason as we passed a very recognizable white-sand beach. I had never told anyone that, and I didn't care if she knew it. I would have said it aloud even if I were by myself.

"And then back home?" she asked.

"Yeah."

"What's the longest you've ever run?"

"I'm not sure," I told her. "I think it's at least thirty miles though. Someday, I want to try to run 100."

I'd never said that to anyone either.

Once we were in Escanaba, I asked how to get to the bus station, but we weren't going there yet. First, she informed me, we needed to stop at Walmart. Walmart, she explained, had boxes for donations of old clothing, which is why she brought all the old stuff. If she'd mentioned it earlier, I might have thought her more rational.

There were no boxes, however, and the white-haired man in the blue vest had no idea what she was talking about. We walked back to my truck with the clothes, and again, I asked how to get to the bus station and when the bus left for Milwaukee. She assured me that the bus was not as exact or as reliable as the tide, and then she walked away with her phone to her ear.

Her friend on the phone, she told me, had given her the wrong bus schedule. She was so, so, so, very sorry, but now we'd have to drive to Menominee, the last town on the Michigan side of the Menominee River another hour away. This time, she apologized and thanked me in the same sentence.

"But what time does the bus leave?"

Salmon are on their way to freshwater to spawn when we catch them, so they die whether we catch them or not.

Somewhere near a town called Fox, on Highway 35 along a breezy, cloudy bay, I could feel my frustration brewing. I could have been a rabbit in a cage, twitching with energy, longing for the first chance to leap away, even if the cage happened to be my truck going seven miles over the speed limit like Dad always suggested was still slow enough for traffic cops not to bother me.

"Are you sure we're going to make it on time?" I asked. "Maybe you should check with your friend again."

"We'll be fine," she said. "You don't worry like this on the boat, do you?"

She had taken off her shoes and her feet were resting on the dashboard. It was 3:00 in the afternoon, and the flight was at 7:00, giving Alice two hours three hours to check in an hour before her flight. I didn't know much about public transit, but I was sure it was slow. I didn't know when the bus left, but I knew there was no time to stop, and there was no going back.

When we arrived in Menominee, I asked how to get to the bus station. She didn't know, so I stopped at a Citgo station to ask for directions. A stoned teenager behind the red counter and bangs down to his nose, said there was no such place. Menominee didn't have a bus station. Without looking me in the eye, Alice went out to my truck, got her laptop, and came back to sit on a case of Coke. She told to wait while she tried to figure out what detail she had gotten wrong. Without a word, I walked out, sat down in the driver's seat, shut the door, and breathed.

I watched her through two layers of glass — my windshield and the window of the Citgo station. Her computer was on her lap, and she was staring at the screen. Her hands were at the sides of the keyboard, but there was no movement. There was no typing and no movement of a cursor, but her eyes were fastened to the screen. I wondered if it was blank. I wondered if anyone had been on the other end of her phone conversations while she had nodded and talked and glanced over at me. I fastened my seatbelt. My hand was on the key. The key was in the ignition. There was still no punching of keys and no movement of a cursor.

I could drive away, go home, deny this trip ever happened, plop down in my bed, and disappear into dreamland. This girl was manipulating me, and if I were to drive away and leave her there, it would only have been fair.

Then again, maybe she was just crazy, and if she were crazy, her behavior wasn't her fault. Maybe she actually believed there was a train station. Maybe she actually believed someone was talking to her through her phone. Maybe, to her, everything she'd said was as real as everything outside my windshield. I stared through it and the window of the Citgo, each layer of glass distorting reality, however slight. I thought of my own social awkwardness, my lack of direction, and how I probably skewed reality myself. Then it dawned on me. *What if I'm the crazy one?*

Before I could decide, Alice opened the passenger door and took a seat. She said she'd find a ride to Milwaukee with some people she knew in Menominee. If that didn't work, she'd start hitchhiking. I thought about her walking on the side of the road, suitcase in hand, clothes flailing about in the wind of passersby.

"No," I said. "Let's get you to Milwaukee."

I drove three hours there, following road signs, listening to Alice's instructions. It was dark by the time we rolled into the city.

Lights and gas stations and more lights and streets and buildings and lights whizzed by as I twitched, and my muscles tensed.

When we arrived at the airport, I remembered Alice had unpacked her suitcase in the Walmart parking lot in Escanaba. The contents were strewn all over the bed of my truck. We got out of the cab, and she started sorting her things. A security officer, on cue, was approaching within the minute.

"Hey, you can't stay parked here," he said to me.

"I know," I said.

Alice kept shoveling things into the suitcase.

"Yeah, you gotta go," he said.

"I know," I said again.

He saw that Alice had nothing accomplished, and I think he took pity on me.

"Okay, I'm gonna give you a minute," he said. "But you gotta make it quick!"

Alice was trying to zip shut the suitcase over protruding clothes when he started to approach us again. In tears, she began to profess how she just couldn't go. She just couldn't. I'd done all this for her, she said, and now she was going to leave me abandoned in Milwaukee with such a long, long, drive home, and there was no way she could ever, ever, ever repay me. She felt terrible, she told me.

"Alice," I said. "Get on the plane."

She hugged me, grabbed an armful of clothes, shoved them into her carry-on backpack, left the suitcase, and dashed away through the automatic doors, articles of clothing dangling from her arms. The security guard shot me a strange look as I drove into the night.

Headlights screamed by me. There were honking horns, semi-trucks, wrong turns, more wrong turns, and more wrong turns after that before I found my way out of Milwaukee. Then I don't know when I made the first, second, or third wrong turn on the way back to Marquette. I wove my way through the back roads and tiny towns with slow speed limits surrounded by hay bales and dairyland. I was often startled by deer crossing and the seldom set of headlights from the opposite direction. My eyes were heavy, and the roads swerved more than my wheels.

I stopped to pee. I stopped to buy beef jerky. I stopped to study my outdated road atlas again. Every time I stopped, no matter the reason, I peered into the back of my truck to convince myself the suitcase and the contents scattered on the floor were real. By the time it was in the light of the sun again, I was less sure.

I rolled into Marquette, parked in front of my apartment building, walked into my one-bedroom apartment with matted-down shag carpet, and I fell asleep with my clothes on.

My answering machine is what woke me. I had, had, had to come out tonight, the voice of a friend informed me. There was a girl I had, had, had to meet. She, of course, was the girl with the white rabbit. The girl was next to me, and Darwin was twitching in his cage across the room.

I don't know how long I'd slept. It might have been six, eight, ten hours, but the girl was still next to me, wide awake.

"All I have for breakfast is some cereal," she said.

"That's all right," I said. "I'm late already."

I had nowhere to go. It wasn't another week until my presentation in my sociology class. I was in front of the room discussing the social ramifications of the debate over Pebble Mine when Alice arrived and took a seat at least five minutes after I'd started. She had returned from her mysterious trip to Orlando.

Starting then, my phone rang several times a day, and it was always her. She would begin speaking and she would keep speaking until the limited time of one minute ended.

"Hey! It's Alice. I'm just calling to see if maybe you want to go on a hike or get some lunch, and if maybe you don't get this until after lunch maybe get dinner later or maybe take a bike ride. I don't know if you've run yet today, but maybe we could go for a run, or maybe you'd be up to run again. If not, we could just make plans to study for the test next week or...."

Moments later, the phone rang again, and she continued.

She started appearing around town too often to be coincidental, even in a smaller city like Marquette. I was leaving for dinner with some friends when her dad's truck almost plowed into me with her behind the wheel. She rolled down the window and asked where I was going next. I told her I wasn't sure, but I thought the plan was to go to the Upfront and Company, a bar down by the shore downtown. I went to a friend's apartment and hid.

If she did catch me on my phone, I said I needed to study, I was having dinner with my grandparents, or I was just about to clean or do laundry. She insisted on joining me in all of these things, and I told her no, not this time. She would be at my apartment in minutes, usually at the door, but one time at the window.

The first time she stopped by my apartment, I said I was just leaving, I got in my truck, and I started driving nowhere in particular. Then she followed me in her dad's truck. When I drove straight, she drove straight. When I turned, she turned. It lasted several blocks as I weaved through streets at random. Eventually, she turned away and I didn't see her dad's truck again.

The next time she showed up, I told her I was going for a run, and as predicted, she insisted on going with me. Alice was usually wearing athletic clothes, so she was prepared, but she wasn't prepared enough. I could outrun her. I changed, locked the door, and started running toward the trail.

Alice wasn't out of shape, and she stayed with me at first, even as I increased the pace. I went faster and faster, but her legs moved swifter, staying with me. I pushed my body harder, kicking faster, racing away. Just when I thought that there was no way out, and I thought that maybe she was too fast, too resilient, she sputtered, slowed, and she was gone, disappeared behind some corner on the Noquemanon Trail. I could make a series of turns, come back to my apartment, lock the door, and pretend not to be home — or I could keep running, which I did.

I started keeping my phone unplugged, so instead of calling, she knocked on the door in the middle of the night, around 2:00 or 3:00. Once, she knocked for over an hour.

I should have confronted her. I should have just opened the door and told her to go away. I should have told her I didn't want to follow me around or to be presumptuous enough to visit me this late, but soon enough I'd be going to Alaska for the summer and wouldn't have to deal with it anymore. It was that day when she caught me in the parking lot of my apartment building. I told her I was heading to the grocery store, and I would be right back.

I was on a plane that afternoon.

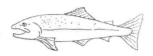

Dad and I are beneath a brailer, hoping some of our body heat is getting shared, shivering as fog drifts over the skiff. The Kvichak is in a shroud, violet from the sunrise, and the tide is low. An attempt to navigate back to Graveyard would most likely lead us straight into a mudflat. Then we'd be stuck there, freezing until the tide was high enough again. I don't know if I'm asleep when Dad tells me there is a fox scratching at the net. The image of red fur, a bushy tail, and four spindly legs is hazy, like a dream, but as the fox tears open a fish from the web in the mud, I know I'm awake because the cold penetrates the bones in my fingers.

In a dream I had three times before I was ten, the house is a pumpkin and Dad is raking leaves on the lawn. My yellow dump truck rolls back and forth against dying grass and its engine revs from my own vocal cords. Dad doesn't see the fox approaching, lunging and leaping, pinning me to my back, clawing and biting my face. He keeps raking the leaves. Then, as though bored, the fox stops thrashing me and walks away, disappearing into the bushes surrounding the lawn. Dad walks toward me with an extended hand, and in his hand is a plastic cassette tape case like the piles of them he and Mom have in the box by the stereo. The case is open and empty, and he tells me it's a present from my mother, which is strange because when he's talking to me, Dad always addresses Mom as Mom.

When I was a kid, we were told at school to beware of foxes because almost sixty percent of death from rabies happen to children, and we'd have to get not just a shot, but a series of shots as though we needed the fear of needles to keep us wary of being mauled by a rabid animal. The outbreak was in 1990, and it affected red foxes in the entire Bristol Bay area. The dream was before the outbreak. The dream was before I learned the Beatles, CCR, and Black Sabbath were pretty cool, and I borrowed the tapes, often losing the cases in the crevice between car seats. The dream was long before Mom and Dad sold the house, beginning my own series of move after move as though the place that I called home would turn into a pumpkin when time ran out.

In cultures across Europe and Asia, Fox is a trickster much like Raven, Coyote, or the Norse god, Loki. There is an ancient Hebrew tale about Fox in a time when the ocean was without life except for Leviathan lurking in the depths. Without subjects, servants, or even companionship, he summoned the Angel of Death. The Angel of Death was to drown one of every species of land creature and transform it into a fish.

Fox, who did not want to die or be a fish, sat on a cutbank, wondering how to escape his fate. Then he saw the Angel of Death's reflection in the water and began to cry. Fox explained to the Angel of Death that his friend, another fox, had been so afraid of the reflection that he jumped into the water and drowned. This reason, he said, is the reason he was crying. The Angel of Death believed the story and flew away. If there was already a foxfish, there was no reason for Fox to drown.

When Leviathan realized that there was no foxfish, he blew angry bubbles from his angry snout. He summoned the catfish and sent her to shore to lure Fox into the ocean. Fox wouldn't chase the catfish, so he sent the horsefish to offer him a ride anywhere he wanted to go. Fox wasn't buying it. Leviathan sent the lizardfish, the dragonfish, and even the fishfish. He sent fish after fish after fish, but Fox was never tricked. From that time forward, Fox was always wary of the shoreline, and there has never been a foxfish anywhere in the ocean.

In Mesopotamian stories, Fox acts as a messenger between one world and the next — like the realm of gods and the world of people, the settlers of land and the dwellers of the ocean, or this roadless region of Alaska and the rest of what's out there. In older Chinese culture, however, Fox is a trickster who takes the form of a woman, bringing misfortune to men who deserve it.

I'm walking from camp to the skiff when a fellow Graveyard dweller tells me Mom was on *the Messenger* on *KDLG*. I have a package from Alice. I stop in my tracks.

"Is that good news?" Dad asks.

"No," I say. "No, it's not."

Back in Naknek, days later, I discover that it is a card and a jar of chocolates. Mom can't let it go that this girl is quite a catch if she's making chocolates, and I shouldn't be so quick to dismiss her. It also turns out, after checking social media, that she has been harassing my friends both in Naknek and in Marquette.

That's when I write Alice a letter back. I tell her to quit bothering my friends. I tell her to quit bothering me. I don't want her chocolates and I am not interested in her. I tell her I slept with a woman the night after I drove her to Milwaukee, which is true in that I was indeed unconscious in a bed with a female, but I don't specify to Alice that there was no sex or even kissing. I want Alice to think I'm an uncaring, deceitful, misogynist pig — that she wants nothing to do with me. By the time I'm finished with the letter, I have at least convinced myself that I'm these things. I sit and stew in my self-loathing until the next opening.

As if on cue by karma, the motor problems begin the next time we're on the water. Max, Erica's boyfriend has joined us for the season. He, Dad, and I have the skiff loaded and ready to head back to Graveyard. Waves crash against the pilings as Dad pulls up to Delta Western's dock for gasoline, and we slam right along with them. Then there is a grinding and popping sound from the motor when Dad tries to adjust our position. The transmission is blown.

Dad is cursing as we drift with the waves into shore, bumping into pilings and boulders. There's a motor in the garage at home. Max and I hold the skiff while he peels his raincoat and lifejacket and stomps up the mud into town in his boots and chest waders. The truck is above City Dock, a couple miles away.

It's been a half-hour by the time he backs the motor down as far as he can with the truck. Max and I hold the skiff while Dad removes bolts from the motor, managing not to drop the hardware into the water. Then Dad and I carry the 200-plus pound powerhouse into the truck and carry down the next one and place it into the right grooves and onto the holes for the hardware while the waves continue to crash into the skiff. After lifting and grunting, trying to align the bolts with the holes for their attachment as the skiff bounces and splashes in the waves over and over again, the motor is on the stern and the fuel line is hooked to a tank and it starts without problems.

By the time Dad drives away with the broken motor in the back of the truck and comes back on foot, it's another foggy day on the Bay, so we make it to Graveyard slow and easy. The fishing is the same — slow and easy. When it starts to pick up two days later, the motor dies after setting the first net. Our neighbor fishermen, the next site over, give us an extra spark plug, and it gets the motor running again.

We make our next delivery to the Pedersen Point tender because the Beaver is leaving and not being replaced. We are already put on limits of 2,500 pounds per permit, which is not nearly as much as we could catch. In town, we get gas and stop at the cannery. Dad complains to them about us not having enough tenders on the Kvichak, and they are unremorseful.

"We don't need your fish," they tell him. "We have a million pounds and you're only ten percent of it."

We're on the water again when the motor starts clicking. It breaks down on our way back to Naknek. Dad waves his arms, blasts the airhorn, and then hangs his raincoat over the lightbar as a distress signal. It's a sign from old times, he tells me, and it turns out to work. A driftboat pulls alongside us.

"Triple A!" he yells.

They tow us toward shore until it's too shallow for them. Then they set us loose, to forge our way upriver. Max, Dad, and I push against the current for two miles, as far as we can go before hitting mud. My legs burn in the water, and I'm sure theirs are burning, too. My clothes are drenched in sweat, and we've all long since stripped ourselves of raingear. When we push the skiff onto the beach, we leave Max with it and walk until we get a ride in the back of a truck. We come back, and change motors again.

Two days later, the motor breaks down again. We borrow a skiff from some other fishermen, spend the night in Naknek, and launch the Purp.

The next day, the Yamaha on the Purp is leaking oil. Back in town, Dad pulls the Evinrude from the Lund to shove onto the Purp. When we get it to the beach, we see that it's too small to push the aluminum skiff efficiently, and it's too small to even fit over the stern. Either Max or I could have told him that, but I know better than to say anything. I whisper to Max that Dad will break the motor before he gives up. After pounding and warping and cursing, Dad forces it, and we finish the season with the motor for the Lund.

There are no more motor problems, and I never hear from Alice again. Fishing slows, and we pack the camp supplies on a calm, clear day. As most people know, sometimes problems build and build until it comes to an explosion. Maybe it's in the form of a letter. Maybe it's in the form of pounding a motor onto a skiff. Like the season, however, these things never really come to a close. I am reminded of this fact the next time I see a fox trotting along a shoreline.

By the time I was 21, before my road trip with Alice, I had decided I was ready to run a marathon. I knew I could run the distance, but I wasn't sure how fast I could do it, and my curiosity got the best of me — so much that I buried my nose into research about it.

I learned that *marathon* was derived from the Greek word for fennel, the yellow, feathery flowers sprawling through the valley where the Athenians took unprecedented victory over the invading Persian army. The Persians were many, and they were masterful warriors on the water, using the tide to surge forward against the enemy. The Battle of Marathon, however, was on land.

According to myth, Pheidippides was a messenger, a soldier who ran from the Valley of Fennel to the city of Athens. He delivered the news and then collapsed to his death. The 1886 Olympics commemorated his run with a race of about 25 miles, and the city of Boston held a similar race the next year, and soon there were other runs to follow suit. It was Queen Victoria who demanded the race finish beneath her balcony in London at the 1908 Olympics, and a marathon became 26 miles, 385 yards.

I had only run one race, the Wellness Run, when I was a college freshman. It was a five-kilometer event organized by Van Antwerp Hall, where I was living with Alan. When the resident director knocked on doors, gathering people for a meeting about it, I thought it was a meeting about running. Instead, he was recruiting dorm rats to hang flyers around town, at the Sports Rack, Downwind Sports, Lakeshore Bike, Quickstop Bike Shop, or anywhere a runner might go. I was a runner, and I knew where I'd go — on the paved path, the side of the road, or the endless network of trails in the hills and woods. Although I didn't mean to help, I was happy to promote running and wellness, and after taking those signs all over town, I knew exactly where and how to register.

On race morning, I was surprised to see that it wasn't just average Joe or college kids with hangovers gathering at the start line like I had expected. There were real athletes warming up, performing dynamic stretches, wearing performance clothing rather than musty sweats. Some of them wore oversized watches with buttons that they braced before an airhorn started us.

As much as I sucked wind and my lungs burned, I was still in the middle of the pack. I wasn't dead last, and I didn't expect to be first, but I thought, for as much as I ran, I would have been at least near the front. Racing, I had decided, was not for me, and I went right back to running just to run. It took almost four years to realize that maybe my body was not conditioned for shorter distances at a faster pace.

I had learned about the watches I'd seen. They were GPS units that runners could use to track both pace and distance in real time. There was no way I could afford one. Other than using the monitor on a treadmill, entering a race was the only way I could have an accurate measurement of how fast I could run over a prescribed distance, and a marathon is the distance I was most curious about.

The Whistlestop was in Ashland, Wisconsin, a neighboring town to Mom and Dad, and I registered as soon as I found out about it online. I didn't know how to train other than to run and run plenty, and I kept training without any structure.

In the weeks before the race, it was fall in Marquette again. Red, orange, and yellow leaves fell from maple and oak branches and piled onto the trail. My shoes shuffled through them, and I caught them in my hands as they drifted down. Temperatures were cool, the dirt was soft but dry, and the days were still long before daylight saving time. Fall, I had learned, was my favorite time of the year to run, and it was a time of year when I especially felt like I could run forever. I made the trip to Wisconsin to see the same conditions.

I remember very little of race morning. Erica was in high school, and she had registered for the half marathon with Max. Dad was still in Naknek, doing HVAC work through the fall. Mom drove us into Ashland from Washburn and Luke was forced to tag along. I took a shuttle — one of a hundred school buses — to the start line in Iron

River. Erica and Max got a ride to the start of the half marathon in the town of Moquah.

The bus ride was quiet, except for murmurs about the weather, other races, or how training had or hadn't gone well. I didn't dare tell anyone the Whistlestop was my first marathon. Then at the start line, the announcer asked first-timers to cheer. It was everyone except for a group in front with muscular legs, lean bodies, and determined faces. I wore a pair of black gym shorts, a red long-sleeved shirt from Walmart, a cross-country ski hat, and a pair of black New Balance trail shoes that later became my shoes for stomping around Graveyard. I had a protein bar and my music player stashed in a fanny pack around my waist.

I positioned myself toward the middle of the crowd, and at the sound of a gunshot, I joined them in a mass of feet flying forward. My feet seemed to be flying forward just a little faster though, and soon I had worked my way, not to the front, but close to it. I put one foot in front of the other, seeing Mom and Luke at places along the course where volunteers handed runners tiny cups of electrolyte drinks, water, and carbohydrate gels.

The trees to my sides and the finely-ground gravel of the corridor beneath my shoes were a blur. On a regular run of more than two or three hours, I would reach into my fanny pack or backpack to grab snacks, but I knew an undigested bite of banana or chunk of granola would go to a lung rather than my stomach. My body was working too hard to process food, and I was caught too much in the excitement to need the distraction of music.

I finished 31st overall, and my finish time was 3:10, two hours faster than what I would have guessed. I had little concept of my speed and distance in those days, but I knew it was faster than I'd ever run before. I also knew I hadn't been suddenly struck with an incredible jump in athletic ability. It was the sound of footstrikes behind me, the site of runners in front of me, and adrenaline from the idea of competition that propelled me faster than normal. I had thought myself motivated on my own, but I'd never run like that without other runners to push and pull me along. I could barely walk for three days.

One of my classes the next semester was *Physiology of Exercise*. Professor Watts was a tall, lanky rock climber and cross-country skier who confessed to believing that the world revolved around endurance sports. Surrounded by jocks, future trainers, and meatheads staring toward the front of the room, I scribbled detailed notes about how the human body adapts to exercise and how nutrition accompanies it. It had been guesswork before, and as I learned from his North Carolina accent talking about the margin of *errah*, it would always be guesswork — but now it would be educated guesswork.

There was a lab component of the class led by a graduate student, and I was always quick to volunteer as a lab rat. We used devices to measure body fat percentage, muscle fiber recruitment, muscle strength, muscle flexibility, and heart rate. Girls giggled at my leaping heart rate as they applied electrodes to my shirtless torso. I told them that I was just excited for the next experiment.

One experiment was a test of VO2Max, the maximum amount of oxygen I could inhale for blood to transport nutrients and hormones to working muscles. Unprepared for class as always, I ran to my apartment, a couple of blocks from the Physical Education Instructional Facility, changed into shorts, and ran back. When I stepped onto an oversized treadmill with an airtight mask, my heart rate was already elevated again. I'd just finished an eight-mile run a half hour before class.

The treadmill moved at a slow pace, a ten-minute mile, but the steepness went up a grade every minute. After ten minutes, I was sweating, burning, and fogging the mask, pointing at numbers on a chart for my rate of perceived exertion. I went from a two to what I felt like was an eleven as a computer screen read the amount of oxygen I was consuming. My classmates shouted words of encouragement as I pushed harder than I'd ever pushed before until my legs gave out and I stood at the front edge of the treadmill, leaning on the panel, sucking air through the mask.

I didn't have the levels of an elite athlete, but I had more than double the levels of an average person. After class was dismissed, the graduate assistant instructor took me aside and asked me about my marathon time and my training plan. My time was all right, but nothing special, and I had no real plan. By the end of the conversation, I was inspired to put one together with the information and the book titles he had given me. I'd been lifting weights for years, thinking of workouts in terms of sets and repetitions, but I hadn't attached the ideas to running.

I had registered for the Journeys Marathon in May, in Eagle River, Wisconsin. The slogan all on its website was *Because Life Isn't a*

Destination, and I liked that slogan even though it sparred with my newfound ideas about structuring training. Mondays, I went to the weight room to strengthen my legs. Wednesdays, I sprinted from light post to light post, jogging easily between the next two light posts. Saturday, I ran for three hours or more. All the other days I took easy jogs and did light cross-training, like biking or using an elliptical machine at the gym. Fridays, I made time for an upper-body circuit. I never knew when another girl would need to apply electrodes to my bare torso.

I was ready to break the three-hour barrier. Three weeks before the race, I started to taper — to take the running down a notch, another notch, and another, to let my body absorb the difficult training I'd put it through, and to be well-rested by the time I drove to Eagle River. I spent the night in the back of my truck on a forest service road, ate sprouted grain bread with almond butter for breakfast, and made my way to the start line.

I began fast and ferocious, and I kept at it and kept at it some more. I strode confidently forward until mile eighteen. I was sure I was going to kill it. Then it started to kill me. My pace wasn't a gradual decline. It was a sudden sputter, as though my gas tank had run out of fumes. I was forced into a painful jog for the remainder of the course, and it was more slow and painful as the mile markers went to 20, 23, and 25. At the finish, my time was five minutes slower than I'd wanted. I walked away from the finish line, limping and disappointed. My lesson was learned, and at the next Whistlestop, I'd have another chance.

The aluminum skiff has no ribs. It has no name. Its surface is cold and smooth, and when we wait for the tide, I sit on top of a brailer, listening to waves splash, wind howl, and seagulls squawk in the near distance. Dad was in the Purp by himself, delivering, when the bow smashed against a tender. I was in the green skiff, picking fish by myself, because we were running out of time. The Purp didn't break apart, but it cracked, and Dad salvaged it with some caulking and sold it last August. Now the new Purp exposes a green undercoat when the paint chips away. We are one of the last operations to begin using an aluminum skiff.

No one is fishing the sites around us, so Dad and I have all four of our nets downriver. The regulatory season is over, which means we're open Monday morning until Friday morning. We aren't even staying at Graveyard. We're riding out against the waves from Naknek, fishing our nets, and going back to the house to sleep. The wind has been nasty every day, but we're catching five to seven thousand pounds every tide, and it's worth the effort. It's worth the pounding against my chest as I pull lines and anchors attached to their chains.

A ribcage protects a person's heart and lungs. It protects the heart and lungs of a wolf, a dog, or a bear. It protects the heart and lungs of a bird, a frog, or even a fish. A fish's ribcage, however, is flexible. My heart and lungs have made significant leaps in their capacity in the last year, and I wonder how much they could grow if my ribs were as pliable as the ribs of a fish. I wonder how much the fishing season undoes the progress of my heart and lungs as I slog through the weeks without real aerobic stress.

Physical stress in the fishing season comes from limited sleep and muscular fatigue. From the bow, I reach down to the water, grab the bridle line tied to the corkline, I lift upward, and again my chest presses against the aluminum. The life jacket around my torso beneath my raincoat is enough cushion for a slow tide, but Dad and I are in the final days of the season. I've pressed my chest into this aluminum net after net, tide after tide, and the tide is running hard. The waves are mountains drifting, their white-capped peaks crashing onto shore. My lower back aches, my forearms burn, and my shoulders are torn apart one more time before the lines are over the bow. Another wave crashes against us.

My ribs break. I don't know yet that they are broken. It's Erica who tells me later, that it's not just a bruise or some simple soreness. For now, I just know that it hurts to breathe hard, it hurts to laugh, it hurts to cough, and it hurts when I first get out of bed. For now, it's a painful spot in the left side of my chest, so I try to lean against my right side or my center, where I haven't tenderized the bone to the point of such weakness.

I hope this pain isn't the eve of my running ability's downfall. In all the warnings of doom and gloom I've heard about running and the damage it can do on my joints, I have explored other endurance sports in preparedness for a day I can't run. I have kept skiing and biking, but I've also tried my hand at swimming. Last August, I bought a wetsuit, bought some books on the sport, and started trying it in Lake Superior. I even started a swimming class at Northern, but I dropped it. The only other students were members of the swim team, and instead of instruction, I was given drills I was expected to know but didn't.

I have tried to teach myself to swim, but guess I have an allergy to it — meaning I can't breathe water. When I was a kid, other kids who were more athletic practiced Sockeye Swim League at the pool. There was no way I was putting on a Speedo. It wasn't a school-sponsored sport, so as far as Mom and Dad were concerned, I was off the hook.

In my first triathlon, I couldn't wait to get in the clear, calm water of that little lake. It was hot onshore, and I wanted to get the first part of the race over-with. Then I discovered it is difficult enough to rotate kicks and arm strokes with turning my head and breathing above the surface, but it's almost impossible while being kicked and scratched and punched in the face.

I may not be a good swimmer, but I share the same fishy ancestor as all other land animals. A fish embryo and a human embryo share the same arch below the head, but when I was born, they closed and became part of my jaw, middle ear, and my ability to speak. My larynx is cartilage that could have been a gill.

In some ways, a fish is more efficient. When my brain stem controls my breath, the message travels from my head to my lungs and back to my head. In fish, the message doesn't have to travel nearly as far. The gills and throat surround the brain. I have a chest, abdomen, diaphragm, and lungs, complicating the route. The message can get lost, causing a hiccup. I'm a hiccup in evolution.

To maintain my athletic endeavors, I have to hope these ribs heal. They should heal, because although my body is not one of a fish, it is like the river. Its molecular structure isn't stagnant but fluid. It's always flowing, and every seven years, almost every cell in a person's body has been replaced. The Keith who started fishing is not the same Keith as today, but Keith is still an ancient word for wood. Bone, unfortunately, is the only part of us that doesn't replace itself at such a rapid rate. It breaks before it bends. Bone has more in common with wood than it does aluminum.

Inside bone, however, as I've learned, is a substance called collagen. It's not like wood or aluminum. It's more like a line between buoys, a line between a buoy and an anchor, or the line on the anchor tied from our bow. When the tide pulls it, a line stiffens and strengthens. When it's coiled on the floor of the skiff, it's weak. As I pull the last line into the skiff for the last time this season, I take comfort knowing it will strengthen again. Someday I will not be able to run, and I will need to be flexible enough to spend more time on different endeavors.

The fishing season had been over for three weeks, and there was no way I should have been running a race, let alone a full marathon. Not only was I out of condition from several weeks without running, but if I breathed too hard, my broken ribs screamed at me. I ran the Paavo Nurmi Marathon, in Hurley, Wisconsin anyway. It was my last year in Marquette, and for all I knew, I would end up teaching in some remote Alaskan village. I needed to race when I could. I could just take this one easy, I told myself, and the pain in my chest would be an effective governor. Then I was caught in the pull of the race, and I went too fast and hit the wall not long after the halfway point. It took me three and a half hours to finish. It took me a week to walk like me again.

It didn't matter. The Whistlestop in October was the *real* race, and I was still determined to run it in less than three hours. The pain in my ribs was less intense by September, and I could sprint harder than ever. I could squat and leg-press more iron plates than I ever had. I could run farther than I'd ever run before, using the kilometer marks on the trail and estimating the distance when I went on the bike path. The pain in my chest lingered just enough for me to notice.

In early September, I ran the Wakefield Marathon and won it. There were only twelve of us, including the race director who I had helped set orange cones around Sunday Lake. I'd spent the night in my truck and had arrived at the course early, Wakefield being just outside of the Eastern Time Zone. The race was nine-and-a-half laps on the paved path around Sunday Lake. It was clear and stagnant, and it looked the same every lap, but the little lump in the course felt more like a mountain every time.

No one in my family was home in Washburn when I stayed there for the Whistlestop again. Erica was a freshman at Northern, and Mom, Dad and Luke were living full-time in Naknek, because Luke wanted to hunt and fish and be a star on the basketball team. I slept in an empty house and woke up ready to push my body to move faster than I'd ever pushed it. I had learned not to push too hard of course, lest I hit the wall again.

I took the bus from Ashland to Iron River, stood in the front of the pack this time, and took off down the familiar limestone corridor. I still didn't have a GPS watch, so I went by the way I felt. If I felt like I was going too slowly, I pushed myself harder. If I felt like I was going too hard, I took it down a notch. The pain in my ribs was my indicator of the proper effort zone.

As I approached the finish line, the numbers on the clock displayed what looked like 2:59. I hunkered forward and moved into a full sprint. That's when the inside of my right thigh spazzed into a cramp and I shrieked as I limped on a leg as stiff as a wooden plank to the finish line. When I was close enough to see it, I realized that the nine was a four. I'd surpassed my hopes by five minutes.

It was my fifth and final year of college — what I called my second senior year. By the winter semester, my ribs were healed, my beard was bushy, and my hair was shoulder-length. In Gwinn, a town 21 miles south of Marquette, where I was student teaching, the kids called me Jesus. I couldn't walk on water, but I was feeling confident about my running ability.

Of course, making time for training was more of a challenge with a full workday and the travel time, but I made it fit. I went to the gym early and I ran in the evening. I had registered for four marathons in the spring, all within five weeks of each other, and I had some training to do. I was only skipping a weekend because of my graduation.

The first of these springtime marathons was in April, in Medford, Wisconsin — the Pine Line Marathon. It was another night in the back of my truck, but this time it was freezing, and the wind was noisy. I was tucked into my sleeping bag, not quite asleep when red and blue lights flashed through the fogged windows. Then the beam of a flashlight was in my face. The cop forced me out of my sleeping bag and onto the dirt parking lot. I stood barefoot and shirtless in sleet as he checked the record of this unkempt 20-something white male sleeping in the park in the back of a red Ford Ranger.

He came back to my truck and told me I couldn't stay here, but Medford had plenty of hotels. He proceeded to give me directions to the Medford Inn.

"Okay, thanks," I said.

I spent the night in the Walmart parking lot.

Sideways-blowing sleet continued into race morning. I had on a knit hat, compression shorts, and a blue, long-sleeved shirt. Most runners were more bundled than me, but next to me was a man with no shirt, no hair on his head, and no hair on his body. He was sinewy, free of visible bodyfat, chiseled like the statue of an ancient Athenian runner. For the first half of the course, I watched his perfect stride and the flexion of his calves.

Somewhere along the course, he, one other runner, and I were called back by a loud voice telling us we'd missed the halfway point. We turned, passed it again, and then another voice told us we had to stop and have our hand stamped so officials know we made it to the halfway point before turning around.

"Screw you!" the Athenian Wisconsinite yelled.

I was the only one of the three of us who turned and had his hand stamped. Then I pulled into the front and stayed there until I won the race. I have always hoped that the cop saw my picture in the paper — bushy beard, shoulder-length hair, and sleepy eyes. The next week, I shaved and snipped my long, curly locks for graduation. Even while walking across the stage and shaking the university president's hand, I was thinking of my next race, and after the ceremony, I went for a three-hour run on the Noquemanon Trail. I still made it to the parties that night, but graduation wasn't a milestone I ever really cared about.

One milestone was the watch. By the time I ran the Journeys Marathon again, the week after my graduation, I had received a Garmin GPS watch as a college graduation present from Grandma and Grandpa. It had settings for skiing, biking, and running, and it would give me immediate feedback on my current pace to the hundredth of a second. At last, I could keep track of my pace. To keep my time under three hours, I needed to run an average mile of 6:50, which I had done before, but now could be consistent and more efficient. Also, I wanted to win.

When it started, I hovered around my desired pace, but two other guys were alongside me. One guy ran to my left. The other guy ran to my right. I looked at my watch to see no consistency. Sometimes it read around 6:30 per mile. Other times it read 6:00. There were times it read close to 5:30. We surged alongside each other for twenty-two miles. Then they shook me away, and I finished in third place, in a time of 2:56. It wasn't my fastest time, and I didn't win — but now I could see how spasmodic my pace could be.

In another week, I would keep a steady pace. I felt should have been ecstatic to finish inside Lambeau Field in Green Bay, but I'd never watched an entire football game my entire life, including the games I'd been to. Jumbotrons and flashing lights and people acting wild in the stands were far more fascinating. My finishing time was a minute faster than my Journey's time.

The last race I ran that spring was in Traverse City, in the Lower Peninsula. Traveling here wasn't a matter of crossing an invisible line or even a river. It meant crossing a massive bridge over the Straits of Mackinac, where Lake Michigan met Lake Huron.

In fifth grade, my state presentation was about Michigan, and I told my classmates about the construction workers buried in the concrete of that bridge, and how it has swayed in the wind to send cars crashing into the Straits. I'd been over this bridge before, but never on my own. As I approached its arch, and the pavement beneath me gave way to metal grate I could see through to the water below, my hands gripped the steering wheel tighter. My fear didn't ease until the bridge began its slope downward onto the Mitten.

I drove along Lake Michigan, into the Mitten's pinky, where cherry orchards led into downtown Traverse City. I slept in the back of my truck at the start line to awake in a sleepy stupor and got on one of the buses packed with runners.

"These buses are all going to the same place, right?" I asked.

The driver nodded.

When I got off the bus, I saw signs and banners for the start of the half marathon, and I knew right away that I was not where I was supposed to be. The buses all went to the same place because the full-marathoners didn't need to ride a bus. Standing at the start of the half marathon, I thought maybe I should just run it. I'd be labeled as DNS (Did Not Start) but I'd at least have some test of speed for myself.

I couldn't do that. I got back onto the bus and told the driver what I'd done. He told me it was no problem. He had to get back there anyway. Then it was just me, the driver, the loud engine, but not loud enough to drown the awkward silence.

"So where are you from?" he asked.

"Alaska," I said, hoping to use it as an excuse.

"Where in Alaska?"

"It's a small town called Naknek."

"I've been to Naknek," he said. "I was stationed in King Salmon in my Air Force days."

When I stepped off the bus, I ran a marathon along a lake far from saltwater, my only real plans being the finish line and the fishing season.

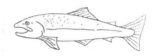

Dad and I are coming back to camp. It's almost low tide, which means we almost can't make it into Graveyard Creek to park the skiff. The bottom scrapes mud as Dad drives us in toward the old, charred pilings of the long-gone dock. I throw the anchor from the bow, Dad takes us onto shore, and we trudge through the mud, up the slope, and onto the boardwalk. Sometimes, when I'm on the loose and decrepit boardwalk, I imagine what it was like in the days that Graveyard was still Koggiung — sailboats pulled into the water, laborers slicing and gutting fish, cooks preparing another meal of corned beef and creamed corn.

Before the final turn to our place is the walkway to what was once the mess hall. It was the busiest of the buildings, so the planks leading to it are most tattered, missing, or loose. It has taken a lifetime coming back here to know where to step. Now the mess hall has no door on its rusted hinges, and the telephone wire across from it hasn't transmitted a message in decades. Rust envelops pipes and machines and canning stoves strewn about Graveyard. Koggiung will never be a village again. It existed for the cannery, and the cannery is nothing but that rusted equipment and the charred remains of pilings.

Then I think about the threat that looms over it, and reality is too sobering not to feel sadness. It's a threat called Pebble Mine. Northern Dynasty is a corporation based in Vancouver, Canada that scouts for locations, digs and extracts minerals, and sells them to technological companies and jewelry-makers. Other companies have come and gone in their involvement, but Northern Dynasty is the corporation that's always been behind it, making promises of job opportunities and economic growth, all the while completely ignoring what would be lost.

Pebble Mine would be the largest open-pit mine in the world, and no open-pit mine has ever existed without catastrophic damage. Even without a catastrophe, chemicals and tailings would slowly seep into the groundwater. It would continue into the lake, into river, and into the ocean. Their methods would use cyanide to leech metals from the ground. Cyanide — what a Bond villain's henchman might use to end his own life lest he is tempted to give away the villain's secret plan for world domination. It's also great at killing seals, otters, beavers, birds, and of course, fish.

Pebble Mine would be a mine for copper, gold, and molybdenum. Molybdenum is useful in nuclear warheads. We've been fighting over gold for centuries, but it's soft and virtually useless. Copper, however, makes pennies, electrical wiring, and indoor plumbing, all of which I use. With my modern lifestyle of gas station stops, smartphones, and using the kitchen sink, I don't know how to stop using them, but Iliamna is the wrong place for a copper mine.

It was an Alaskan company that first discovered these precious metals in the ground next to Lake Iliamna. A stealth operation drilled holes and sampled soil to see just how much of it was down there. Northern Dynasty took over the exploration after the new millennium, and by 2005, it was all theirs. In 2005, all of us knew what the Pebble Mine was going to be. Lake Iliamna is a glacial lake, spanning over a thousand square miles of clear, glacial water. It is the headwaters of the Kvichak and Nushagak River. The Pebble Mine would be right on it.

Since the project has gathered public attention, more anti-Pebble stickers have been placed on driftboats, skiffs, bumpers, and the back windows of almost everyone's car. It has a simple design.

It's the words PEBBLE MINE circled in red, with a red, slanted line over them. I have one of the stickers on my own bumper.

Sure, I recognize the irony of it. A car is made of metal that had to be mined, including the copper wiring in the stereo system. I display my opposition to the Pebble Mine, and I'm fairly conservation-minded, but I fly planes, I drive, and I use boats to fish — all of which use fossil fuels. The amount of petroleum products used in our industry is preposterous, not just to catch our fish, but to transport them across our planet.

The Pebble Mine is more disturbing and unsettling to me, probably because its potential for catastrophe would be direct, sudden, and quick to say the least. I do also recognize that it's troubling because in those direct, sudden, and quick ways, it would affect me. Thousands of mines have wreaked havoc on half the watersheds in the American West, and I haven't paid attention, let alone done anything about it. In Michigan's Upper Peninsula, I've watched a similar debate over sulfide mining in the Yellowdog Watershed Preserve, and the only debate I attended was for extra credit in a class.

It isn't just a natural habitat under threat. Those salmon spawning in Lake Iliamna are depended upon by canneries, family businesses, and guides. Entire towns exist because of fishing. Without fishing, in a place like Naknek, there is no job at the counter at the post office. There is no position to teach at school. There is no need for a grocery store, an airport, or a road. Jobs in administration, management, retail, accounting, the welding done on boats, carpentry on summer cabins, and transportation in and out of Naknek disappear.

Yes, when the salmon are gone, bears die and seals die. Yes, when the salmon are gone, whales and birds die — but when the salmon are gone, the people are gone, and when the salmon are gone, Naknek becomes another Graveyard.

When Odysseus was presented by the Lotus-Eaters with a fruit that would erase all his memories of home, he didn't take it. He didn't want to forget Ithaca's vast lands for hunting with his bow and his loyal dog, Argos. He didn't want to forget his wife, Penelope or his son, Telemachus. He didn't want to forget Ithaca's lone mountain, waving forests, or even the wild boar that left a scar on his foot. Remembering it, however, never meant that he wanted to go back there. It took a decade for Odysseus to return to Ithaca, but not without opportunities. It was almost as if he could have clicked a pair of ruby slippers together and arrive home in an instant.

After Odysseus and his men escaped from Polyphemus, he gloated and shouted his own name, practically begging the cyclops to retaliate with a curse. When he had a leather bag of the winds, instead of pushing the sails home, he left it lying around with the hired help who opened it and set the ships off course. When Odysseus and his men were trapped on Circe's island, he waited an entire year before bribed her with his sexual prowess in exchange for their release. When the Sirens sang their deadly, temptuous song from the water, all men but Odysseus plugged their ears. Instead, he told them to tie him to the mast so he could hear it without being drawn to his death. I think Odysseus was always listening to the Sirens, traveling further into his journey rather than just sailing home.

Part of me wanted to find a conventional path, and part of me wanted an odyssistic life, but whatever it was that I wanted, my own journey had reached a screeching halt. I was living in the basement at Mom and Dad's house in Wisconsin. On one typical day in this chapter of my life, Luke finished another day at Washburn High School, walked home, opened the door, walked downstairs to take his new puppy outside. Then he saw me, in shaggy-haired, unshaven glory, in sweatpants, watching an episode of *Batman: The Animated Series* from his black gaming chair, which I'd placed as close to the TV as possible. His black labrador puppy was in my lap, chewing on an empty beer bottle.

"Phoebe, no!" Luke said, yanking it from her mouth.

"She's fine," I said. "Now get out of the way."

"God, Keith," he said, rolling his eyes. "Get a job yet?"

"Nope," I said. "But it looks like school's out."

He shrugged, silent. He knew what was coming next, and he hated it. I got up, stretched, and went over to his Spanish teacher's house. We'd been dating, and Luke was embarrassed.

I wasn't as lazy as I appeared. I'd spent most of the day running and filling piles of job applications, stuffing them into manilla envelopes, and sending them around the country. By the time Luke was home every weekday, my brain and body were fried.

I couldn't complain about it. I was the one that didn't want a job right away. I wanted a life of wanderlust, wherever the wind in my sails may take me, battling cyclops, and talking to gods and ghosts. My college friends were starting careers, getting married, pumping out kids, parking in their suburban driveways, sitting on the couch after work, beer in hand, watching a football game, content in what I saw as a mundane existence.

When I was still student teaching, the last requirement for my degree, in my half-hour drive to Gwinn every morning, I had begun plotting how to get off-track. Even though I begged to differ, Northern's registrar had insisted my half-assed effort was enough for a diploma, and I had to figure out the next step. I started mapping a trip across Mediterranean Europe, beginning the journey with the Athens Marathon, the original course.

After graduation, and after fishing, but before the basement days, and before Athens, I stayed in Naknek until September, running alongside the Alaska Peninsula Highway, always moving faster toward the mountains than back toward town. Beyond those mountains wasn't college anymore, but a faraway journey across the Atlantic and across Europe on the northern side of the Mediterranean. First, I was staying in Alaska to run the Equinox Marathon in Fairbanks.

For the first time since I was a teenager, it was after August and I was watching the world go by from a TV screen in Naknek. I watched American favorite, Ryan Hall struggle in the heat of the 2008 Summer Olympics Marathon in Beijing. I watched Sarah Palin ask if she could take off her governor's hat while she said Alaska's ballot initiative to prevent any new mines was a bad idea. She was announced as John McCain's running mate the next day. My vote for Obama was confirmed.

Before the Equinox, I stayed for about two weeks at Riel and Norm's apartment in Anchorage. They were working nights as bouncers at a strip club called Fantasies on 5th. When they went to work, I slept on an inflatable mattress. While they slept, I ran on the bike path, wary of the occasional moose. During the day, we watched movies, loitered at the mall, and hung out at Bosco's Comics. Sometimes — but not at Bosco's Comics — beautiful women appeared from the liquor aisle or the kid's cereal section with hugs for Norm and Riel. Working at Fantasies seemed like quite the gig.

After every one of those hugs, however, Norm and Riel had a story following it with a disturbing story. Fantasies clients often followed the women home with flowers, framed photographs, stuffed animals, and marriage proposals, and not in any kind of way that was cute or uncreepy. Then there were the women's own stories of alcoholism, cocaine abuse, prostitution on the side, and domestic violence. Part of Norm and Riel's job description was to walk these women home. Although I'd celebrated birthdays and bachelor parties a time or two, I realized that I wanted nothing to do with strip clubs.

When the time came, Mo and Smiley drove me from Anchorage to Fairbanks in their Toyota they had kept stashed in Eagle River. We drove eight hours through mountains, rivers, moose, and of course the Alaska Pipeline pumping its black sludge across the state. It flew from the backseat windows as I thought about my journey ahead.

Yellow leaves had been falling in Naknek, but there were more bare branches than leaves in Fairbanks. The marathon began on a grass field in the Skarland Trails area, and the course immediately took us up a hill, onto the rugged dirt trails toward a mountain called Ester Dome. Mo and Smiley met me at various checkpoints, cheering as I didn't keep any kind of steady pace but enjoyed the unexpectedness of rugged terrain. I finished the race with sorer legs than I'd ever had before, and they were splattered in mud.

The next day, I boarded the Alaska Train with my trashed legs and sprawled out on a bench seat to watch the mountains and clouds and yellow leaves as a blur. As the last flagstop railway in the United States, the train stopped for backpackers and hikers along the route. Unkempt beards, ratty hair tangled beneath knit hats, the smell of aged sweat, boarded the train. There was a Kerouacian or Londonian romance to it, but I didn't yet know jack. Although I didn't think I was as smelly, or half as crunchy, they seemed like people who didn't want to be stuck moving in one direction, but then again, here we all were, on the same train heading toward Anchorage.

After my flight from Seattle to Minneapolis, Mom drove me to Washburn. Greece was still more than a month away, and I bided my time. Then it was Whistlestop Marathon weekend again. I had not recovered from the Equinox, but I was compelled to run anyway. It was the weekend that I first met the Spanish teacher.

My Athens trip was booked through a travel agency. The agency's plan included the marathon, a two-night stay at a hotel, and a shuttle from the airport. Jet-lagged, I rode in a limousine to the hotel with Tim, a young businessman from Boston with a business suit, a business, haircut, a business watch, and a business demeanor. He was on the same itinerary as me.

"So, you must have run Boston," I said.

"Nope," he said. "Just Philly. I'm not qualified."

Tim said he had just three days in Athens before he had to get back to his wife and his job, and then he turned the conversation to me, and I told him my plans.

"So, you have no job, no obligation, and you're in Europe the next six weeks?"

"Yeah," I said. "It's going to be interesting."

"Oh, it's going to be amazing!" he said. "It doesn't matter what you do!"

His nose twitched and he grinned a toothy grin that wasn't a business grin.

At the hotel, I shared a room with Nick, an army guy from Oregon who was stationed in Germany. Through the travel agency, choosing the roommate option saved some money, and if I was going to spend several weeks sleeping in hostels after the marathon, I needed to get used to the idea. Neither Nick nor I were sure of the purpose of twin beds when they were pushed together into one, but we were happy to have separate sheets and blankets.

The three of us and the rest of the group, maybe a dozen Americans from half a dozen states, took a tour of the nearby streets, the Temple of Zeus, and the Acropolis with its ancient temples and view of a city sprawling into forever. Everywhere we turned was another ancient structure. Even the streets near the hotel had ancient ruins around the corner.

In the morning, a bus took us to the Valley of Marathon, where the Athenians had taken victory over the Persians. Instead of soldiers unsheathing swords and bracing shields, there were runners tightening shoes, performing dynamic stretches, and applying Vaseline to nipples and groins. The voice on the speakers spoke first in Greek, then in English, and then in Japanese. While I waited in line for a porta-potty, a woman who didn't want to wait released the Kraken in the open.

I wished Nick, Tim, and the others luck in their race. Then I found my way to the start. In an event as large as this one, not one, two, or a handful of runners were in front of me. There were thousands of them. There may have been millions as far as I was concerned, milling and swirling, waiting for the moment to begin the surge toward the finish line.

As the crowd began moving, I began pounding my bones into the pavement. Heatwaves were visible, and as the crowd spread, the pavement seared my soles. Within the first three miles, we circled around the Marathon Tomb, which wasn't much to see other than a grass mound and a statue of what I presumed was Pheidippides.

There was no way that Pheidippides had included this loop in his own run unless he was trying to shake off some swooping buzzards. I wondered if the memorial was put there to commemorate the Battle of Marathon or if it was put there after Queen Victoria added the extra two miles, 385 yards. I couldn't wonder anything too long, since I was in a hurry to run fast, and I was distracted by at least fifteen Kenyans swooshing by me on the other side of a rope. They had already run all the way around the circle.

We ran south along the Petalioi Gulf, but too far away from shore to see it. Then the course swept north and took me past the Athens International Airport, back into the city of Athens with its honking horns, disgruntled drivers, and cigarette smoke indoors. My lungs burned and blood rushed from my brain. I detested the aid stations handing runners entire bottles of water. As hundreds of them lay wasted on the street, I thought of the patches of plastic floating in the ocean. I thought of the petroleum used to make plastic. Even with the desert in my throat, I couldn't justify taking an entire bottle for a single guzzle.

My legs hurt and sweat soaked my eyes. The marathons over the course of this year, the mysterious nature of my future, and the heat were all eating at me. I thought maybe Athens would be my last marathon. It seemed appropriate to end where it all began. I could stop running, settle into a career, find a mate, spawn, and die.

Then I saw the Olympic Stadium, where the finish line would be waiting after one-half lap around the track. An orchestra was performing, cameras were flashing, and endorphins were once again surging as my feet hit the forgiving surface of polyurethane. I wasn't sitting in Naknek, watching the world go by from the other side of a TV screen. If I quit, I'd never experience these kinds of moments again.

Tim, Nick, and I went out on the town to celebrate, six sore legs set loose on ancient streets, hiking bar to bar — first among tourists, and then into narrow streets where locals drank. Between several beers and too many shots of ouzo, we forgot we were sore, and we forgot we were strangers. Nick wasn't ready to get married to his girlfriend, he told us, but the military would make life more affordable if he tied the knot. He asked Tim, the married man, for advice, but Tim was more occupied with the slender, blond bartender. The more he drank, the more occupied with this girl he became, and the more frequently his nose twitched.

"Do you have a girlfriend?" she asked.

When his nose twitched again, I couldn't help but stare at his teeth. They were too white and too straight. They were like he needed to gnaw on a shrub to wear them down.

"No," he said, which was technically true.

"I'm not bringing this girl home with me," he kept saying to me, his nose spasming. "I'm just having fun."

He was right. He wouldn't leave with her, but it wasn't up to him. She flaunted, but she winced every time he wasn't looking. Somewhere during all of this back-and-forth, Nick took a cab back to the hotel. Tim asked the bartender to come with the two of us to the next stop, and she said the bars were closing. When he asked if she'd like to come back to his room, it was the last we saw of her.

As Tim and I stumbled along the streets, my quadriceps hurt with every step. I longed for my hotel room where I could collapse into the twin bed next to Nick who had been there for hours. We hailed a cab and Tim asked about what I had planned for the rest of my time in Europe. I told him I was heading to Olympia first.

"Nah, fuck that!" he said. "Stay here and find some pussy!"

I rolled my eyes as the cab stopped. I paid, and as we stepped onto the pavement, my quadriceps hated every second of it. My feet and legs were in ruins, but the last steps into the hotel and to the elevator would be worth these last moments of pain.

"Keith," Tim said. "You have two choices."

I knew what he was thinking. There was a strip club around the corner, and he'd been talking about it for two days. The thought of it alone brought his nose into a tantrum of twitches.

"You can go back to your room, or you can go around the corner with me!"

I was tired, and as of two months ago, these places had left a bad taste in my mouth. It was the wanderlust, the fear of missing out, and probably the alcohol that led me further down the rabbit hole, so as Tim danced toward the promise of women taking off their clothes, I inched toward the doors.

The place was dark, dingy, and shrouded in smoke. My shoes slipped on the dusty floor. Two of every three dimmed lights were broken. Men of all ages with handfuls of paper lurched forward from stools at the stage. Fantasies on Fifth, or even the Great Alaskan Bush Company, was a classier place than this hole behind the hotel, and my head spun like the flashing colored lights through the smoke.

Right away, two women sat at our table, put hands on our shoulders, asked our names, and complemented our handsomeness in Eastern European accents. When the host, who looked like someone's sleazeball grandpa, asked if we'd like to buy the ladies a drink, I shook my head. I recalled the first time I had ever gone to one of these places. He'd told me that if you get a drink, sip it slowly or else you have to pay for another one. He had also told me that the women get drinks for free.

Tim, when asked about drinks, leaned back in his chair, and said, "Hell yeah!"

Two glasses of ice with a splash of liquid arrived. It was too blue to be anything but Gatorade or antifreeze. The women pretended to sip the drinks, pretended to be interested in us, and then Sleazemo Grandpa put the bill on the table, which was 280 euros. For the first time all night, Tim's goofy grin faded. He leaned forward with the bill in his hands, and for just an instant, Tim was sober again. He stood and took Sleazemo to the side, in a dark corner next to the jukebox while I stayed seated, my arms folded over my chest, avoiding eye contact. On the stage was Sasha from Slovakia, stripping stockings, stilettos, and her real name.

"Taken care of," Tim said when he sat back in his chair. I don't know how he did it, but he had talked our way out of the bill. Then one of our new friends asked if he'd like a lap dance, and careless twitchy

Tim was back, led into a dark corner by a near-naked Romanian woman pulling him by the collar. Her glass of cartoon-colored sugar water remained on the table next to the other one.

"You don't look like you want to be here," our other new friend said to me.

"Not really," I said.

"Why don't you go to bed?"

"My friend," I said. "He wanted to come."

"How long have you known each other?"

I looked to the floor. "A couple days."

She rolled her eyes. "Go home. He'll be fine."

I worried about leaving him. In his stupid, drunken, horny, twitchy state, he could be robbed of his driver's license, credit cards, and his passport if it was on him. Sleazemo Grandpa might call his sleazemo cronies, have him taken into the alley, and have the twitch beaten out of him.

Then I thought of the blonde bartender, and how every time she turned around and he stared at her butt, he turned right away to me with that grin and that twitch, checking to see if I was looking, too. I thought about the massage place in Boston that he had told me about, where he frequented, where happy endings came first. I thought about how Tim had a wife, a house, a successful career in accounting, and how he had to lie to maintain it all.

Running, he had told me, was an outlet for him. It was something I understood all too well, but now I understood that running wasn't enough for him. He longed for wild nights and sexual conquest, but these appetites had been stifled and caged by the conventional path. I couldn't help but wonder if the conventional path held this same result for me. I took one last look at Tim, grinning ear-to-ear in a chair as a naked, female body grinded against him in exchange for cash. Without guilt, I stood, walked out of the strip club, and went back to the hotel. I was on a bus to Olympia in the morning.

I spent the next two weeks traveling Greece by bus, stopping in villages and places between villages, where sometimes I was alone on some grassy, Grecian landscape, hoping the guidebook was up-to-date with its schedules. The bus always arrived, no passengers or driver speaking a word of English. I traveled to Delphi where the Oracle had provided prophecies to kings, where scholars were told to know thyself at the Temple of Apollo, and where Athena was worshipped inside the Tholos. I went to Mount Olympus, where Zeus and other gods were presumed to watch our planet. Sometimes I walked between villages, alongside sheep and their shepherds.

Meteora was my ultimatum in Greece. I had first seen pictures of it while shoving pizza down my face at D&D, and I had recently discovered it again when researching places to visit. As the server at D&D had explained, and as the web confirmed, Greek Orthodox monks lived atop gigantic pillars of rock towering into the sky. In the pictures, they sat in wicker baskets and lifted themselves to the monasteries with a pulley system. I stayed the night in a room above a restaurant in Kalambaka, a town at the foot of Meteora. Breakfast was fruit, nuts, and Greek yogurt, which I guess was just yogurt there, and then I hiked the trail through rocks and greenery and descended into the pillars.

Fog drifted over the monasteries and towers of stone, and it still had a pink hue from the sunrise. Some monasteries were on gigantic stone monoliths, only accessible by baskets I'd seen in pictures. Others had bridges to them. It looked like a painting. Then I stepped into one of the monasteries, and a monk was talking on a cell phone. When I walked out, a busload of tourists slowed to take their pictures. My trance was lost. It was time to make my way to the coast.

The ferry to Brindisi, Italy was late. I slept in the terminal until midnight, and I boarded in the dark and floated across the passage between the Adriatic and the Ionian Sea, among Ithaca, the island of Odysseus. I couldn't remember if it was a real place or not, but I realized it didn't matter. Ithaca was his home, and the idea of home was founded in myth. Home is where the heart is, but my heart was inside my chest.

This idea was all-the-more apparent after my connecting train was late in Catania, and there were no more rides that night. As I paced back and forth across the platforms, la polizia were booting out the homeless. Anyone dirty, unkempt, or layered in blankets was forced to leave. Then they approached me, and although I had joked about it, I understood for the first time that in a technical sense, I was homeless, too. Perhaps we're all homeless.

As I wandered the city, none of the hotels fit my budget, so I kept wandering until I stumbled upon a plaza with bars and clubs and young people partying away the night. I sat on some steps, and decided I'd stay there — but I couldn't ignore the desire to sleep and the fear of being robbed, so I moved into the narrower streets and alleys, looking for a box, a dark corner, or a reasonably clean dumpster. At last, I wandered into the garage of an apartment building. Underneath the staircase was a dark closet with a dirt floor. It didn't look like anyone used the space. I crawled inside of it, shut the door, leaned against my pack, and fell asleep.

It wasn't restful sleep. It was the kind of sleep where dreams are interrupted by reality, and reality is interrupted by dreams. I dreamt I was fishing, and the fish kept coming, even though it was time to go back to school. I needed to get back to school so I could run, but when I got there, there was no more school.

When my eyes opened in the dark, I didn't know how much time had passed. I pushed open the door and poked out my head. The garage had no man-door, and I looked for a button or a lever to no avail. I tucked myself back into the closet, and I waited for the first footsteps and the sound of the garage door opening. When I heard it, I burst from the closet, sprinted by the car, and ran for the first time since the marathon, all the way to the train station.

Tim was right. It didn't matter what I did. I was a speck moving across our planet, and if I didn't end up on my flight from Madrid, the consequences would be quite insignificant. In Dante's *Inferno*, Odysseus himself reveals a story in which he never returned to Ithaca but spent the rest of his life wandering. He reveals this information, however, while he is in the eighth layer of hell. I suppose Dante was trying to say that, at some point, a wise man accepts the idea that *home* is a physical place where he belongs.

For the next month, home was a room at a hostel, room to let, or some other hole in the wall with holes in the wall, somewhere in Italy, France, or Spain. I was a Catalano in Catalonia, but it was certainly not my home.

When I came back to Wisconsin for the holidays, that wasn't home either, but there I was, applying for any job teaching English I could find. It wasn't the desire for fulfillment or beginning a career that drove me. It was the desire to be out of the basement, and take a step forward, no matter where it happened to be. When my relationship with the Spanish teacher came to a screeching halt, I was motivated even further. Although Washburn was a beautiful town on the edge of Lake

Superior, there was nothing beautiful about being a college graduate living in his parents' basement.

Out of desperation, I accepted a job in a small town in the middle of Kansas.

One theory suggests a one-way migration of meat, like mammoth, moose, muskoxen, and caribou, first brought predators across the Bering Land Bridge to Alaska. People and wolves alike chased animals down for sustenance, and when the prey migrated, so followed the predators. Another theory suggests there a longtime, seasonal migration between the two continents — an ebb and flood of feet flowing back and forth across a landmass that became a narrowing isthmus.

"Keith," Dad says, pointing down the beach. "Look."

The two of us have just finished setting the second net of our two lower nets, at our sites closer to Naknek and Bristol Bay. I've hooked the outside buoy to the bow, and now we're waiting for the tide to rise high enough to set our other two nets upriver. Dad is pointing at a lone caribou standing on a sandbar a few feet from shore. He's far away, but I recognize the animal by the magnificent set of antlers branching over his head. The sandbar is not much bigger around than his body, but as the tide flows upward into the Kvichak, the water ascends toward his hooves.

"I think those are wolves," Dad says. "See them?"

I didn't spot them right away, but he's right. Onshore are two figures, watching and waiting as the caribou's sanctuary disappears. With every breath, every hunger pang, and every drop of drool from canine jowls, the caribou is closer to making one of two choices — drown in the current or be taken down for food.

"Wow," I say. "I've ever seen a wolf before."

Although I've never seen one, let alone a pair of them, I know a few things about them. Wolves in their natural habitat, that haven't been transplanted, target the sick and weak caribou and help keep the herd strong. Sometimes there are more wolves, and sometimes there are more caribou.

Sometimes wolves act as scavengers, picking scraps like the seagulls swooping our net, but they always prefer their own kill. I've been eating caribou since I had my first set of teeth, and I understand and share the taste for it. As a kid, Mom told me not to gnaw on the bones when I dug my teeth into them, trying to savor every last strand. I never listened. Sometimes I still chew on a chunk of grizzle for the better part of dinner before I deem it safe to swallow. I depend on my canine teeth.

Sometimes I went with Dad when he hunted caribou — by fourwheeler, snowmachine, or boat. Once, we were on an overnight trip up the Kvichak when the tide reached our feet in sleeping bags. We moved the tent and packed it wet in the morning. When a hunt was successful, Dad hung the carcass from the ceiling in the garage and skinned and butchered it himself. He had to chase away dogs who love to lick blood dripping down. Then Mom made steak for dinner with a side of potatoes, pasta, or rice. Then, if there was any wolf in me, I'd let it off its leash.

It's hard to think of any of the dogs we've had —Mosie, Auggie, Bonkers, Cooch, Murphy, Phoebe — with their big brown eyes and floppy labrador ears, descended from wolves. Wolves teach their pups how to stalk prey, and pounce with stiffened front legs to grab its throat by the teeth and collapse its windpipe. Murphy chases planes flying by the house, barking like it will entice them to come closer.

The only dog in the family I can imagine as a wolf is Chrissy, the chihuahua, who I've seen more often than any dog growl and bare her teeth, and she tears apart a scrap from the table the way a wolf tears apart a caribou. One time Murphy took off after a caribou from the beach at Graveyard. He disappeared for an entire day, as he often does, but the only animals he ever brings home have already been killed. Our front yard is often littered with severed legs, antlers, and one time a frozen chicken still in its plastic wrap — which of course we ate.

The first animal I killed, other than a fish or a mosquito, was a willow ptarmigan with Dad's .22. I carried it back in the back compartment of my fourwheeler. We ate it for dinner. Even though Dad said I was one helluva shot, I never got much into hunting. Either the instinct isn't in me, or it's not one I have unburied. Luke, on the other hand, loves to hunt and fish. He's traveled all over the country for fowl and furbearers and fills his freezer with meat.

In the Wilson household, caribou, moose, sockeye or king salmon, and maybe the occasional ptarmigan is standard protein at dinnertime. Still, chicken, turkey, and pork sometimes find a way onto our plates. When it's easier for wolves, they feed on carrion. When it's easier for people, we find food at Costco in Anchorage.

The difference is when wolves choose the easier option, they clean our planet of food already going to waste. When we choose the easier option, it is an option created by other people. Cattle are rallied into corals, roped, castrated, branded, and raised for the butchering. Chicken and turkey chicks are shoved onto a conveyor belt and raised in shoebox-sized coops. Pigs are slung slop until they are fat enough for slaughter. When people choose the easier option, we create a soft, sedentary, less-sustaining meat, and make more waste than we can clean.

I like to think we're more like wolves than cattle when we fish. As these two wolves wait on the beach, the fish splashing into our net are far from domestic. They arrive from cold corners of the ocean, contributing to a cycle created not by people. I like to think that it takes a wolf of a man be a commercial fisherman or a runner, but the fish we catch are future fillets and contents of cans on shelves in stores we'll never shop.

Without us, no salmon would make it into a shopping cart, next to a bag of potatoes, package of pasta, or a box of rice, wheeling its way through aisles of price tags. Without us, no salmon would make it across a conveyor belt behind a cash register, into a paper or plastic bag taken to a kitchen from which we would never eat. Without us, the salmon that have made it this far would likely arrive at the headwaters, spawn, die, become fertilizer for plants and food for scavengers.

At the same time, without a farmer in Idaho, we wouldn't have potatoes to eat with our caribou steaks. Without a combine in Kansas, we wouldn't have wheat. Without a ranch in Montana, we wouldn't have Black Angus. The wolves on the beach will never see a potato, a grain, or a steer, but they don't need to see it.

No human is a lone wolf. We are all too codependent. We romanticize wolves because we share similar motives, but wolves learn and adapt without altering their environments. They kill without guns, spears, clubs, or rocks, and they eat without refrigeration, stoves, or microwave ovens. These two wolves on the beach will never depend on wolves devouring livestock in Oregon or ranches around Yellowstone.

As the water closes in on the caribou, the wolves take small steps backward, patient for him to choose death by collapsed windpipe over death by a windpipe full of water.

"Let go of the net," Dad says and starts the motor.

We charge toward the wolves, chasing them up the mud, behind the bank, into the brush. After there is no sign of them, the caribou wades to shore. He saunters down the beach, moving along, and vapor drifting all around him. Then we head upriver to set our other two nets.

There is no sign of the wolves, but it doesn't mean they aren't around. Wolves have been around me my entire life, but I had never seen one, let alone two, until today. Although we don't see it happen, our interference has probably only delayed the inevitable kill. They'll spring from their hind legs, their jaws will clinch the caribou's windpipe, and they will devour him alive. He'll kick until they have devoured a carcass. First, they will have their fill of muscle and organs. Then the seagulls, eagles, and other scavengers will take care of the eyes and the remaining strands of meat. The tide will wash away the bones.

Clark Kent was raised in the fictional town of Smallville, Kansas, but Lucas, Kansas was too real for me. It was a small ville indeed — off-center, a little to the east, and just south of the Republican River. If I had chosen a place to live by throwing a dart into a map of the Lower 48, I had barely missed the bullseye. The center was a forty-five-minute drive away, the same distance from the bizarre formations at Rock City Park, the World's Largest Ball of Twine, or the Sternberg Museum.

At Sternberg is where I realized Kansas was once part of the ocean floor as part of the Western Interior Seaway, splitting North America into three sections. I visited the dinosaur exhibit, including a robotic tyrannosaurus rex that reminded me of a childhood toy, but I stood longest in front of the museum's most famed fossil, the Fish-Within-a-Fish, a Gillicus skeleton inside a Xiphactinus skeleton. By the time I lived in Kansas, the only significant body of water nearby was Wilson Lake, a dammed reservoir where kids told me old houses still sat on the bottom. Even though the Lake and I shared a name, Kansas made me feel like the Gillicus, trapped inside a place that I wasn't supposed to fit.

Upon my first arrival into Lucas, I was welcomed by the World's Largest Souvenir Travel Plate, a satellite dish painted with bright colors and miniature murals. I'd rolled into town on fumes, parked at the gas station, and started to fill my tank. Another truck parked on the opposite side of the pump. Out stepped a driver with ratty long hair, a scraggly mustache, tattered overalls, and no shirt. He pointed to my Alaska plates and asked about Sarah Palin. I told him that, no, I didn't know her, and no, I hadn't met her. Then he told me he'd vote her for anything, man! Anything! As he made predatory howls into the sky, his eyes were as bright as the headlights that had hypnotized me for sixteen hours of driving.

The principal and his wife met me at the K-18 Cafe where they served fried chicken, fried chicken, and fried chicken with a side of potato salad. He had told me not to bother bringing any of that salmon stuff to Kansas, because he was allergic to fish. He also told me that I was going to gain weight in Lucas, because the cafeteria cook was the best cook in Kansas, and she made the best corn dogs I'd ever seen. It was as though he relished the idea, and he bragged about the history teacher having gained thirty pounds his first year.

When he had hired me over the phone, he also told me the position opened because my predecessor had been caught in a sexual relationship with a freshman boy. I kept the nervous jokes to myself when he said the school mascot was the Cougars. The temptation left me as he went on to complain about some parent causing a stink over prayer at school, and the next thing you know, some commie isn't going to want to pledge allegiance to the flag. I didn't say a word.

On our way into the K-18, two teenage girls were on their way out. The principal stopped them in their tracks. "What are you ladies up to? Causing trouble?"

"We were just wondering if our new English teacher is hot," one of them said.

The principal, without skipping a beat, said, "Can't you judge for yourself?"

When they realized who I was, the two disappointed girls, red-faced, stared down at the floor and scurried away to their table.

"So, what are your interests, Keith?" the principal asked. "And don't say highschool girls."

I told him I ran marathons. It wasn't something that I often told people, but I needed to change the subject, and I had registered for the Kansas City Marathon, so he'd be seeing me training on the shoulder of the K-18 Highway between Lucas and Luray.

"Hmm," was all he said.

Luray was ten miles to the west, where I rented a two-bedroom apartment in a four-apartment complex across from the Luray Cemetery. The principal had told me the neighbors across the street were quiet, and when I first got to the apartment, I understood his joke — but the rest of the town was just as quiet.

In the quaint, brick-sided, shoebox-shaped building, the history teacher stayed on one side of me with his wife and son, and a deliveryman stayed on the other side as a home-away-from-home. On the far end was Leroy, a big ol' redneck of a redneck, always wearing overalls, a plaid shirt, and a baseball cap. His two pickup trucks were parked in front, each with a gun rack against the back window.

Leroy often sat in a folding chair on his concrete stoop, grilling hot dogs and hamburgers, and plotting how to drag the other tenants into a one-sided conversation. Leroy a retired oil rig man who told me about the good ol' days when pansy-ass tree huggers weren't all over your ass for an eensy weensy little spill here and there. I told him I was happy when it wasn't in the ocean, because I liked seafood.

Leroy didn't. Leroy hated eating meat that wasn't American ranch-raised beef. He liked to hunt, but he'd give away the meat, which was nice because sometimes he gave me pheasants. I roasted them and picked out the buckshot as I ate. Sometimes he liked to drive all day, he told me, scanning the roads for rattlesnakes, beating them to death with a shovel. I didn't want to eat rattlesnake. He told me that was okay. Nobody did.

Living in Luray meant living between Paradise and the Garden of Eden, as a sign advertised on the way into town. Paradise was a town up the road, and the Garden of Eden attracted travelers on the K-18 highway into Lucas. I never made it to Paradise, but when I visited the Garden of Eden along with other tourists, Adam and Eve welcomed us as angels and Indians — as they called them — watched from their perches. A tour guide explained all the concrete statues in the yard, including a laborer crucified between a doctor, lawyer, preacher, and capitalist. The statues were constructed during the final days of one Samuel P. Dinsmoor, a veteran of the Union arm who was mummified in a coffin with a glass lid in a limestone mausoleum. When I gazed down at his dry, scrawny remains, as the final attraction of the tour, I wondered if he was the only person from Lucas in favor of the Union.

The Grassroots Arts Center was the other tourist trap, so I felt compelled to see it. I was led through a collection of scrap metal sculptures, mosaics of chewed bubble gum, a pile of rocks, and a car constructed of pop-can pull-tabs collected over the course of decades. The final exhibit was in a house a block over. The woman with the permanent smile, who lead the tour, even though I was by myself, drove me there. Lining the walls were Barbie dolls with Batman's head, Ninja Turtles with pinwheels for arms, baby doll heads with Legos for eyes, melted Fisher-Price People, and other mutilated remnants of my childhood memories.

The first day of school was scheduled on the same day as a funeral for a former school custodian. Everyone on staff went to the funeral but me, so every student at school was in my classroom. I was 24 years old, at my first day of work, and I was in charge of an entire school. There were only thirty-seven students, but I heard more racist comments about black people in those first three hours of the day than I'd ever heard in my life.

"The guy who freed the slaves got shot in the head," an innocent-looking freshman boy said. "Shouldn't that teach you a lesson?"

Another freshman boy came out as gay within two weeks of school, and he was harassed until he was never seen again. Rhetoric from other teachers, although not all of them, was that he was better off to be away from the other students. After a while, I started thinking that maybe if I said I were gay, I could get fired, and I wouldn't have to be in Kansas anymore.

I still had a way to escape every day after school. I drove back to my apartment, changed clothes, and ran toward Lucas. Again in my life, I found myself running back and forth on a gravel shoulder. The difference was that this road didn't end. I could keep running. It was 1,500 miles to the ocean east or west, but only 800 miles to the south. Still, I could get there with enough persistence — or, if I had decided, I could get in my truck and drive and tired, sore muscles or a hungry stomach couldn't stop me. I could go anywhere I wanted. At least that's what I told myself, and I proved it to myself by going to Kansas City in October, one state over, across the Missouri River.

The Kansas City Marathon was on my birthday, on the Missouri side. I stayed at a Motel 6 on the outskirts of the city, in a room with unmade bedsheets and pubic hairs on the shower walls. Instead of complaining to the desk, I unpacked my sleeping bag over the top quilt. I went to bed a 24-year-old, woke up a 25-year-old, and ran 26 miles, 385 yards through the streets of Kansas City. I was an adult with a full-time job and adult responsibilities, but I could still run. I didn't have to choose between them.

Two weeks later, on Halloween night, I was trotting along the gravel shoulder toward Lucas from Luray when a sudden jolt of pain surged from a spot on the left side of my leg. It was iliotibial band friction syndrome, and it lasted for months. Back then, I had no knowledge of massage or foam rolling or even the correct stretches. I applied ice to it several times a day, but it still flared into pain at random times.

"Okay, class," I'd start. Then my leg buckled, and I'd hobble to the nearest desk to lean on it.

It continued until December. The road was endless, but inflammation would surge, and I was forced to stop. I had a debilitating injury preventing me from exercise, something I had always thought was an excuse people had. It was an excuse for aging teachers with gray hairs, which I had begun to find in my beard.

It was still the first semester when talks were in full force to close Lucas-Luray High School due to budget cuts. Then we had a meeting, and it was official. It was consolidating with Wilson High School, five miles away in the town of Wilson on the other side of Wilson Lake. In a twist of irony, Mr. Wilson would not be carried over to the new school. I held my enthusiasm inside. It was disappointing to be losing my first job, and it was even more disappointing to see an entire school disappear, but selfishly, I couldn't wait for the excuse to leave. In the meantime, I waited for the end of the first semester for two weeks of reprieve.

'Twas the night before Christmas break, and all through the apartment, nothing was stirring — not even me. I was sound asleep until my heart raced with the realization that school started in ten minutes. I threw on clothes, chugged a protein shake, and sat behind my steering wheel to see I still had an empty tank. It had been empty for a couple of trips back and forth between Lucas and Luray, but with my refusal to get out of bed ten minutes earlier, there had been no time to stop.

Somewhere between the two towns, I was going 55 miles an hour. Then it was 45, 35, and 25. It slowed until it stopped, and my only reaction was a sigh. As the yellow bus appeared in my rear-view mirror, and I sat helpless as it got bigger and bigger until it slowed, stopped, and the windows flew open, familiar faces of students laughing. I told the driver I'd be fine. I was just out of gas. After the bus disappeared down the road, a local stopped by and told me he could leave a tank in the back for me. In the meantime, he could give me a ride to school.

Every class that day heard me tell the story of Icarus flying too close to the sun with his wings of wax. The wings, I explained, were the gasoline. The sun was the school, the place I was trying to reach. I had running clothes stashed in my classroom, which I changed into to get my truck at lunchtime. I didn't have time to change back before my first afternoon class, and the adult teacher and the wild runner merged. The next time I drove, I drove back to Marquette and Washburn, visiting family and friends. I skied on the trails, my IT band friction syndrome not affecting the motion.

By the time I came back to Kansas, I was able to run again. It wasn't for long distances, but I could run. Soon I could run a mile before the pain recurred. Then I could run almost three. By the time I knew I could run five, I would run two and a half miles and turn around and run two and a half more. I knew how to time the pain's return, and I didn't let it get me until I was back on my doorstep.

By February, my injury faded into non-existence. I drove to the Post Oak Trail Marathon in the woods outside Tulsa, Oklahoma. Excited, I took the lead, and I stayed in the lead for 25 miles, through trees and over dirt, the kind of running I sorely missed. I was in full bliss until a volunteer stopped me in my tracks. He told me I'd made a wrong turn. The guy in second place had followed me. I turned, tripped over a rock, and he helped me to my feet.

I'd been running a decent clip, but suddenly I was stumbling, and could only hobble forward. My mind and body were more connected than I ever believed as I struggled. On my way through the weaves in the woods, I saw the lodge where the race started and finished. My body begged me to cut through the trees and be done. My ego wouldn't let me. I kept going and finished in third place. I licked my wounds and drove away. Maybe I should have won, but I was happy just to be running long distances again.

I was back in Kansas, about 45 minutes away from Lucas when the passenger side front tire tore open on the asphalt. The key to open the spare tire broke in the rusted slot, but I tried anyway, and it broke in half. I stood on the side of the road, cars rushing by me as contemplated my next move. Wind ruffled my jacket every time a car whizzed by me.

I dug into my passenger-side glove box, found a number of my expired free roadside assistance, which led me to the number of a place in Salina open on Sunday. A wrecker arrived and pulled my truck back there. I rode in the cab to the shop where I left my truck and walked away. I called the principal to ask for a personal day while I waited for my truck, but he was in Salina anyway, so he gave me a ride back to Luray. I had to tell him the whole story. He thought I was weird, but he wasn't mean. He even had an extra truck to let me drive. The math teacher, who commuted every day from Salina, took me back the next day.

In the spring, I was in Hays, Kansas watching *Iron Man 2* at the theater. Early in the movie, the lead characters made a scene on a racetrack in Monte Carlo, France where I'd been not long ago — but it seemed like a distant dream now. I had begun a career, and I could still travel and run, but for some reason, it seemed every time I went somewhere to run, a wrench was thrown into it. I was in the land of interconnecting roads, still watching the world through a screen.

The movie was interrupted by a tornado. First, they interrupted the audience with a warning and started it again, but by the time the villain first attacks the hero, we were being told to evacuate to the restrooms. I sat on the floor with strangers, both men, and women, including the workers. They confessed to hoping their cars would blow away so they could collect the insurance money. I confessed to bringing in outside food.

Outside, the tornado tore through town, and I hoped my truck was still there, but part of me wanted to go outside let the tornado lift me and carry me somewhere over the rainbow. Every time I ran, I wondered if a tornado would sweep me away. When I ran the Eisenhower Marathon in April, I ran like the faster I ran, the sooner I could move out of Kansas. I crossed the finish line in 2:49, and it was the first time I collected prize money.

I was applying to jobs all around the country with nothing but letters of rejection as a response. Meanwhile, the principal encouraged me to apply to the eighth-grade job in Russell, the county seat. I didn't apply, but they scheduled an interview anyway, to which I went. Then they offered me the job. It was a smaller workload, and Russell was a town with a grocery store and a movie theater. It would have been better, but it still would have been Kansas. I didn't have another job, but I had already had my heart set on leaving. Although it was somewhere new and different, and attached to roads, there was something all-too-familiar about this feeling. There were roads leading in and out, but I couldn't help but feel an unbearable yearning to leave, and to be part of a world outside of it.

It wasn't the racism, bigotry, religious fundamentalism, or the extreme right-wing ideology that I didn't like. In the isolation from people I could relate to, and in isolation of being stuck in one place, there was something a little too familiar about it. I knew what this place was when I first arrived. I suspected it the first day I was there, the first time Leroy saw my license plates, and he looked up from the hot dogs on his grill.

"Alaska, huh?"

"Yep."

"I've got a question for you."

"Yeah?"

"Do you know where Naknek is?"

As I realized is the case in much of small-town America, there are places like home.

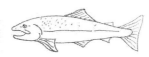

Most days on the Kvichak, a peanut-butter-and-jelly sandwich sits in my stomach, bacteria and enzymes breaking apart its protein, carbohydrate, and fat, working to make them efficient as possible for my body to refuel and repair itself. A peanut-butter-and-jelly sandwich is a treat, but it's not ideal for function. It has the three macronutrients, but it lacks vitamins, minerals, phytochemicals, and other micronutrients to help my body endure the season.

When I'm far away from here, I'm running, and I'm choosing my own food, I allow myself to trust what our planet has provided. Nuts, seeds, grains, fruit, vegetables, fowl, fauna, and fish have fed people farther back in time than anyone can measure. Then we began altering food. Grains were pulverized, fermented, and made into bread. Fruit was smashed into and jelly. Nuts were roasted, salted, and crushed into butter. Preservatives were added to maintain freshness. Refined sugar was added for sweetness. Plastic contained them as they were trucked across highways and put onto shelves at Costco.

It's early in the fishing season, and my stomach is unsettled, still not used to Graveyard food, but the Kvichak is calm in these moments between dusk and dawn. The sun peeks over the horizon and glows over the water beyond Graveyard, where the Kvichak Bay narrows into the Kvichak River. Red light fades into a violet sky, and pink puffy clouds expand into what look like explosions frozen in time. Each ripple in the water teems with color radiating from the sky. Red sky at night means sailor's delight, and red sky in the morning means sailors take warning, but it's late June, the part of the summer when the line between sunrise and sunset is as indistinct as the shoreline.

For now, the weather is pleasant, and the tide is in its ebb. The flood brought thousands of pounds of fish to our nets, and the ebb is abundant, too. Fish are piled into the brailers, and the same warm hues of the sky and water gleam in their silver scales. Their struggle is over. They've kicked and splashed and gasped in the dry air and breathed their last breath. We pick them all the same, toss them into a brailer, and they are weighed by the scale on the crane on the tender. They are making their one-time journey to their natal streams, and we are people putting an end to it.

When I was a kid, and Dad took me hunting, he always made it a point to reiterate that we only kill to eat or to keep from being eaten — Rudyard Kipling's law of the jungle. We kill caribou to eat them. We kill ptarmigan to eat them. We smash mosquitoes against the wall at Graveyard to keep them from eating us. Sometimes we take a fish back to Graveyard for dinner, but we kill them by the thousands, delivering almost all of them to one tender or another.

I tell myself it's still going to be food. I tell myself that it's still going to be eaten, but I've seen how wasteful people can be at a table. Pizza crusts, half-eaten hamburgers, and bones with strands of chicken still attached are scooped into a trashcan, filling yet another plastic bag ready to be hauled to a landfill.

By the time we get back to Graveyard, I'm hungry and I couldn't push away if I tried. I eat everything in front of me. I always take what I'm going to eat and then eat what I take. If I take too much, and my stomach is full and uncomfortable, I finish it anyway. If something unexpected arrives at a restaurant, I eat it anyway, whether or not I want it, and whether or not it's bad for me. When other people can't finish what they've ordered, even if it's not something I want, I often finish it for them. When I cook for myself, I put on my plate what I intend to eat. To control myself, I put the rest of it in the refrigerator before I even sit down.

We're at the table at Graveyard when Dad tells me about when he was my age and he shot a squirrel for fun, felt immediate guilt, and held a funeral for the departed rodent. He dug a grave and buried the squirrel in the dirt. Somehow, Dad went on to slaughter more squirrels and groundhogs and chipmunks and tiny birds and felt the same immediate remorse.

"And that's the time in my life when I was killing lots of shit and feeling bad about it," he tells me. Since then, he has decided to stop killing without reason.

Hundreds of thousands of salmon later, I'm not sure where this lesson stands. I have no real sense of guilt over it. Salmon are abundant, and Bristol Bay is a sustainable fishery. More than I want to know goes to waste, but any guilt I feel is the same guilt I feel for switching on a light, knowing coal is burning at a power plant, contributing to air pollution and climate change. It's the same guilt I feel when buying another pair of running shoes undoubtedly sewn together by some starving kid in a sweatshop in China. I don't know why it's always China. It could be anywhere. It's an intellectual guilt, but emotion is absent. Acceptance of injustice and constant damage to our planet has been instilled by the culture around me.

People didn't always process food. In Ancient China, for instance, people ate rice pure and whole, unbleached. They ate it with meat from fish, fowl, and furbearers, with vegetables. Now they have McDonald's like everyone else. Corn was once the backbone of culture in Central and South America. A kernel of corn is a kernel of corn until it is tossed into vats with millions of other kernels, its shell removed, its fibers destroyed, its fructose isolated and concentrated into syrup swirled into a batch of preservatives and smashed raspberries.

The people who first arrived on Bristol Bay's shores, and the shores of its rivers and lakes, ate the same salmon we catch. When we take a fish to Graveyard for dinner, or lunch, or whatever the meal is called at the time of day it happens to be, it's a fish I savor and enjoy more than any other food. Wild salmon is an elite superfish with the strength and endurance to forge miles upriver through a gauntlet of predators after years thriving in the ocean.

I eat it even when I'm nowhere near here, because it's a natural, sustainable source of protein. I can tout its omega-3s, taurine, niacin, B vitamins, choline, pantothenic acid, biotin, and potassium. I don't get these things from a factory, a farm, or a peanut butter and jelly sandwich. I get it from this water and take it back in a cooler. I don't get to run much during the fishing season, and I can't stop other people from wasting it, but I know that when I am running up or down some paved road or rugged trail, the power of wild salmon swims through my bloodstream.

"Where are you going today?" The Border Patrol officer at Port Huron, in Lower Michigan near Detroit, snatched my passport from my hand. I told her I was on my way to Buffalo, New York.

"What's in Buffalo?"

I was on my way to Boston.

"What's in Boston?"

I told her I was running the Boston Marathon. She was not impressed. She scowled the way she then scowled at every answer I gave her. I lived in Michigan. The truck had Alaska plates because I grew up there. I had indeed been outside of the country recently. I was in Peru and Guatemala, in fact. The truck was in Wisconsin at the time. A year ago, I was living in Kansas.

Four officers tore apart my truck. They unzipped bags, opened my CD cases, searched under the seats, and removed the contents of my cooler. Then I was escorted inside to a waiting room where two officers pried at me for information. If I were going to lie, I would have simplified it, from some kind of beginning to a neatly-tied end. They wanted a straight story, but the truth wasn't a straight line — like a year for me had never been some arbitrary measurement between January and December. A year went from one fishing season to the next one.

The Aztec and Maya didn't design their calendar like that either. It was composed as a cycle ending with the winter solstice of 2012. Some people were anticipating an alien invasion, some kind of a spiritual awakening, or the day of the rapture. The date was still almost two years away, and some people couldn't be told that like the twelve on a clock, the date was just a notch signifying another cycle aligning our planet, its moon, the sun, and the other stars in the sky.

The Maya understood that our planet's rotation does not take an exact 24 hours like the tide does not change in an exact six. A year is not 365 days, which is why every four years, the Gregorian calendar has an extra day in February. The Egyptians and the Greeks had a handle on solar cycles, lunar cycles, our planet's orbit, and the movement of constellations, but the Maya, the Aztecs, and the Inca had an even more precise handle of measuring it. Although annihilated by Conquistadors, these groups of people were more advanced than me in more ways than I can even imagine. Give me a thousand years, and I could never create, invent, or measure what they created, invented, and measured.

It was not long after the fishing season when I had arrived at the airport in Cusco, once the capital city of the Inca Empire. Lines of drivers in tiny cars yelled "taxi!" out the windows, and I crawled into one of them with my backpack next to me. I asked for a ride to the language academy where I had enrolled in a course for certification to teach English as a foreign language. I didn't want a career that *allowed* me to travel. I wanted a career that *encouraged* me to travel and live in exotic places.

My lease on an apartment started Monday, but it was Saturday, so I had reserved a bed in a hostel somewhere uphill from the academy. I flung from side to side as the driver tugged the steering wheel and we zipped around razor-sharp turns through an ancient city of white bricks and grass-thatched roofs. He honked his horn, ignored stop signs, and weaved through hundreds of identical cars performing hundreds of identical actions. We swerved around old ladies peddling crates of alpaca sweaters, children playing soccer in the street, and tourists taking pictures. I'd given up on finding a seat belt by the time he parked in front of the academy, and I handed him ten Peruvian soles. He had asked for eight, but two of them were for getting me there alive.

The academy was on Avenida del Sol, the Avenue of the Sun, one of the busier and bigger streets downhill of the main square, Plaza de Armas. A sign in English pointed me down the stairs where a gringo about my age was in the human resources office, speaking Spanish to two younger women. After they left, he welcomed me, gave me directions to the hostel, and told me about places to eat around the Plaza de Armas. A taxi, he told me, could take me there if I couldn't find it.

"I think I'll walk," I said.

At Plaza de Armas, conquistadors had long ago torn down an Inca temple to build a Cathedral, and other, smaller churches were built beside it. From the fountain in the middle, I could see a square with its edges as places of worship, gift shops, bars, and dance clubs, what the people there called discotecas. There were places to order Peruvian fare like ceviche de trucha, carne de alpaca, or papas fritas. There was also a McDonald's. Tourists toured, beggars begged, and vendors stepped in front of me, stopping me in my tracks.

"Massage, amigo? Massage?"

"Ropa de alpaca, amigo?"

"Special massage, amigo? Special for you"

"Restaurante, amigo?"

"Marijuana? Cocaine?"

"No, gracias," I said to all of them.

In my uphill trek to the hostel, streets narrowed into cobblestone alleys until they steepened into steps. Plaza de Armas was over 11,000 feet above sea level, but the city climbed high into the ruins of Sacsahuayman, well above 12,000 feet. The air thinned as I ascended, and I sucked air with every forward lunge.

The hostel bar was inhabited by a motley crew of twenty-somethings from different countries. I ordered food from a lanky Australian kid with a purple mohawk. A girl from Vienna and a guy from San Francisco brought me into their conversation about travel, existence, the meaning of life, and the Brazilian Brahma they convinced me to order. One pint turned into three, and at 12,000 feet, three was like six. I puked in a bathroom stall and went to my room where there were two sets of bunks. All of them were empty, so I took a spot on the bottom, closest to the door. An hour or two into the night, I felt movement under the sheet.

"Can I help you?"

"Gracias," the girl said.

"For what?"

"Gracias," she said again.

I got up, turned on the light, and she screamed as she bolted from the door. I didn't take it personally.

In the morning, the academy called a cab to whip me across another seat through Cuzco's streets and alleys. I realized that in Cuzco, the richer neighborhoods were at a higher altitude and the poorer ones were toward the bottom. My place was in a yellow apartment building on Calle Huancaro, downhill from downtown, somewhere around 10,000 feet, where rain flowed from the top, fruit and potatoes were hauled in rickshaws, barrels of garbage were burned on the curb, and the occasional dead dog lay in the street.

I was on the third floor of four. The kitchen window overlooked homes on the hills where sheep wandered over piles of garbage. The bedroom window overlooked the street on the other side. From that bedroom is where I discovered that the Cusqueñans were awake and active at around 5:00 AM, the same time they went to bed. They hooted and hollered from nights of drinking, and cars honked on their way to work. Peru's elections were soon, and cars drove back and forth, campaigning with loudspeakers.

If I wasn't awake after that, I could always electrocute myself by touching the electrical wire wrapped around the showerhead. In Peru, I was a tall man, and I bumped my head on it more often than not.

If I didn't, the water was always cold, because the wire didn't work well. By the time I left my apartment, I was awake and alert.

It was a three-mile hike uphill to the academy where I'd be from 9:00 to 3:00 Monday through Friday with twelve other twenty-somethings without jobs in an American recession. Our classroom was upstairs in a big room with a big table where we'd practice adverbs, adjectives, and dangling participles before practicing teaching them to others.

It was a full-immersion style teaching of English with demonstration as the prime teaching tool. Most of the time, we practiced on each other, but sometimes students were brought into our class as guinea pigs — which may be a bad example considering I'd learned that roasted *cuy* was an upscale, Peruvian dinner.

"How are you today?"

"What is 'today'?"

"It is not yesterday," I said, pointing behind me.

"It is not tomorrow," I said, pointing forward.

"It is today," I said, pointing toward the ground.

"Floor?"

At lunch time, I lived on quinoa, goat cheese, and black beans at a vegetarian place up the street, or ceviche de trucha across the street. Fifteen Peruvian soles was the same as about five American dollars, and it bought a pile of pickled trout on top of yams, corn, tomatoes and onions. Nights and weekends, I went to the pubs with classmates.

I ordered an alpaca steak for dinner one time, vomited all night into the toilet, and I missed a day of class to eject fluids from two ends. The steak was delicious, but I should have known not to order meat after seeing steaks and chickens slung over lines at the markets, warm in the sun. It didn't stop me from trying the roasted cuy, which arrived on the table complete with eyes, teeth, and claws. Those were the only parts I didn't eat.

Class was long and brutal, but I would have preferred to feel well enough to attend the day I missed. Once, it was canceled due to protests in the streets. We arrived at a metal gate over the entryway, and for once, no cars were on the street. Instead, there were rocks and chunks of cinderblocks people had thrown in protest of a high water bill from the city. No one in my class was sad.

A party at the academy celebrated finishing the program and attaining our certificates. Drinks and snacks were provided in a ballroom where colorful lights circled and flashed to a mass of bodies wobbling to awful American pop and hip-hop. It was like a middle school dance, but with alcohol in the open — teachers and students alike drinking it.

Out of nowhere, a bouncy Cusqueñan girl grabbed my wrist and pointed to another Cusqueñan girl leaning against the bar with her arms crossed.

"Go," she said. "Talk."

That's how Cat with a 'C' introduced me to Kat with a 'K'. Kat with a 'K' was the manager of a clothing store on a square near Plaza de Armas. A friend of hers was a singer in a metal band, playing the next day in Aguas Calientes, the gateway town to Machu Picchu. I met her at the Plaza, boarded a nine-passenger van with her, my backpack, and ten other Peruvians. Then I listened to distorted electric guitar, heavy drums, and a roaring, female voice belt hardcore Spanish lyrics. After the concert, we had dinner and spent the night at a hotel in town.

When we arrived at the ancient city abandoned by the Inca and reclaimed by the tourism industry, it was shrouded in fog. As we explored the ruins and hiked the trails around it, the fog dissipated until Machu Picchu was in clear view from the trail above it. Postcards and magazine advertisements could never capture it. I'd seen nothing like it since I looked out over Meteora.

Some classmates and I had planned a trip to Lake Titicaca, and when Kat and I were back in Cuzco, I was on a bus to Puno soonafter. It might have been 100 degrees on that bus. I was thirsty, sweaty, and I still had occasional bouts of diarrhea I blamed on the alpaca steak. Tiny TVs presented *the Passion of the Christ*, a movie with Aramaic dialogue, complete with Spanish subtitles at the bottom. Then they showed the movie again.

My gut was angry, and my brain hurt from dehydration, but as Jesus was whipped, cut, sliced, and nailed to a cross, in a film gorier than *Friday the 13th,* there were times during that bus ride I might have traded places with him.

We stayed with a family on an island with no electricity. The people spoke Quechua, an ancient language of the Inca, as a first language. Spanish was their second one. They fed us quinoa soup and goat cheese, and in the morning, we climbed to the summit of an island more than 13,000 feet high, where one clockwise circle around some ancient ruins was supposed to remove curses and evil spirits. I wasn't sure about that, but after one lap, my gas was gone. My diarrhea never returned either.

When my new friends parted ways to teaching positions in different parts of Latin America and back to their homes in the States, I stayed in Cuzco and continued my relationship with Kat. I took Spanish lessons at the academy, and Kat taught me more of it in the evenings. In turn, she was learning English from me. She suggested I try getting a position at the academy, but I never did. I saw myself becoming stagnant again, and a familiar longing was returning.

Registration for the 2011 Boston Marathon was coming up, and I knew it would fill within the hour it opened. Continuing this path in South America was one adventure. Going back to the US and running the Boston marathon was another. I was on my laptop at the exact second that registration opened. It seemed like an easy choice. Teaching English in South America paid about 300 dollars a month, and it was near impossible to attain a work visa, necessitating a once-a-month hop across a border.

Boston filled within not just the hour but within minutes. When I found out I was accepted, I signed and faxed a lease for an apartment in Marquette. Just to say I had used the TEFL certificate, I found a six-week volunteer position in Antigua, Guatemala starting in November. I didn't tell Kat.

My relationship with her seemed to be getting more serious all the time, and I told her we should slow down. It wasn't because I didn't like her. It was because every day I didn't tell her I was leaving, the guiltier I felt. The faster time ran out, the worse it was going to be, and the worse it was going to be, the faster time ran out. When I finally did tell her, I never saw her again. My final month Peru was on my own.

November was the rainy season. Water didn't collect in the Plaza or the richer neighborhood of San Blas. It ran downhill, to my apartment, where the streets were rivers, where garbage and dead dogs floated down the current, washing onto doorsteps. When I wasn't in class, I spent my time wandering the city, working out at the gym, and eating in restaurants with their Peruvian prices. Other times, with a bag of groceries, I walked down the hill, waded across the street, and went upstairs to cook and go to bed early.

I'd been sleeping more than 14 hours when a door opened into the bedroom.

"Hay una señorita aquí para ti."

"Huh?" I heard what he said, but in my grogginess, I had forgotten flying to San Salvador to Guatemala City and then riding a bus to Antigua where I was staying with a host family. For the most part, I was having a hard time believing there was a señorita here for me.

He repeated, more slowly this time, "Hay una señorita aquí para ti."

The señorita took me to the school, explained how to get to Alotenango, where I would be teaching. She left me at the studio apartment above a restaurant downtown, where I was paying rent. It was on the same street as big hotels, fancy restaurants, and a supermarket where I bought my food.

Antigua was refreshing. It lacked honking horns and thick blasts of black exhaust and vendors backed off with a simple shake of my head. I slept late, ran, went to the gym, and walked to the city market where pirated movies were sold for ten quetzales, barely more than a dollar. Next to the market is where school buses from the United States idled, each with a man hanging out its door, yelling the destination of the bus in a yodeling stream of Spanish.

I had to find the one yodeling, "Alotenango, Alotenango, Alotenango!"

Three quetzales went to the driver, and I took a roller coaster ride through several villages to the Municipalidad de Alotenango, where the school was at the bottom of a hill of cobblestone, next to a church. It was a gray, concrete box. A blue dumpster was in front of the door, and in front of the blue dumpster was a man rolled up in blankets, asleep on the cobblestone. Inside, there were three classrooms and a bathroom that hadn't been cleaned in years. The classrooms had cinder block walls painted yellow. A whiteboard was in front of columns of desks for a class of 20 students

Class began at 2:00, but the first student didn't walk into the room until at least 2:05. One by one, kids ages five to seventeen arrived with backpacks and found seats. Some of them could exchange pleasantries in English. Others had never spoken a word of it.

Somewhere around 4:35 the adults arrived for the afternoon class at 4:30. Their skill levels were just as diversified, but not as much as their ages. There were eighteen-year-olds, middle-agers, and one 86-year-old woman. Nobody arrived on time. Maybe they treated this way because they were only a few generations away from having used the Mayan Calendar. There was no consequence to wasting something that never ran out.

After my volunteer time, I ventured deep into a corner of the country by bus, exploring the ruins of Tikal and ruins hidden places in the jungle. There was one village to which I rode a van over several miles of wet, bumpy dirt to a village on the river. There, I paid a man named Carlos to drive me upriver through vines and brush in his boat. I stepped onto the secluded shore in a lagoon archipelago, heard deep growls in the trees.

I turned to Carlos.

"Monkeys," he said.

It was the only word in English I heard him say. I was relieved that they were not jaguars. Somewhere, deep in the jungle surrounded by a lagoon, listening to roars, thinking every stick in the trail was a snake, I felt alone with my primal self. I began to run, hurdling over logs, embracing the sauna effect of the humidity. The desire to run was not just a means of escape for me. It was a compulsion even when I had escaped. It was not a guilty pleasure. It was a necessity. Running in Boston would be a celebration.

Upon my return to Antigua, Erica and her boyfriend, Andrew joined my last ventures in the country. We got lost trying to find a road to Montenegro, always somehow winding up in the city of Chimaltenango as though it were the same road every time — whether it was pavement or winding gravel. It seemed I was always following the same roads back to the same places. We made it to Montenegro and its hot, black sand beach where we were kept awake by roosters and Guatemalans playing music from their phones. Erica and Andrew left me at the airport, and I was back in Marquette. The two of them would return soon to move to Salt Lake City.

When I was back in Marquette, it felt like I never left. I was back in time for the ball drop from the Savings Bank Building and its copper-coated clock tower. I was in a familiar, comfortable place as the Gregorian Calendar started again.

Time itself, however, did not start again. Grandpa was on his deathbed. He had been struggling with Parkinson's disease for years, even years before anyone else knew it. He was a doctor and had diagnosed himself. When Erica, Luke, and I were kids visiting Florida, and Grandpa was talking funny, we thought he was just trying to make us laugh again. Measurement of time could start again, but time would never reverse, even as often as it felt like it did. He died on the first day of the year, one day before his birthday.

That year's ball drop in Marquette was a notch marking birth, death, and a new year, but time itself kept moving. There was still the rest of January, February, March, and April. April is when I stood in front of border security in Port Huron, remaining as still as possible while a drug dog was instructed to search me. He was much more interested in the sticky residue of melted candy on the floor, and the officers soon let me go. I was off to New York, and then to Massachusetts, where there was a start line in Hopkinton and a finish line in Boston. It was one place where thinking in terms of a start to finish made sense.

A line, or a rope as most people call it, is twine woven, braided from one end to another. It twists and turns in a neat pattern, but the ends need to be tied, taped, or seared together, or it unravels. We use lines to tie nets to buoys, to tie to the tender to deliver fish, to tie ourselves to Erica's skiff when we wait for the tide or the next announcement on KDLG

"This is the Alaska Department of Fish and Game in King Salmon with an announcement for commercial permit holders in the Naknek-Kvichak District."

When I started fishing, we were "fishermen." Then we were "fishers." Now we're "permit holders." The announcements broadcasted over KDLG have changed the terminology, but it's still the same job. Set the nets, let the salmon hit, pull along with a skiff, and deliver them to the tender.

Erica was 21 when she moved her operation to the Kvichak section and started staying at Graveyard with us. The room across the hall from the Doctor's office had been vacant since Mom quit fishing in 1984, and Bob had his own room apart from his female coworkers. Erica hired Mary, her college friend, and they stayed in that room. They were the only all-woman crew at Graveyard, and probably on the Kvichak. Erica's site was directly next to ours, and although we had separate operations, we lived together and operated on the same schedule. Male or female doesn't matter. Andrew, my soon-to-be brother-in-law, fishes with Erica now, but she catches just as many fish as she did with Mary.

It takes three Wilson men — Me, Luke, and Dad — to bring the net across the skiff. It's not even July and the nets are sunk. The corks are below the surface, and we wouldn't see the buoys either if the water weren't glass calm. Two earlier deliveries have us at over 12,000 pounds for the tide, and the fish haven't quit. Sweat soaks my baselayer as we pick over 6,000 pounds more.

When there's an hour left to closure, Luke and I roundhaul as Dad drives us forward. Luke stands in a brailer, pulling the leads. I stand in the bow, pulling the corks. Both of us are thigh-deep in fish as we pull and pile the nets on top of nets and brailers. There is nowhere else for them to go, which is why Luke is standing in one. There is no freeboard above the surface — just a pile of fish and net, and three Wilsons with the fruit of their labor piled between the bulkheads of a 21-foot skiff, the Evinrude E-Tec pushing us toward the tender.

After waiting in line behind several skiffs, the skipper tells us the hull is full, and we watch the last fishermen, fishers, and permit holders drive away. The crane operators stomp the lids closed. There's another tender coming at midnight, they tell us, with the flood, but that's four hours from now.

Erica and Andrew arrive behind us, and the crew invites us all aboard. At first, we lay down on the deck. Then the crew invites us into the cabin where they feed us fish filets and steamed rice. Inside, it's warm and dry. There are the comforts of home, like a refrigerator, a microwave, laptops, and a TV, but as we enjoy a meal and conversation about our lives in the Lower 48, it's hard to ignore the wind gaining momentum outside, raising the waves with the tide.

When the new tender arrives, the waves are menacing. We put on our rain gear again, and step into our skiffs. Waves thrash against us on the way over to the new vessel, and we lose fish over the sides as we bounce our way to it. Luke's eyes are wide and fearful. Dad and I have been here before, but Luke is the smart one. Then the motor cuts, the skiff jerks, Dad swears, and I turn to see we've run over a piece of line floating in the water. He bends over the splashwell as we drift upriver, untangling the mess in the propeller while I keep watching for things we could hit.

Andrew and Erica cut in front of us and tie to one side of the tender. Another crew ties to the other side. We are left waiting, bouncing in the waves, and I watch Erica's skiff slam into the tender almost sideways — even the bottom crashing against it. My muscles tense as I watch the weight unloaded from their skiff, and I'm sure Luke and Dad feel the same.

After they drive away, I tie our skiff to the tender. We slam against it, repeating the same motion as Erica's skiff. Dad ties the stern line, and we begin our delivery. As the waves slam us against the surface, against the tender, the clips on the crane bounce once or twice before we can fasten them to the loops. When the first brailer is clipped and untied from the skiff, it rises against the lights, empties, and lowers back to us. With a thousand fewer pounds on board, gone from the bow, we rock lopsided in the water. The sooner we can get another brailer out of here, the better chances we have not to swamp.

Then there is a siren on the other side of the vessel. I hear it over the wind and waves and men shouting. Luke freezes. The crane operator disappears. The attention of the crew is on the skiff on the other side of the tender, where two men have gone overboard. The skiff remains lopsided. It rocks and splashes in the waves, and splashes into the stern are bigger now.

"Hey!" Dad yells up to anyone who can hear. "We gotta get more fish out of here or we're gonna swamp, too!"

The scale from the crane is still lowered into our skiff, and I start clipping the next brailer to it. Luke is frozen.

"Luke!" I say. "Brailer! Come on!"

I can't hear what Dad and the skipper are shouting back and forth through the wind, but Dad starts untying the stern line.

"Keith!" he shouts. "Untie! Skipper says we're going to calmer water!"

I release us. Then water dumps into the stern.

"Hey, we're sinking!" Dad yells. "We're sinking!"

Fish float toward me. The motor is underwater. I've untied, but the line is still in my hands, sliding through them. I tighten my grip and feel it burn through my gloves.

"I'm bailing," Luke says. I know he doesn't mean the bucket when he crawls to the side and climbs aboard the tender.

Metal crashes against metal. Splashes between vessels tower above me. Waves keep dumping into the skiff. My hands burn as they tighten harder around the line as I slip into the dark. In my peripheral vision, I see Dad climb aboard the tender, too. I'm alone in the skiff, drifting away, dead fish floating against my hips. Dad and Luke's voices are somewhere in the lights.

Luke says, "Screw the skiff, Keith! Get up here!"

Dad says, "Damnit, that's my son!"

I keep drifting into the darkness, and for a moment, the waves are silent — almost still. My mind must have gone black. I don't remember tying the tangle into the net, into the mess on the floor, holding the skiff against the current, but I look down, and it's there. It's not a bowline or a keg knot or even a granny knot. It's a wad of line woven back and forth and around itself in some kind of mess that's somehow holding.

I've done what I can, and now I need to get out of this skiff. I step toward the tender, but my ankle is wrapped in the line. My face splashes into the floor. I taste salt. Water pours down my neck. The bail bucket floats by me and disappears. I flap and kick, but it's futile. The more I move, the more the line tightens. Water keeps pouring toward me. Water is all I see. Now I realize, surrounded in the dark, that I've come face to face with the tide. I know it won't wait, but I can't help but whisper.

"Not now."

With one jerk of my foot, my shoe flies away and disappears. I crawl to the side, and the crew lifts me aboard. From the deck of the tender, I watch the skiff sink and flip. The fish are gone. The skiff flips again and again, bouncing in the waves. Everything is gone — the plastic food box, the toolbox, the metal slides we use to pull the net across the bow. For a moment, I see the empty gas tanks floating behind the stern. Then they disappear into the dark with everything else. I feel empty.

Dad yells, "No!"

Luke remains a statue.

I fall to my knees.

The net hanging from the crane is a wadded mess of lines and ruined web. The other net is behind it, and my muscles clench with the thought of the splish-splash of another fish getting caught in it. Somehow, the skiff doesn't go anywhere. The skipper barks orders, and the crew works like they'd practiced this a thousand times, to tie the skiff tight against the tender.

Inside the cabin aboard the tender, Dad says he needs to sit down before he falls down. The two men who went overboard are safe with us. It's them who give us a ride back to Graveyard. The waves are hellacious, and a skiff full of fish would never last through these conditions. Back at Graveyard, Erica and Andrew are still awake, hoping we'll make it there.

If we had arrived at the tender first, she tells us, and if they had watched what happened to our skiff, they would have tried to take their fish back to Graveyard and delivered when it was calmer. They would have died, she tells us. They were saved by a piece of line brought by the tide.

I'd been living in Marquette again for almost a year in another one-bedroom apartment. I was skiing, biking, and running new and old trails, and taking substitute teaching jobs for extra cash, hoping to find a permanent position. Of course, hundreds of other Northern graduates were doing the same thing. Even though I was free to spend my time the way I wanted, and I was running faster than I'd ever run, I couldn't shake the awareness that I wasn't accomplishing anything.

I was taking classes at Northern to keep my teaching licenses active. They were undergraduate history classes with eighteen, nineteen, and twenty-year-olds, including a kid I had taught as a student-teacher. When classmates talked during a lecture, or they complained about the workload, I couldn't help but shoot dirty looks and wonder what the hell was wrong with them. Then I remembered their age. I'd even taught one of them and remembered that he'd been a pain in the ass. Maybe I had made my own progress, but maybe I was going backwards.

Erica had graduated from Northern, and Luke had finished high school. He was attending college at Bemidji State in Northern Minnesota while Erica was on her way to medical school. Seeing my siblings, both younger, moving in the direction of their goals and aspirations fed my longing to seek my next job in my next town. It was the best of times and the worst of times in my tale of different towns and cities.

I had run the Boston Marathon the previous spring. A month later, I ran my first 50-miler at the Sulphur Springs Trail Races in the woods nearby Toronto, Ontario. I had run several 50-kilometer trail runs, and 50 miles had been on my to-do list for a while. Give me a trail run at any distance, I had discovered, and I'd take whatever rocks, roots, climbs, descents, and obstacles like fallen trees the trail gave me. Racing on pavement had a specific science and tried-and-true formulas.

When I was training for Boston, I looked forward to it, but the goal of my finishing time loomed over me, and anything that disrupted the training was a source of anxiety. The risk involved was alluring, but also menacing, even though no one would really care but me. Running an ultramarathon, any footrace longer than a marathon was more about overcoming the inevitable pain, exhaustion, and other obstacles I would experience. When I ran Boston, my time was 2:47, one minute faster than I wanted. When I ran the Sulphur Springs 50-miler, I finished in just under eight hours and took third place. Each type of race had its own appeal.

I was currently training for the Philadelphia Marathon. The race was in November, giving me enough time to train after the fishing season left me out of condition. It was also a flat course close to sea level. When looking for a time and place to set a new personal record, it fit my criteria.

I ran intervals on paved streets, sprinted on treadmills, charged up hills in quiet neighborhoods, and performed squats and lunges on a rubber floor. Every other weekend, I ran a half marathon somewhere nearby. The other weekends, I ran long and slow. Then I flew to Philly, checked into my hotel room, saw the historic Eastern State Penitentiary, the Liberty Bell, Independence Hall, and Edgar Alan Poe's house in the middle of the projects.

The start of the marathon was at the Philadelphia Museum of Art, where Rocky famously ran its steps to the top and danced the way

I used to dance before I was announced as "now wrestling." I sat atop those steps calm and reserved, watching the sun rise above the crowds at the portable toilets. When the race began, I blasted forward again on east coast streets, and I finished in 2:42.

Back in my hotel room, I ordered a large pizza and plopped myself flat on my back with the box on my chest, shoveling my favorite dietary vice into my piehole. Then I saw the news. One runner had been a quarter-mile from the finish line when his heart failed. Another runner had collapsed on the pavement just after finishing. Neither of them survived. I remained flat on my back with the luxury of cheese and refined white flour forcing my overworked heart to work even harder, and suddenly I wasn't so proud of my time anymore.

During the flight itinerary back to Detroit and then up to Marquette, I couldn't help but question my purpose behind running these races. Running itself, I understood somewhat. It was the need to challenge myself, to put myself through physical struggle, and to keep myself sane and healthy. Running a prescribed distance as fast as possible, however, was demanding — and described by others as insane and unhealthy. It wasn't a metaphor for life. I wanted life to be long, but I didn't want it to be fast.

Grandpa was gone, and Grandma was not feeling well. She was living alone in her condo overlooking Marquette's Lower Harbor and the old Ore Dock. She had her good days and bad days and Mom was regularly making the drive from Washburn to help Aunt Christine take care of her. My responsibilities were reduced to taking her dog, Gino, for a walk. I would take the shaggy little Shih Tzu on the paved loop around the park and along the Lower Harbor.

After Philly, it was Mom who asked me if it was the race Candice had been training for. I didn't know. I'd never even met her. All I knew was that Candice had taken a teaching position in Chignik Lake, a village on the Alaska Peninsula with a school in the Lake and Peninsula School District. It was a place smaller and more remote than Naknek. Before I took my job in Kansas, I had been exchanging emails about a position there, teaching English — but I liked running and racing too much to resign myself to village life, so when it came down to that or small-town Kansas, I chose the place that was no place like home.

Candice was from Pennsylvania, and like me, she was a runner. When she moved to Chignik, she kept running. Although getting to a race would mean taking time from work and a series of plane tickets, she had registered for yet another one. She was running when the wolves killed her. I was in Kansas, longing not to be there.

I wasn't in Kansas anymore, and I wasn't in Naknek either. I supposed my compulsion to race would remain mysterious, and I decided to keep embracing it rather than question it. After Philly, and after skiing the American Birkebeiner for the first time in four years, the snow was melting, the sun was warmer, and I was bursting with energy when I ran. This energy was dampened, however, with knowing that even though I was fast, I was also going nowhere. Springtime meant the clock was ticking toward the fishing season, which brought a level of uneasiness when I didn't know where I would be afterward. Marquette felt like home more than anywhere else, but I didn't feel like I belonged there. Even though I was living in my favorite place to live, I knew I couldn't be there much longer. Teaching positions were opening again, and again I started applying to them all around the country.

Before I moved anywhere, I was running the Salt Lake City Marathon in April. Erica was living there with Andrew. He was working and she was using her time to study for the MCATs, practice new recipes, and train for the marathon. She knew it would be hard, and she might hate it, but she said she wanted to experience what I seemed to love so much. If she hadn't said that, I probably wouldn't have registered. My sights were on the Ice Age 50-miler in May.

Grandma, otherwise positive and rosy-eyed at all times, was not a fan of Erica taking her time between college and medical school. She said Erica would lose her momentum. I knew better. She was the valedictorian of her high school class, and she graduated with honors from college. Erica, a Norse word for ever-powerful, was ever-determined no matter what she was working toward. Now she had decided to run a marathon, so that's what she was going to do. The two of us walked to the railway station in downtown Salt Lake City and rode to the start at the University of Utah.

We hugged and then seeded ourselves into the crowd. I had told her to just keep putting one foot in front of the other, and she'd get to the finish line. It wasn't a joke. Sometimes it's really that simple. The race began and the course turned into a canyon road and descended into turns through the streets of the city. It was hot and hilly and definitely a difficult marathon. After I crossed the finish line, I waited with Andrew for Erica. After she crossed the finish line, she walked with us on wooden legs to a table with water and bananas, and I could tell it was a hurt she hadn't expected. She'd be sore for days, but we still made the trip to camp and hike around Zion, because that's what she had planned.

When I was back in Marquette, I kept applying for jobs, and I kept training for the 50-miler. If I couldn't make myself useful by continuing an actual career, at least I could spend my efforts on something meaningful to me. Then I took a phone call from a school in Montana. The superintendent said he'd like to interview me.

Then Grandma was gone. Mom was in town, and she called me from the condo. She and my aunt Christine were with her. After Mom's phone call, I had a Skype interview within the hour. I didn't allow myself the tears. I changed into a shirt and tie and wore pants just in case I had to stand up during the interview. I was offered the job the next day. I took a 50-mile jaunt through rolling hills and woods on the Ice Age Trail in Wisconsin. Then I did plenty of crying when I packed up my truck and headed west.

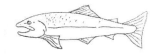

Salmon swim toward the east into the Kvichak, toward the rising sun. We watch the wakes trail behind fins on the surface, but we see nothing below them. The water is too disturbed with mud and sediment. From where they swim, we don't know exactly. It's from somewhere in the Pacific, maybe verging on the Arctic.

"What is it like up the Kvichak River?" Matt asks, again licking the salt from his lips, never having been near the ocean. "How far does that river go?"

Matt is Luke's college friend, and he is our crewman this year. Luke has decided to work at the Bear Trail Lodge in King Salmon, guiding vacationers and celebrities, helping them land the fish of their dreams with a rod and reel.

Matt wears a camouflage hat with his short red hair matted beneath it, and he has a smile yellowed, perhaps from too much sweet corn. He stands with his arms straight and puts ketchup on everything, including a cut of grilled filet of fresh king salmon, and

I can't help but stare every time the red paste spatters on the sacred flesh of the coveted species. Matt is a farmer, a hunter, and a fisherman — an outdoorsman from Illinois who lives in Bemidji, Minnesota. He has an appreciation for where food comes from, and he is truly excited to be here.

Dad explains to him that the Kvichak pours from Lake Iliamna, the largest body of water in Alaska. The village of Igiugig is at its mouth. Along its shores are also villages like Kokhanok, Newhalen, Iliamna, and Pedro Bay. Lake Iliamna is where they want to dig the Pebble Mine.

Even after the grueling trip from the Lower 48, Matt wasn't the least bit groggy when he, at last, reached the King Salmon Airport but radiating that smile. In the skiff, he never stands quiet and still, but he learns quickly what action corresponds with the next, and he works hard on board. He knows how to use his back to reef on the leadline, pulling fish toward him. Then he straightens his back, lets the fish dangle down, and problem solves the gills out of the mesh. If it drops from his hands, he bends down, picks it up, and tosses it into one of the brailers behind him. He's a natural.

"Saltwater," he says, licking his lips. "It's real!"

At Graveyard, when the first of the wind arrives, the Visqueen windows flap and flutter, and the bushes are brushed sideways against the tundra. Dad wakes up Matt and me hours before it's time to head check the nets. The motor guard, the protective bar around the stern, is around one of the wooden pilings in the mud. We can't simply wait for the flood and drive away, because our anchorline is wrapped into another anchorline and our bow will be dunked beneath the surface, taking the other skiff with it. Graveyard is a frenzy of fishermen on the beach devising lifts with boards and rocks. Then the chainsaw arrives and cuts the piling, sawdust spraying like the splashes of crashing waves.

As the wind gathers more momentum across Bristol Bay, and it funnels itself into the Kvichak, we don't put nets in the water, even when it's open to fishing. The danger is not worth the reward. Instead, we remain hunkered down at the hospital, watching branches torn from bushes and landing on the porch. We have more time to sleep, but the wind howls too loud. The storm lasts for two days.

Days later, the sun has returned, and the wind is gone. Between checking nets, Dad spots a log on the surface, shining in the sun, but it's not a log. It's the Purp. I reach beneath with the boathook to grab for its anchorline, or anything I can grab. It takes three, four, five tries before I get ahold of anything. Dad ties it to the stern, and he drives forward, wrapping the line around the Purp, and he cranks the motor. I watch the Purp rise to the surface, waterfalls dumping from its sides. Water is up to its rims and Dad keeps driving to keep it above the surface. Dad waves his arms at Andrew, who is fishing with his friend Kurt, and their skiff pulls alongside of us.

"What do you want us to do?"

Dad is in full-fledged fishing mode. "I want you to take Matt and put him onboard the Purp with the bail bucket."

Andrew pauses. "I don't think I want to do that."

"How come?" Dad yells. "Why not?"

"Pull it into the beach," Andrew says. "Let it go dry."

"No," Dad says. "Put Matt on the Purp!"

Even Andrew knows fishing mode, and he concedes. With both our skiffs still moving, Matt climbs aboard with Andrew. He doesn't hesitate for a second. Then Andrew drops Matt onto the Purp. It seems like a bad idea, but we all know Dad will accept no other option right now. I don't know if Matt thinks anything of it.

"Whatever you do, don't stop bailing," I say. We all say it to him in one form or another as he steps into the sinking skiff.

With the Purp following, Dad drives in circles as Matt bails like hell. He scoops water and dumps it back into the Kvichak, and scoops more of it as the Purp's wake and our wake together swirl into what looks like a whirlpool forming. It gushes against the sides of both skiffs. I know that if, for some reason, the motor fails, the Purp will dive back below the surface along with the kid from Illinois. When the Purp is almost empty, Dad stops, and it stays afloat on its own. Matt looks up, sweat shining on his face. I don't know if he ever stops smiling.

When I was still 22, I met a girl at a party. When this girl wasn't interested in a guy, she told him her name was Anne. She gave me her real name, but she lost her interest in me by the time I was 29. I don't remember the first thing I said to Anne, but I remember shaking a Magic 8-ball with her, playing a game of foosball with her, and making fun of her friend who talked way too much.

Before the end of the night, Anne and I were finishing each other's sentences — by which I mean we were combining magnetized words on the refrigerator when her friends told her it was time to go. A friend of mine drove them to their next party, and when he returned, he asked me why the hell I didn't ask for her number. She was upset about it the whole ride, he told me.

It was mostly my shyness that had kept me from asking for her number, but it was also the way her friends whisked her out the door with barely enough time to say goodbye. Besides, I didn't have a cell phone back then. Getting a girl's number meant finding a pen and a crumpled receipt to shove back into my wallet. Cell phones were for slaves to technology, man.

The next day, I was searching for Anne the old fashioned way. I used my laptop to find her on Facebook. Still in its early days, the social media site required a legitimate college email account, and only students at the same school could communicate through it. There were no privacy settings or multiple pages on someone's account. A page had a spot for a picture and places to list specific interests like hiking, running, sushi, napping, and the movie *Failure to Launch*. Anne was easy enough to find, so I sent her a private message and asked for her phone number that way.

We had coffee. The date went well, and when I dropped her off at her apartment, she told me that if I wanted to go out again, it would be her treat. Naturally, I left a voice message asking if she'd like to go to the play on campus with me, but I never got a call back. I guessed it didn't go that well after all.

A few months later, she wrote on my Facebook page.

I saw you running in the wilderness today.

I sent her a message right back. It turned out that she had returned my call. My answering machine hadn't recorded her message, because Alice had filled its memory. I asked her if it would be weird to go out again after all this time.

It wouldn't be, Anne wrote back. *I would like to go out again... but my current situation is really not going to be too pleasing to you. I would like to explain myself if you don't mind... I started dating this guy a while back, about the same time I met you.*

It was supposed to be nothing serious but we started hanging out a lot and to make a long story short, I got pregnant the first time we slept together (and used protection). It was pretty shitty. So he more or less took off, and I am due in July. Sounds trashy I know, but it was really a stroke of bad luck (or a bad guy) at the time I guess.

Anyways, there will be no hard feelings on my part if you don't want to hang out, but I just wanted to give you the scoop.

I didn't see Anne again for five years.

When I was 27, I was living in Marquette again. Anne and I had exchanged messages on occasion over the years. She saw me graduate from Northern, travel through Europe, live in the basement in Wisconsin, teach in Kansas, spend time in Peru and Guatemala, and move back to Marquette. I saw her leave Northern, finish a nursing degree, raise a son, and move to Key West with a new guy.

I was in Key West with my family for the New Year. The first night there, we ate at the hotel restaurant, and I ordered fish tacos. They were not okay to eat. They were not salmon, mind you. I puked in the toilet and spent the next day lying in bed, which was time to contemplate contacting Anne for no other reason than the fact that I was in Key West. That's the second time I got her number.

After a family dinner on the pier, we wandered around town while Anne and I texted back and forth as she made her way toward us. I stood on a step to make myself seen and dialed her number. Then I heard her voice for the first time since we had coffee. Then I saw her.

There was nothing bizarre about it. It felt as casual as it should have felt. We picked up our conversation right where we had left off. The difference was now she had a five-year-old son, she was a nurse, and she had recently ended her relationship with the guy who had brought her to Key West in the first place. Even though we enjoyed our night, and no one pulled her away this time, it still felt abrupt when she left me under the canopy of the hotel. I told her I hoped it wasn't another five years before we saw each other again.

It wasn't. She visited me in March. We hiked along the Dead River Falls, we had dinner, and we went back to my place. She didn't come in. I was too bashful to ask. Once again, I watched her drive away. By the time she told me that she wished I'd kissed her by the waterfalls, she was back in Key West.

After the fishing season, I was in Marquette one more time to move out to Winnett. Even though Anne was working things out with the other guy, she visited me again. On our way to go camping, with one tent in her Jeep, I asked her if the other guy knew she was with me. She said he didn't. She also said she wasn't about to start a dishonest relationship.

We hiked, we swam under waterfalls, we drank beer around a campfire, and then we crawled into the tent. With three feet of empty space between us, we fell asleep. In the morning, I confessed how hard it was to keep my distance. She told me she felt the same. I reached out my hand. She reached out hers. We lay there with joined hands for what could have been fifteen minutes or hours. Then we said our goodbyes in Marquette before she drove across the Mackinac to the Lower Peninsula where she had moved.

I was with friends at the Ore Dock Brewery on its opening night when the text message appeared on my phone. *Six years late and a day short of us I'm no longer obligated to anyone. Can we start anew?*

It *was* too late. I moved to Winnett, Montana.

Winnett was less of a town and more of a glorified trailer park. My own trailer was directly across the street from the school, and the commute from my bedroom to my kitchen was longer than my commute to work. It was explained to me that as the seat of Petroleum County, Winnett was the only town in the county. It had less than 500 people, less than 200 of whom lived in the actual town.

Surrounded by rolling hills and sagebrush, I distracted myself with teaching, coaching the cross country team, and training for the Seattle Marathon at the end of November. I was teaching five different lessons every day. I was leading workouts. I was doing my own training early in the morning and after practice. I didn't have cable, I didn't have Internet, and in Winnett, my cell phone didn't even have service. Mom, Dad, Mo, and Smiley visited me the week previous to the marathon. They all said I was too skinny, but I'd never been in better shape to run a marathon.

Race morning in Seattle was ideal. It was cool and calm, and I was absorbing the athletic energy in the air. I warmed up on the soccer field by the start just as I'd told teenage runners to do. I seeded myself at the front still jumping and kicking and staying loose.

Then it started, and I drove my body forward through those first streets, onto the bridge to Mercer Island, and back toward the city.

Within the first half of the course, I went from being the eighth runner to the fifth. By the time I reached Seward Park, I was the fourth runner. If I could catch whoever was in front of me, I would be in the top three of a big city marathon. More important, at this kind of pace, I was going to reach my longtime goal of breaking 2:40.

I didn't recognize the same landmarks at first. It was the runners around me that sent fear down my spine and down my legs. There had been a turn, where I joined a steady stream of runners that I had assumed were running the half marathon. Plenty of courses I'd run joined merged with half marathoners at some point. They were moving slow, and there had been no arrow or sign or volunteer pointing which way to go. Then I realized the number bibs around me were blue. My bib was blue. I had made a wrong turn.

Anger and frustration were pushing through my muscles. I looked at my watch, and I was running faster than five-minute miles. I thought I'd warp myself into superspeed and surpass my expectations. Maybe I'd even reverse time and go back to where I was supposed to go the other way.

Then I saw my watch hit 26.2 miles in less than 2:40. After all the training, I'd done everything I'd set out to do, but it didn't matter. It didn't count. My ego was smashed into pieces, and my muscles were feeling the pain. At the 3:03 mark, I crossed the finish line with emotion constricting my throat.

On the subway to the airport, I stared at my flip phone. I was showered, melancholy, and on the way to the airport. For the first time in months, I sent Anne a text message. I said I wanted to see her. Right away, she told me she wanted to see me, too.

I was in Marquette for my winter break, but she didn't drive up. I didn't drive down either. It might have been fear of committing an eight-hour drive to a maybe. It might have been fear of wasting more time on a heartbreak. At midnight, on another January 1st, I was with some friends as a ball dropped from the Savings Bank Building in downtown Marquette. By 1:30 AM, I was alone, registering for a 68-mile run in California.

I ran that race, testing my endurance farther and further than I'd ever tested it before. It began in fog drifting the way it drifts over the Kvichak River when Dad and I can't make it back to Graveyard. It drifted like me drifting from place to place. Then I realized it wasn't fog. It was clouds, and I was ascending above them. The course was, of course, up and down many of the Santa Monica Mountains. By mile 35, I was climbing over a rocky peak of a mountain when my inner thigh cramped. I pushed through it, but then it got worse again and again.

Soonafter, there was supposed to be a station with water. There was an empty table instead. By then, my hydration pack was empty. I'd been depending on the aid station, but the volunteers had not yet arrived. The cramps weren't stopping, but there was nothing to do except push my body as the heat intensified. Every time the muscle in my inner thigh refused to relax, I stopped to stretch it. It was a driver passing by a road crossing who rolled down his window and asked if I needed anything.

"Water," I croaked, and he threw me a bottle. It was gone in seconds. I could feel my liver and kidneys being reconstituted like those animal-shaped spongy toys that expand with water. The cramps got better, but they didn't stop until I had some electrolytes in my system. I made a mental note to carry electrolyte capsules next time.

By mile 50, the sun had set. All was dark except for the beam of my headlamp illuminating the sagebrush along the narrow trail. Every step I took was a step farther than I'd ever run before, and I pressed into the night. I was nowhere near the front, but I wasn't there to win or even be competitive.

I'd entered this event, I told myself, to tear apart my body and split my open my soul. I needed a crack large enough to reach in and stir and distill my doubt, fear, and insecurity. These feelings fought each other. Then they joined forces. Then they fought each other again. I let them swirl around, slicing and clawing and biting at me.

I already knew that I didn't want to be in Winnett. I was sure that I wanted to be with Anne, but there had to be an even simpler answer. What direction was I supposed to take? I crossed the finish line, ate a plateful of pancakes, and passed out with my head on a picnic table. I was back to work on Monday without any real answers.

I was going to Marquette for a wedding in May. I asked Anne to be my date. She accepted. On the last day of school, I packed a bag, hung my suit in the back window, locked my trailer, and made the journey back to the Midwest before flying to Alaska in June.

She made it. I stood in the wedding, which meant I was with the groom and the other two groomsmen all morning. I was in the ceremony in the afternoon. Then I was at their table during the reception. It was after the ceremony, after the reception, after all the years of messages, phone calls, and traveling back and forth, when we kissed for the first time under the stars. We took a cab to her friend's vacated apartment, and we laughed as we walked down the hallway.

There would always be good decisions, bad decisions, right turns, and wrong turns. There would always be mistakes to make, and sometimes there would be opportunities to correct them. I looked at my life, like many people look at their lives, as a course full of surprises. Putting myself through grueling runs was one method of digging deep to try to find my own answers.

Maybe here lay another reason why I had always counted on one certainty, as I thought about after the Seattle Marathon when I was sulking in the hotel lobby.

"How did it go?" a runner had asked me

I told him about my mistake, and he told me how sorry he was to hear it.

When he asked where I was from, I told him I was living in Montana, but I grew up in Naknek, Alaska.

"Naknek?" he said, surprised. "I fished out of Graveyard one season, early in the 90s."

There were right turns and wrong turns, but all turns eventually took me back to Naknek.

Since Naknek has no hospital, babies like me are born in Anchorage. Our mothers have to know when to anticipate labor, so they know when to get on a plane and fly across hundreds of miles of tundra and mountains, to the nearest available hospital. There used to be a closer hospital — out the mouth of the Naknek River, and up the Kvichak, in the village of Koggiung. There are people in Naknek alive today who were born in the same hospital where Dad and I sleep, before the village lost its cannery to a fire, before it burned to charred pilings in the mud.

The two cemeteries were there decades before the fire. One cemetery is an Aleut burial site. The other one is full of laborers who built the cannery, most from China and the Philippines, who fell victim to the influenza and smallpox epidemics of the early 1900s. Sometimes their skeletons are exposed in the eroding cutbank.

Our bedroom at Graveyard is a patient room, where many of them died. I don't think about it much. Most often, Dad and I get to camp, make a peanut butter and jelly sandwich, brush our teeth, and fall asleep in my bunk as fast as possible before returning to the water three or four hours later. I wonder if the crewman, Dan, thinks about it. I know I'm getting older when I've seen generations of crewmen. The summer before I fished, Dan's dad John made the wooden cork fish on Dad's birthday. Its painted eye still watches us from the wall above the table.

Growing up, I often stayed up late reading after bedtime. When I knew Mom and Dad were tucked away in their bedroom loft, it was safe to turn on my lamp and turn the pages of a book until my eyelids were heavy — which always took too long. If I heard footsteps down the stairs, I turned off the lamp, threw the book under my pillow, tucked my head under the covers, and faced toward the wall. I could never keep my eyelids still when I forced them shut, so if Dad decided to check on me, I needed to hide my face. Mom was more lenient about my nocturnal habits, and during the fishing season, when Dad wasn't home, she let me stay up late watching mindless monster movies on the SciFi channel — movies where the dead burst from their coffins, climbed above the dirt, and walked among the living, eating their brains.

If I allow myself, I still fall into a pattern of sleeping late and staying awake late — but I value sleep too much to truly enjoy the luxury. It takes serious discipline for me go to bed early. I count breaths, take melatonin tablets, drink herbal tea, and avoid the screens of TV, phone, computer, or at least I wear yellow-tinted glasses that block the blue light allegedly disrupting sleep hormones. It's all so that I can rise at a reasonable hour without struggle. Because I struggle to carve myself into this pattern, I take pride when I accomplish it. Because I know the hurt in my frontal lobe on a morning after a night of insufficient rest, I avoid temptation to break the cycle.

During the fishing season, I have no trouble falling asleep. I never valued sleep this much until I started fishing with Dad. The rest of the year, nighttime is for sleeping and daytime is for being awake. During the fishing season, the time to sleep is when the fish aren't hitting. We set our nets with the flood and then the time between high tide and low tide is not quite six hours. In one day, we go to bed and wake up twice, the times shifting slightly but unnoticed. After a week or so, I lose track of whether it is morning or evening.

Sometimes when I hear the alarm clock at Graveyard, for a moment, I don't know how old I am, who is president, or what crewman is working with us. Part of my brain doesn't even recognize the sound that wakes me, even though it's all-too-familiar. I've heard it since I was eleven years old when I started commercial fishing with Dad.

The sound of the alarm clock pulses through my frontal lobe. My entire body clutches in desperation to any final seconds of sleep. I dream of going to college, running a marathon, buying a house, moving through the stages of life until I'm awake. Whether I'm eleven, twelve, twenty, or thirty — when I hear the intruding, unnatural sound of the alarm clock, it is summertime, and it is fishing season, when the natural stages of sleep are never satisfied.

Salmon are headed upriver to spawn, die, and continue their cycle. I'm up the Kvichak to catch them, collect my check, and spend the rest of the year far away, spending the earnings far away. Most of these fish I never see again — with their wide, lidless eyes grafted into the harder flesh of their heads. When I leave every year, I take a cooler of frozen fillets for myself — without spines, skin, eyes, cheeks, eggs, milt. All of that goes into a bucket, into a grinder, and into the river for the gulls. The eyes are always the first part to go.

One time, I watched a chunk of home-canned salmon fall onto the pavement of a parking lot of a gas station somewhere in North Dakota. The fish slumped like I sometimes do in the bow, holding the net, falling asleep standing up. During one more trip across the country, part of me was still waking to the pulse of the alarm clock and the squawking of seagulls. My rice cracker remained plain and sad. That fish didn't deserve to be there.

Sometimes I think if hell is real, my version would be experiencing every death of every fish I've ever killed. Whether or not a seal or a seagull gets them, by the time we get to them, they are usually dead, strangled by their gills by a nylon square hook. Sometimes a square hook is over the gills. Sometimes the fish has splashed into three or more. Sometimes they thrash themselves into a tangled mess I have to unwind, flip around, flip back and forth, and then push to the floor with my thumbs and middle fingers. Sometimes they're still alive, but then they drop to the floor and they flap against it until stillness. I don't even need to look at them anymore. It's all muscle memory. When I hear the alarm clock, and the thought of sitting up and walking and working isn't as painful as the thought of opening my eyes, wonder if I could keep them closed all day.

Like all fish, salmon have no eyelids. To rest, they find spots of slow-moving water, and drift without resistance, like pumice floating on the surface of Naknek Lake or Lake Iliamna — bodies of water where they are headed to spawn. Whether or not this act of rest counts as sleep remains outside of human definition. Patterns of rest, however, in any type of fish, are abandoned in times of migration or spawning.

When I hear the alarm, I keep my eyes closed as long as possible, even as I open my hands. The muscle fibers in my fingers and palms are swollen, inflamed, full of scar tissue from picking fish after fish, tide after tide, day after day, week after week, year after year. Their skin is cracked, and a layer falls away as I rub my fingers together. I clench both fists at one time. Then I alternate them. I clench my fists until enough blood flows in and my hands feel functional again. They'll be at work again soon enough.

I lay like a fetus when I sleep, like when I was more fish than man. When I'm awake, I shift to a position flat on my back. I still sleep on the top bunk where I've always slept — before I was even born. It's the same bunk where Mom broke her arm, pregnant with me. Without opening my eyes, I could climb down this ladder, walk through that medicine closet, and put my peanut butter on pilot bread without pause.

When I do open my eyes, the peeling, off-white paint looks like eggshells shattered against the ceiling with an empty light socket in the direct center of it. I stare at the cracks three feet above my bunk until I hear Dad rustle out of his sleeping bag below me. Before climbing down the ladder, I look out the window to my left. A wood pallet is nailed to the other side of the wall, covering the bottom six panes. The bottom three are hard plastic, and the middle is Visqueen plastic, and a draft is streaming through the cracks. The bushes are higher than they used to be, swaying and brushing against each other.

I climb down the ladder, and my feet, still in the wool that I never bothered to remove, touch the rug. The rug is an extra square of carpet from my childhood bedroom, a bedroom where I haven't slept in decades. The carpet used to be sky blue. Now it's sky gray, the same color of small streaks in my beard. Dad's entire beard is the same gray.

Sometimes I wonder if the alarm clock jars me, not because I'm being jarred out of sleep, but because it is a reminder that time is running out for me to decide if I want to continue the operation when Dad is done. He says he's done when he is 70.

The truth is that I don't love fishing as much as he does. Given the choice, he would have been born into it, but given the choice, I wouldn't have been. If he had the choice, Dad would have been born in this hospital just to spend more time fishing. He's old enough that he could have been. There are people in Naknek, alive today who were born in this room, opening their eyes for the first time. Someday, for me, it will be the last time.

It was August in Marquette. Anne and her son went home, and I started driving back to Winnett. In the spring, I had signed a contract for a second year, so I was alone in my truck, driving west.

The trees of Minnesota's Paul Bunyan State Forest were blotting the sunset when the throttle stopped working. I pressed it tight against the floor with no connection to the transmission. I coasted as far as possible, landing in the driveway of a trailer home, not unlike mine in Winnett. I sighed, shrugged, and loaded my backpack with a few things, and rode my bike into Walker, the next town. I checked into the first hotel I saw and called a repair shop in the morning. They didn't have the right parts, so I waited for First it the driver two days.

Part of me didn't feel stuck. I'd choose this town over Winnett any day. I spent those two days running and biking along Leech Lake, wandered the touristy downtown full of fishing t-shirts. I don't know if it was more torturous or liberating knowing that I could stay here, rent a place, find a crappy job that paid more than teaching, and run to my heart's content. I could do that in any one of these towns I'd passed. I could do that in any town I would pass afterwards.

The truth was that I could do whatever I wanted, and what I wanted was to wait for the repair work in Walker and then head right back to Michigan. Of course, that's not what I did. After my truck got a new transmission, the forest turned to rolling hills and hay bales which gave way to the 400-mile monotony of I-94 between Fargo, North Dakota and Glendive, Montana. Then there were the endless tan fields of black cattle, each one destined to be chopped up and put on someone's plate. Every car I crossed had a driver, and every town I passed had a story. My story was going to continue in Winnett.

Even though driving forward was my own choice and my own action, I hoped the tires would fall off or the axle would break. Somewhere along the tan, rolling hills of eastern Montana, inside the confines of my little red cab, I let out a deliberate scream. I screamed until there was no air in my lungs I screamed until I hyperventilated. In those moments, I felt temporary relief, so I gasped in some more wind and screamed again.

Within 45 miles of Winnett, as though the weather were reflecting my emotions, a western wind howled as the sky darkened and churned. Then there was the hail. It started small, and then it accumulated until it was heavier hail than I'd ever seen. White, round chunks of pure ice pounded the windshield. It scattered across the road, bouncing and rolling like white marbles. Able to see nothing else, I pulled over in front of a gate to yet another field of cattle as the hail crashed against the roof and windows. Then I watched the side-view mirrors shatter. First it was the driver's side. Then it was the passenger's side. With boxes in the back blocking the rearview mirror, I made it to Winnett without being able to see anything behind me.

Surrounded by sagebrush and fields of cattle, the painted white 'W' loomed from the red rim rocks towering over town. The sun was hot, and the small grid of paved streets was void of vehicles. The inside of my trailer had retained the smell of musty carpet. The school across the street had work for me to do.

The first weekend back, I went to Billings to trade in my Ford Ranger for a Subaru Crosstrek. In another week, I parked it at the airport and flew back to the Midwest via Dallas. I arrived at the Detroit Metro Airport well after midnight in the middle of a thunderstorm. As we were held captive inside the fuselage until the lighting stopped, Anne was inside the airport, talking to me.

"Sorry about this," I said. "I can't wait to see you."

The fuselage flashed as thunder roared, vibrating the floor, the walls, and the seats. Passengers all around me screamed.

"We just got hit by lightning," I said.

"Sounds like it."

When I got off the plane, Anne took me back to her house and her child in the suburbs. It was as though I had been rerouted onto the conventional path, placed right where I should have been at my age. All we needed was a white picket fence. It was sterile and mundane, but it was comfortable, the way it was supposed to be.

It was after the wedding back in Marquette, the reception on the water, when a cousin asked, in the context of marriage and the future, "So, what do you think?"

Anne was in the near distance, standing in her dress against the backdrop of the sunset reflecting on Lake Superior.

"I don't know," I said. How could I?

In the morning, Anne again drove south without me. I again went back to Winnett. I kept coaching, teaching, and training harder than ever for the Seattle Marathon.

Anne and I talked every day, but we wrote letters anyway. Letters, as she had put it, were more intimate, thoughtful, and heartfelt than a text or social media message. I talked about what the future might hold. She talked about what she knew it held, which was parenthood, a steady job, and living in the suburbs of Detroit. I couldn't wait to talk about it when she came to visit in October.

She didn't come. It was too hard to get away from work, she said. Anne would come to Seattle instead. Instead, I received packages from her in the mail, including a birthday card her son had made. It was a picture he'd drawn of the three of us.

A few days later, there were two more envelopes in my post office box. I opened them right away. One was from her and one was from her son. He had handwritten the addresses himself. I opened his envelope first. Inside was another birthday card on which he had drawn a picture of Anne and I with exaggerated tongues intertwined around each other. There was a circle with a line through it with *NO KISSING* written firmly in big letters below it. I laughed. Then I opened up the other envelope, and I wasn't laughing anymore.

The crossroads between the post office, the Kozy Korner Cafe, and the general store, where I could buy canned corn and frozen spinach, were still and lifeless. At the same time, it all moved too fast for me to sit up straight.

> *The logistics aren't in our favor*, it said.
> *We don't know "us" well enough to make a big decision*, it said.
> *I don't want to be in a long-distance relationship*, it said.
> *I just feel like I'm waiting, and I can't wait anymore.*

It was a lonely night in the trailer, but I realized that it was always a lonely night in the trailer. Even before this night, Anne and I would often finish a conversation, and I would first notice that it was nighttime. Engrossed in conversation, I'd never turned on the lights. I was alone in the dark, but I'd been alone in the dark the entire time. I'd kept looking at the future, the trailer's long walls mere shadows of a distant past, its details already blurred and faded by a fallible memory.

Anne didn't come to Seattle, and race day brought more of those dark, churning clouds to my life. The wind blew 30 miles an hour with gusts up to 40. It was a headwind most of the time, and other times it was a side wind. It pushed against me at the start line, it pushed against me in those first couple miles where it channeled between all the tall buildings around me, and it pushed against me the entire way. My cheeks flapped on the bridge to Mercer Island. On the way back into the city, it nearly blew me into other runners.

There was no way I was going to finish as fast as I wanted, but I could pour everything I had into this course. I could channel the emotions, and all that hard training, to get this thing right. Fourteen miles into the race, after the lap around Seward Park, I made a right turn. In another twelve miles, I crossed the finish line with my family waiting for me. I'd made peace with Anne ending our relationship, or so I thought.

A few weeks later, on Christmas Eve, in a guest bedroom of Mom and Dad's newer house in Washburn, I opened my laptop to take a look at Facebook. There was a picture of Anne, her son, and a guy — and it wasn't an old friend or relative of hers. It was exactly what I thought it was. My stomach churned, emotions erupted, and after a few heated text messages, I never heard from her again.

I met with Anne's best friend at a pub in Marquette. She told me everything I didn't want to hear but everything I needed to hear. Anne had waited until I got the letter before her first date with the guy. There was nothing I did or didn't do to push Anne away. I just wasn't there, and Anne didn't want to wait. She didn't cheat on me, but she sure didn't waste any time.

Then someone familiar walked into the pub, and my heart sank into my stomach. She walked over to the bar, started conversing with a group of women, and I was brought back to miles of pavement, blurs of headlights, wrong turns, and a white rabbit.

It was Alice. The last time I'd seen her was more than five years ago, with a brief glimpse of her walking to the stage at our graduation. I looked away then, hoping she didn't spot me. I did the same thing this time — not in fear of being followed or stalked or questioned or even confronted, but in my guilt of the words I'd written her all those years ago. I'd broken Alice's heart, and it was only fair that someone did the same to me. It was part of life.

I thought I was over it. Then I learned the whole truth from Anne's friend while I was back in Winnett.

Keith, there is more to this, but I don't know if I should tell you.

Well, now you kind of have to, I wrote.

I know, but this is really going to hurt you.

It's going to hurt me not to know.

I don't know how long I waited for it.

She's pregnant.

I stared at the screen, motionless. I felt something inside me festering. It was the familiar feeling I'd had in my last trip with my truck. I put my face into a pillow and screamed.

I didn't run much after that. I'd registered for the Kentucky Derby Festival Marathon in April, but my motivation wasn't there. I was waking up mere minutes before work. Never mind trying to get in morning miles.

I'd run in the evenings, but somewhere down the road, my airway would become constricted by my own emotions and my own questions. Why did I think it was going to work with Anne? How could I have fallen for someone like that? Why did I think she was my way out of Winnett? Was that why I'd become so attached to the idea of a life with her? Did I just think she was my way out of Winnett? I needed to snap out of it.

I was at my desk after school when the custodian stopped at my door and said I had visitors. I wondered whose parents were here this time to complain about a low grade or a missing assignment. Then I recognized Mr. and Mrs. Bakun.

The Bakuns had retired and left for Montana when I was in middle school, and now they were living outside Bozeman. When wind got to them that I was teaching near one of Mr. Bakun's hunting spots, they decided to stop by, and when I told him I was teaching PE, he asked if he was using any of his old tactics.

"Yeah," I said. "I do the freeze thing."

In elementary school, we'd enter the gym running. Then Mr. Bakun would yell, "Freeze!" and we'd become as still as possible. Then he would tell us to skip, hop, gallop, or run again, telling us at random times again to "Freeze!"

Just then, I realized that I'd been frozen, and Mr. Bakun was here to tell me to run again. I finished the marathon in Kentucky in 2:49 —a miraculous time considering the lack of any real training.

I started applying like crazy for new teaching positions. At the same time, I had been accepted to a master's program back at Northern. Mom and Dad drove their little trailer across the country to move me out of my big trailer. When I still hadn't been offered a job, they hauled it to their barn in Wisconsin. It would be there waiting for me when I came back to the Midwest for grad school.

Then I got an email from the personnel director of a school district in Oregon. He insisted that I come to the job fair in Missoula, where he'd be. I almost ignored the message. Living in Marquette again, just one more time, would make me happy. It would be a chance to regroup, reconnect, and reset the mess I'd made.

I drove to Missoula anyway, put on my best teacher clothes, practiced my best teacher lines, and walked into the job fair at the University of Montana campus. I was keeping my options open.

The first person to approach me, of all the recruiters, was from Dillingham. I said thanks but no thanks and found the Oregon guy. After a quick conversation, he put me on the phone with the principal at one of the high schools in the district, and I was offered the job right away. He told me to go have a beer and think it over. I didn't get a beer, but I went for a walk outside. It was 10:30 in the morning.

As much as I wanted to be in Marquette, moving to Oregon would feel less like living in the past, and among the lakes, mountains, trees, and even some athletic culture, Oregon had always looked like a place I'd like. I signed the contract and differed my plans for grad school.

After the last day of school at the end of May, the Montana High School Track and Field State Tournament was in Great Falls. With the team and the other coach in the van, I took my own car packed with the remaining possessions from my trailer.

I said my goodbyes from the tournament, and I took a detour north, into Canada to run the Calgary Marathon, and once again, I found myself at a border crossing, telling my life story to someone who didn't want to hear it. I was asked to get out of my car to answer some more questions, but some other guy was causing such a scene about a DUI from his distant past, that they told me I was clear to go.

On race morning, my GPS watch froze. No matter what buttons I pressed, the little round screen read *6:58 AM* every time I looked at it, and I kept looking at it right through Canada's national anthem. Instead of getting frustrated, I embraced the idea. Even though I hoped to be faster than three hours, I couldn't concern myself exact times or what was *supposed* to be.

I had to run the marathon the way I used to run — with the feeling in my legs, the flow of my sweat, and the pounding of my heartbeat to monitor my effort. When someone shouted "freeze" there was no one to say "run" but me. I moved forward by feel, I didn't make any wrong turns, and I finished in 2:59.

Salmon swim with aerodynamic fins, their tails swishing, propelling them from the ocean into their natal freshwater lakes and streams. Led by scent, and perhaps a sense we don't understand, they are on their way to continue the pattern of rebirth and regeneration. My voyage home is a little different.

"Take off your shoes! Take off your shoes!" A bulging belly stretches the TSA uniform to the verge of explosion, and I hope the x-ray machine can't detect the words in my head. *Explosion*, I think again. I'm not sure what irritates me more — this rule existing in the first place or this lady in front of me who doesn't know it, as though it hasn't been in place for decades. The line moves, one foot forward at a time, civilians stripped and questioned, possessions thrown into the machine. I'm in the place between one world and the other.

Maybe it annoys me because I am all-too-aware of my dependence on material possessions. I had them moved from Winnett to Mom and Dad's barn in Washburn, and that's just one of the times I've moved. Every time I've moved, I've cursed my own accumulation of things, but I keep accumulating them. On my way to Naknek, I pack a few essentials, knowing I already have most of what I need waiting for me there. It's none of TSA's business that I have protein powder, vegetable powder, or a bag of almonds in my bag.

I take off my shoes. I take off my belt and my jacket, too. I turn my pockets inside out. Paying for the flight wasn't enough to empty them. I confirm there are no liquids in my carry-on luggage after I put my Ziploc bag full of three-ounce containers in a plastic bin. It can't be napalm if it's small, I guess. I step forward, put my hands up, and millions of bullets of radiation penetrate my organs. Then my bag is deemed fit to move forward, or I'm chosen to be searched further.

Paying attention to the news overwhelms me with natural disasters, terrorism, human injustice, and constant damage to the environment. Like too many people, I've been desensitized to it, but I don't like being accused this way — treated as though I'm guilty until proven innocent. Like anyone, my values and opinions are too many to give fair and equal attention. Attention is lost to running or skiing or planning another trip. I would never claim to be an activist. I'm not one for starting a war, raising picket signs, or even confrontation in general, but threats to clean water are more piercing than the radiation TSA uses to hunt for suspicious tubes of toothpaste.

American sewers used to drain into rivers without a thought from people. The Hudson River was too toxic to allow swimming. The Cuyahoga River was so polluted that it was on fire. Farms, lawns, and golf courses spill pesticides into water every day. Oil, gas, and salt accumulate on pavement and wash into watersheds. Then there are oil spills — but with the threat of Pebble Mine overshadowing Bristol Bay, I can't dwell on all the other problems caused by water pollution.

Plastic accumulates from grocery bags, used bottles of detergent, straws, and broken toys no longer wanted by kids or parents. It is all from what people throw away, and most of it is plastic. Teachers told me to cut plastic six-pack holders into pieces. Otherwise, an unsuspecting seagull swimming on the surface of the ocean could be strangled. One of those six-pack holders could choke six seagulls at once for no other reason than me wanting an unnatural surplus of sugar in my bloodstream. We're all part of the same food web, and plastic is undoubtedly in my bloodstream, too.

I was proud of my ability to tear the rings apart with my bare hands. They were fish-picking hands, and they could hold my bodyweight while I did more pull-ups than any other kid. If the advice inspired me in any way, it was to drink more sugar, so I could tear apart the rings. The intent was in the right place, but the message was wrong. With all the missing eyes, gills, and guts in nets we had seen, no Naknek kid I knew was concerned about the survival seagulls. The plastic itself is much direr to our ability to live. Cutting it into pieces isn't the answer. Smaller pieces sooner become undetectable particles.

Charybdis, who threatened Odysseus and his men, is sometimes personified as a maelstrom spiraling in the ocean, pulling people from their ships into the underworld. Maybe it's an inaccurate depiction, but people foresaw a spiral of death lurking in the ocean. In reality, its existence is of our own doing. It's a vortex of our own trash, poisoning life in the ocean, poisoning us.

Plastic is just refined petroleum which is just algae and plant life that lived on our planet millions of years before people existed. Maybe it's justified when it returns to destroy us in our search for convenience. Use it once and throw it into a receptacle, usually made of plastic. Then it kills us.

Even Naknek has changed in the age of information, even though the internet in every household is limited by bandwidth. In the age of addiction to the internet and smartphones, I'd like to say retreating to Naknek every summer is a time when the rest of the world disappears from my attention, or that it's at least limited, but Mom and Dad pay for both internet and satellite TV at the house.

Even at Graveyard, we listen to KDLG broadcasting Morning Edition, NPR, and the World Cafe. Michael Jackson's death, and plenty of shootings and terrorist attacks, including the shooting in Colorado at the latest Batman installment, *The Dark Knight Rises,* I heard first on KDLG, over a peanut-butter-and jelly sandwich.

At the Borough Building in Naknek, I'm trying to be more active in my stance for protecting clean water. A guy in front of me, Dad, and other members of the community at the Borough Building paces back and forth on the floor in his jeans, his suited colleagues behind him at folding tables. He tells us that he used to blow up oil rigs in the military, and they didn't leak. We have no idea how oil rigs work, he tells us. I understand well enough that when they blew up in the desert, on land, it wouldn't be dispersed into water. Media has both surged and faded in its attention to oil-drilling in the Alaska National Wildlife Refuge, but as awful a spill there would be, it would not be as devastating as it would be in Bristol Bay.

Our oil company friend tells us that our argument about sustaining a natural source of food is invalid. He's just going to put some chemical on it to make it taste better anyway, he tells us. He says that we have to understand, that as people, that's just how we are. I hate to admit I think he's right, but I also understand a spray of lemon, and a pinch of garlic and a sprinkle of oregano isn't toxic. That's what I usually use. He tells us our concern about the oil freighters bringing invasive species stems from paranoia. It can be prevented, he tells us, but he doesn't offer an explanation.

When he finishes, a blonde woman in a pantsuit stays seated at her table behind him, behind her microphone, and tells us, just like Pebble Mine advocates tell us, they will do everything possible to prevent environmental catastrophes.

The problem is that people can only prevent catastrophes they can predict. No one predicted an oil freighter would crash near Valdez and cause one of the largest spills in history. No one predicted the spill in the Gulf of Mexico. No one predicted an angry band of disillusioned Muslims would hijack commercial flights and crash them into one tower after another. If someone did predict any of these events, shame on that person, because not everything was done to prevent it. As people, we give ourselves too much credit in our ability to predict the future, to mitigate consequences, and to understand how much we don't understand the ocean. We seem to make sacrifices anyway, in the name of corporations.

Corporations are not people. They are not fish. They are not life, but they act like it. They feed and grow and migrate and thrive, but they only exist in belief, and it's the belief in money on which they feed. They are like great white sharks, lurking, breeding, never sleeping, always waiting to devour their next prey, but they exist only in our imagination. Oil companies want to drill in Bristol Bay, and Northern Dynasty wants to devour the headwaters of the strongest, most sustainable wild fishery in the world — but these companies don't really exist. Figments of our imagination, corporations, and the value of money have chewed their way into being an actual, physical threat.

The irony is that belief in money is what keeps me coming back to Naknek. I catch the fish. I eat them. I also eat steak and kale and quinoa. I eat what I never saw grow or live. I see rice, dead in the grocery store, and I give the store something that only exists in imagination. Then I take home the rice, boil it, and eat it. It's real rice, and it goes well with a piece of wild Alaskan salmon, drizzled with lemon, rubbed with garlic, and sprinkled with oregano.

People can be wasteful of food, but people are most wasteful of seafood. Imagine a net scouring the tundra, scooping bears, caribou, moose, and squirrels. Then imagine eighty percent of the meat left to rot. Restaurants can't sell bears, caribou, moose, and squirrels from the tundra, but they can sell salmon from Bristol Bay. Bristol Bay fisheries are sustainable, but not all fisheries follow a sustainable model. That's why a restaurant can serve shark fin stew while the rest of the shark rots in the ocean. Some people will organize themselves and defend rainforests, wetlands, and even deserts, but the ocean is too often ignored.

A picture of our planet taken by a satellite shows rough patches of green surrounded in blue, because most of the surface is ocean. Alaska is called the Last Frontier, but the space beyond our planet is called the Final Frontier as though we're already finished with the last one. We've explored the Final Frontier, too, and our planet's orbit is littered with our trash. We have not even tapped into the unlimited possibility of outer space, and the possibility of what's out there is beyond our comprehension and understanding — but the ocean, too, is called the Final Frontier.

A lack of understanding does not mean the ocean is untapped or untouched. Pollution is pumped into it every day. Plastic islands float and swirl on its surface. Carbon emissions heat the atmosphere, speed the melting of ice caps, and accelerate the rate at which the water level rises. We use floating boxes of wood, aluminum, or fiberglass, find life, and scoop it into nets and traps. Then it's served with a little lemon juice, garlic, and oregano — or chemicals if it is so desired — if it makes it onto a plate at all. Worldwide, fishermen toss eighty percent of their harvest overboard. They cut nets that drift forever, killing everything and anything in their paths. In the United States, about half of what does make it onto a plate is scooped into a trash can and hauled to a landfill.

The Alaska Department of Fish and Game has regulated Bristol Bay's salmon fishery for decades, allowing it to return strong, often stronger than it was before. Wild Alaskan salmon is the most sustainable seafood, and maybe the most sustainable source of meat, on our planet — but Fish and Game can only do so much. Pollution can poison them. A missile launched into the ocean can annihilate them. The Pebble Mine could destroy their spawning grounds. An oil spill could suffocate them.

When it's open to questions and comments at our meeting, we all have our say. Dad says we need to, as people, find a way to use less oil rather than finding more of it. He says the salmon are a much more precious resource. Petroleum won't feed people. It might bring shipments of creamed corn and SPAM, but we have salmon right here, right now. The risks of climate change and damage to our planet is everything these oil people deny.

From another part of the world, the fight over clean water at Standing Rock, for instance, caught my attention in a painful way.

It wasn't my home, and I had no intention of traveling there for the cause, but I saw people gathering to stand, as it went, with Standing Rock. They were there to stop the pipeline, and they were sprayed with firehoses, pelted with bean bag cannons, and pepper-sprayed in the face by law enforcement. The officers were not serving the people but a figment of their imagination.

Many of us believe in stopping oil companies from ravaging precious resources to enable the poisoning of freshwater and the horrors of climate change. Many of us care about it more than most things, but most of us are not activists. Most of us are not there in person to stop it, as much as we believe in doing so. I'm just another fisherman listening to another advocate of an industry that will destroy the fishery.

I fear the day if and when Northern Dynasty or some other company sends in the troops to Lake Iliamna. There may come a day when the conflict over the Pebble Mine boils down to a standoff, face-to-face, people-to-corporation. Law enforcement may be obligated to take the corporation's side, armed and poised with pepper spray, tasers, tear gas, napalm, and bullets, rubber and otherwise. There may come a day when the only thing stopping the headwaters of the Kvichak River from being ravaged with poison is people courageous enough to stand in front of an army. If that day comes, I wonder if I would be there. I wonder how many people would be there with or without me.

I crossed the US-Canada border into Eastport, Idaho. My car was stuffed to the gills.

Among the empty booths and utter lack of traffic, there was one officer at the crossing.

"You moving from Alaska?"

I was moving from Montana.

"You have Alaska plates, and your car is full of everything but the kitchen sink," he said. "What's your story? Make it quick."

I had taken a detour into Alberta.

"Get a little lost?"

I'd gotten lost plenty, but this detour was on purpose.

"Okay," he said. "Where in Montana were you living?"

I told him that I was living in Winnett.

"On purpose?"

I still wasn't sure.

"Have a nice day, Mr. Wilson."

The road from Calgary had looked kind of like Winnett, but it looked like Kansas, too — brown and covered in hay bales. In Idaho, however, there were mountains and lakes and evergreens, and not just potatoes. I couldn't wait to get to Oregon with even more mountains, lakes, and evergreens.

Then the landscape transformed again. The trees turned to sagebrush, and the mountains became sparser. I'd researched Klamath Falls as a Marquette-sized town with the things I liked in a town, like a brewery, a bike shop, a Thai restaurant, and a running store with a yoga studio. It was also within a reasonable driving distance to the Oregon coast, Mount Shasta, the Redwoods, Portland, and San Francisco. Crater Lake was less than an hour away.

Klamath Lake welcomed me into town, and although it looked pretty and blue, I'd read that no one swims in it because it is covered in algae. Then I discovered that Main Street was run down, with its fair share of empty buildings. The first human being I noticed was a guy my age with sagging pants and a sideways cap. Maybe I wouldn't fit in here after all, but it was still no Winnett or Luray or Naknek. It wasn't great, but it wasn't terrible. It was an appropriate place for someone like me.

The first people on the Link River, I'd read, had named it Yulalona, after their word for movement back and forth, but it was a trick. It was too far from the coast for tidal currents. The wind pushed its water so that, on the surface, there was an illusion that it had changed directions. Now, even the name Klamath Falls was misleading. The Klamath River and the Link River once had salmon runs as strong and as powerful as that of the Naknek, the Nushagak, or the Kvichak — but like the Columbia, Snake, and Klamath, the Link had been dammed.

I spent the first night at the Maverick Motel, next to the Klamath Basin Brewery, where the beer was good, the food was awful, and the server was a cute girl.

"So, you just moved here?" she said. "Why?"

"What do you mean why?" I said.

"There's nothing to do here," she said.

I retrieved my house key in the morning, moved my car into the garage, and moved everything in it onto the ragged shag carpet of the living room. I took a cab to the airport for another fishing season. I was heading to Naknek earlier than normal because there had been no tickets available at any later date. It was after I'd gone through security, after I handed over my ticket, after I put my backpack in the overhead storage compartment, after I sat down, and after the plane was in the air when the pilot made an announcement.

"Ladies and gentlemen, good evening. We'd like to thank you for joining us on the last flight out of the Klamath Falls Airport. It's been an honor…"

I didn't hear the rest of it. I was busy trying to process the fact that there were no flights back here. I didn't panic either. I could find a way back easy enough. I could fly into Medford, a ninety-minute drive away, and rent a car. That's what I did after the season.

In August, I attended orientation at the district office. There were fifty-two of us in that room, but Mandy was the one I noticed. She was cute, blonde, well-dressed, and intriguing. On the second day of the orientation, I sat at the table where she had been sitting, but she arrived late, and my plan was foiled. Soon I learned she was working at my school, where we were formally introduced by the principal.

Mandy told me that she was from Payette, Idaho, a town on the other side of the Snake River, separating Idaho from Oregon. Mandy had graduated from the College of Idaho, where she played soccer. She went on to work as an accountant and auditor before tiring of spending her days hunched over a computer screen in downtown Boise. She quit to spend three months in New Zealand. Then, like me, she shrugged her shoulders and went into teaching. She was teaching business and technology. Her uncle was the guy who had recruited me, and he'd recruited her as well.

School was in session a week when Mandy, the other new English teacher, and I made plans to meet in the Fred Meyer parking lot to go climb the nearby Mount Thielsen. Mandy was there that morning, but the other guy was a no-show. The three of us hadn't bothered to exchange phone numbers, so after a couple of laps around the parking lot, the two of us decided on a closer destination. We drove to Crater

Lake and climbed Mount Scott together. Mandy might have thought that I had arranged it this way.

All over Oregon, I was running in new places through the mountains, woods, lakes, and streams. I was winning races, too. Mandy and I explored the coast, the trails, the Redwoods, and the nearby cities. It was somewhere around Lake Tahoe that she agreed that she was my girlfriend, even though I had to ask because Mom kept asking me.

Work, however, was not as great. Kids got under my skin. My first period had forty seniors, and few of them seemed to like me. They stared at their phones and whispered when my back was turned. Students didn't understand the purpose of the lesson. Students weren't engaged. The vice principal punched these details into her laptop from a desk in the back of the room.

After a friend's wedding in Michigan, I spent most of the night on a bench in the PDX airport, listening to the same announcement about leaving unattended baggage over and over again, contemplating my career as a teacher. I'd been in this airport many times, and I was once again in a place between places. When I made it into school for afternoon classes, and my substitute went home, I was tired, groggy, slow-moving, and definitely not teaching to the best of my ability. The vice principal wrote it in her notes.

Most kids didn't seem to connect with me. The vice principal didn't seem to respect me. Klamath Falls wasn't all it was cracked up to be. I signed my contract for another year anyway. There was more to this corner of the country that I wanted to experience. I was enjoying traveling to nearby places, and I was enjoying my developing relationship with Mandy.

A couple weeks before that next fishing season, I was running a 50K trail run at Smith Rock, outside of Bend. Mandy watched the start of the race, and then she headed to Mount Bachelor to ski. As I ran the winding switchbacks up and down the dry heat of red rocks, she was somewhere on a mountain that I could see in the distance, swishing over the snow in the grasp of gravity. For days like those ones, I would stay in the grasp of Klamath Falls.

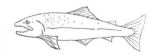

Waves chop. My stomach growls. My eyelids are heavy. The tide has pulled the web tight around gills, and it cuts like cold, steel knives into my gloves. A wintery wind blows from the north. The only warmth is from the red glow in the distance, illuminating the waves accumulating with the flood. It reflects against the aluminum, but the cold lingers long after we finish picking. My fingers are almost frozen as I untie the last line from the last buoy after the nets are in the skiff. Rain soaks beneath my raincoat and sweat seeps into the wool layer against my skin. Muscle fibers in my back and shoulders are torn to shreds.

I lean on the edge of the bow as I yank an anchor from the bottom. The claws we now use are not as heavy as Big Bertha, and there isn't mud globbed between flukes, but claw anchors act as scoops and sometimes I lift small boulders.

The wind is getting stronger, and the waves bigger, and they pound my feet into the floor. The claw slips between my hands back into the water, so I tighten my grip and pull the line again to the chain. Then I jerk the chain several times to splash off the rest of the mud before lifting the claw into the bow.

Sometimes I think the waiting, as Tom Petty would say, is the hardest part. Then there are the tougher times, when there are too many fish to handle, when it's too foggy to see, when the weather is bad, and I change my mind. It's the question over what is more difficult — a mental or physical struggle.

When I land at the Ted Stevens Airport after the season, I notice a family munching on Doritos, slurping Coke from plastic straws, adding to their redundant mass as they shuffle through the terminal. The youngest boy wants a toy. The mother complains that Starbucks isn't open yet. Everyone has their own struggles, but I doubt these people were outside in uncomfortable weather during their Alaska trip. First, I feel disdain for these people. Then I have disdain for myself for being judgmental.

On the next flight, a woman complains to me about the fan above my head freezing her and she would appreciate if I turned it off, thank you very much. Part of me wants to yank open the emergency exit door, let the wind gush into the fuselage, and show her how warm it feels to be inside after that. I scold myself for thinking this way. She can't help it. She doesn't know what she sounds like. I remind myself that a soldier returning from Iraq might feel the same about me complaining about heat.

In college, it bothered me to hear complaints about the remoteness of Marquette and Michigan's Upper Peninsula. It was an entire three entire hours to a Green Bay Packers game or the nearest Best Buy, and it just wasn't fair that it was so far. Marquette didn't even have a Meijer, they'd say. Now it has both of those stores, right by the Target and Walmart that were already there.

When I was a kid, I walked home uphill in 40 below, shoveled snow, had to pump gas by actually pumping it, didn't have cable TV or internet, and didn't get a trophy for missing eight out of ten layups. I am a millennial, meaning I belong to a generation with a reputation of softness and safe spaces, but I think I've been an old man since I was 20.

What people complain about, what people find uncomfortable, and what people appreciate has nothing to do with our age, however. I don't think it has to do with inherent nature, either. It's a matter of perspective. My disdain is not toward people I see as soft. It's toward seeing that softness in myself. Without my upbringing, I might be whining about no Starbucks, too. Without the hardest parts of fishing, I would be just like them. I might be overweight, reading comic books, and watching science fiction movies in all of my spare time instead of just some of it. That's my personality. I might have never run a marathon or gone willingly into temperatures below 32 degrees.

Even in Naknek, stable electricity, plumbing, and paved roads, have made it easy to slip into comfort and convenience. Too many of us are too comfortable, which is a reason to put myself through a struggle. Maybe it's not my place to address, because I'm not a single parent working three jobs just to feed everyone at the table. I'm not without access to shelter or born into a third world nation, living with dozens of people in a house with no windows, eating a half cup of rice every three days. Then again, maybe it is my place because I've been so fortunate and putting myself through a struggle is a reminder. It helps me appreciate the life I have.

Without discomfort, and without a struggle, it is too easy to lose connection with our passions, our primal selves, or an appreciation for the comforts we do enjoy. Struggle is crucial. Running is a simple route. I tend to think of the fishing season as a detriment to my running. It's time away from the practice of it. It's a time where I eat processed. It's a time of irregular and insufficient sleep. If I weren't a fisherman though, I might not be a runner.

Fisherman don't have a year-round job restricting them to a desk or an office twelve months of the year. They might be finishing another fishing season somewhere else, or they might be migrants and vagabonds. They don't want to spend 40 hours, five days a week, surrounded in white walls, waiting for their two days of beer and watching TV until it's time to go back.

It's not a judgment for me to make about people who follow that road. For the longest time, I wanted to live in a linear, conventional way — go to college, begin a career, and then keep that career until retirement. After my first European adventure, I tried hard to follow it. It didn't work.

Like long-distance running, the fishing season is when I dive into a deep part of myself like it's a hole in the ocean. Even after the longest, hardest, toughest slogs of running, I can eat wholesome food, stretch tight muscles, ice sore ones, take a hot shower, and lay on a soft couch. My Lower 48 life is easy. A six-hour run is tough, but a fishing season is tougher. I can leap with reckless abandon into either of them, and when I manage to swim back to the surface, I have gained another piece of myself.

When I run, and lactic acid burns, and muscle fibers are worn to the bone, I remember how hard fishing can be, too. When the insides of my gloves are soaking in cold sweat and there are thousands of pounds of fish to pick from the net, running seems easy. The physical training that I do conditions me, but it doesn't always last to the final mile. It takes something else for the ability to dig down to my full potential. As much as I complain to myself about losing aerobic capacity during the fishing season, it strengthens my capacity for struggle. It's what I pull out of the nets that pushes me through it.

When I was a kid, I imagined being Superman, because I wanted abilities out of this world, but then I realized that I was more like Batman. He didn't have super-strength, x-ray vision, or the ability to fly. Instead, he had determination, discipline, and a neat utility belt with all kinds of neat gadgets. I wasn't a billionaire, and I have never been great with gadgets, but the biggest difference was that he had direction. Running had been my only real direction, and I didn't even always get that right.

A movie called *Batman v. Superman* was released into theaters during my second year in Oregon, and I was disappointed when it wasn't received well. Ben Affleck's Batman fought Henry Cavill's Superman in a visually-stunning yet plot-deprived film. Oregon didn't bring out the best version of myself, and that movie did not bring out the best version of my fictional heroes.

In the movies, in the comic books, and in the cartoons, to become the ultimate version of himself, Bruce Wayne practices meditation with monks atop monolithic monasteries, he dukes it out with scroungy lowlifes in stale, concrete boxing gyms. He masters ninjutsu from the greatest sensei in Japan. In Universities across Europe, he studies psychology, criminology, and chemistry, but he never finishes a degree. He takes the knowledge he needs and moves on. Once a skill set has been attained, he finds the next one. In the pages of the comic books, these scenes only appear in a quick panel or two, always in flashbacks, often in grayscale. Bruce Wayne's journey is a mystery blown into fragments. The symbol of a bat is only the punctuation of his journey. Maybe my symbol was a salmon.

There is one version of the Batman story, when this journey has ended, and Bruce is bleeding to death in his study after a failed battle in the streets with a pimp and a gang of prostitutes. He asks the memory of this father what is missing from his mission. As if on cue, a bat crashes through the window, shards of glass splashing to the floor. The bat lands on a stone bust of his father and stares him in the eyes.

"Yes, father," he says. "I shall become a bat."

This version was always a little too much for me — not because it seems unrealistic for a bat to break right through glass, but because no epiphany in my life ever just hit me like that. By the time I was thirty, I had everything I wanted, and I was doing what I wanted to do, but it definitely didn't come crashing through a window.

I wouldn't say that I was living a dream. I'd say that I was living like I'd expected to be living by the time I was 30. I was living in a two-bedroom house with a garage and a yard with a fence opening onto the paved bike path. I either ran on the path one way or the other, or I crossed it and ran up the street to Hogback Mountain, reaching the top for a view of the city. I was also dating Mandy, who was always up for an adventure.

I felt like I had arrived at the finish line of a small-town marathon, but I'd realized that life is more like a track meet — a series of different events and skills. I could jump as high as I can, leap as far as I could, and drive myself forward as fast as possible toward the end. When I got there, I could experience that of bliss, but that moment would always be brief. Soon, I was back, trying to keep up with work, but there were always ungraded papers, unentered grades, and lesson plans that needed revision. It all disappeared when I ran, and I wanted to keep outrunning it.

I had registered for the Boston Marathon again. Ever since the bombings, I had wanted to go back and prove I wasn't afraid. I was, however, afraid to ask for time off work. I saved enough comp time to take a day off, but out of fear of the administrators refusing my request, I took a sick day.

I stayed in the same hotel I stayed in five years earlier on Friday and Saturday night, in Danvers, close to Salem. Like I had done five years ago, I explored the town where the Salem Witch Trials had taken place. *The Crucible* is a play I had taught, about those trials, about how people were accused of witchcraft and executed for no reason. It was a story I appreciated about rage boiling inside the containment of a small town.

Sunday night, I stayed in downtown Boston, in the Seaport District. I walked along the paved shore, the boats, the fish smell, and the piles of net and line reminded me of a Naknek cannery, but with a metropolitan city behind it. The first time that I ran Boston, America's fastest marathoner, Ryan Hall, was one of the top contenders. I watched the back of his head take off with the other elite men. The second time I ran Boston, I had seen him in advertisements for Alaska Seafood. I met him at the expo, told him I was a commercial fisherman in Alaska, and I appreciated the ads. He told me that he used to think about commercial fishing in Alaska.

The first time I ran Boston, two years before the bombings, I stayed in a hotel in Medford, not far from the start line in Hopkinton. The hotel offered a shuttle into the race, which was a separate operation from the official shuttle busses in downtown Boston. I left my warmup outfit on a bus that shuttled it to the finish line for me. Then, I was escorted into the first corral of the first wave by security. I began the run right after the elite men. I kept a perfect pace and felt like a superhero as a consistent crowd from Hopkinton to Boylston Street chanted, cheered, and pushed me to what was then my fastest time.

The second time I ran Boston, two years after the bombings, there were no private shuttles, and I had to wake up hours ahead of time like everyone else. There were no bag drops either. At the start area, all of us wore clothes we had to either throw away or donate. Runners were dressed in tattered sweatshirts, pants with splattered paint, garbage bags, and flannel shirts found in thrift stores. We looked like fishermen or cannery workers walking on the side of the Alaska Peninsula Highway.

It was another bright, cool day just like I remembered it being the last time, but security was elsewhere. Then I started and felt just as good as I did the first time. I was at a steady 6:10 per mile, feeling conservative. My energy was high, and my spirits were optimistic. Then I felt something in my foot. It was like a pearl forming underneath the place where most people have an arch. My flat feet had never given me problems before, but there was a problem now, and it didn't get better.

None of it got better — my spirits, my energy, my pace, my foot. Nothing could shake the pain, and the pearl grew into a golf ball. It wasn't bone or connective tissue, but muscle — something that would recover quickly, but it was costing me precious minutes. I thought it might be my shoe, but if I stopped, it would cost me more. I looked at my watch, saw that my time was doomed anyway, and I did what I had never done in any run that wasn't at least fifty miles long. I stopped, pulled over to the side, and took off my shoe.

A passing runner yelled at me not to quit. I thought, *I'm not quitting*, but what came out was "I'm not finishing!" I shuddered at the words from my own mouth.

When I kept running, I knew it wasn't my shoe. The golf ball had become a watermelon beneath my foot, pounding my missing arch.

In the shower room at the hotel gym, steam crept across the floor, the walls, and climbed to the ceiling, floating like phantoms and their whispers to give up running. My consciousness was levitating in fragments, spinning and fluttering around my being. Surrounded in fog, gushing water, and moans of the pained, a wise man spoke.

"People always want to know why we do this, don't they?"

"Have you ever come up with a good answer?" I asked.

"Nope." The wiseman was naked, holding shampoo.

Yes — a wise man indeed. It's the lack of answers I found appealing. Plenty of my life demanded explanation and reason. Answers didn't always come, and when they did, it's wasn't always because there was a question. As my thoughts gathered, and my distilled soul settled into stillness, finding itself as one again, stronger than before, I remembered some of the questions I did have.

"We have no obligation to anyone other than ourselves to do this," he said.

I didn't say anything.

"Right now, it seems like a good time to be done with it."

I shrugged. "Then we always register for another one."

When I got on the plane in Boston, I'd come to terms with the results of the marathon. Watch any runner, at any event, who lingers around the finish line too long. This person has no direction. This person gazes into space and absorbs the results of the recent effort. This person needs to sit down and have some electrolytes. Then the post-race blues hit, and soon enough it's always time for the next challenge. I kept running, and I even kept racing, but I never ran a marathon again.

Before the principal and vice principal took me into the office to discuss whether or not they would renew my contract, I had already enrolled at Northern for the third time in my life. I was going for my master's degree, but I didn't care about that. I didn't know if I would ever teach again. I just needed to start over. I needed to be back in Marquette. I also needed Mandy, but she was moving to Sun Valley, Idaho. Both of us wanted to continue our relationship, but neither of us knew which direction it would go.

After the summer, and after the fishing season, after I'd helped Mandy and her parents load a trailer, I was alone again. In the darkness of 5:00 AM, my car crushing its own axle from the weight of material possessions, I backed out of the garage and watched the address on the front of the house fade from the beams of my headlights. Most of my things were left in a storage unit behind me, and the distance in front of me was through the looking glass I called a windshield. As the sun ascended into the eastern Oregon sky, heatwaves slithered off the pavement and I questioned what was real. The last time I had been on this road, sunrise was in my rearview mirror.

Of course, I did get to see Mandy again before I continued to Marquette. I had enough time, and Sun Valley was a detour worth making. Mandy was still trying to find a place to live, so she was staying at an Air B & B place. I stayed there as long as I could. Then the morning of emotions arrived, and this time, I really was alone again.

I was doing what I wanted, but I wished that there was some kind of sign that I was making the right choice. I'd had everything I'd wanted. Now I was leaving it to start over and reconnect with myself. It was all on me, without a Batman, Superman, or naked wise man in a shower room to be a symbol, and example, or a guide. As I watched another sunrise from my windshield, I crossed the Idaho-Montana border and traveled back in time.

After having made this trip a few times before, instead of going straight to Bozeman, I decided to take the extra few minutes into Big Sky, where I'd never been. The town and the resort, I discovered, were off the beaten path, and I had to slow for mountain goats as Lone Mountain appeared in my windshield. It was around noon, and I was hungry for lunch. The GPS map on my phone had suggested a Thai restaurant called the Lotus Pad, so I parked my car at the town center and started walking. It was at least a five-minute walk, but my drive was long, and the streets were empty. I needed to move my legs.

I regretted stepping away from my car's air conditioning as the sun burned and heatwaves were visible on the pavement. Other than a man, a woman, and two young girls, no one was around in this off-season ski resort town. I was focused on the directions on my phone, but I could see this family to my right had also reached the intersection of Big Pine Drive and Rainbow Trout Run.

"Do you know where the Blue Moon Bakery is?"

The man of the family had turned to face me. I looked up from my phone to see Ben Affleck waiting for an answer, gray streaks in his hair shining in the sun.

Somewhere far away, a bat must have crashed through a window, scattering shards in all directions.

"Keith," Luke says. He fishes his own operation now, next to ours. His skiff is tied to us, waiting with us for the tide.

"How much time do you think you've spent sitting in the skiff, waiting for the tide?"

"Like," I start, "in my life?"

It's a good question. How much time, sitting in the bow of a skiff, my foot on an anchor, staring at the corks for a bob or a splash, contemplating existence, life, death, and the universe, have I spent waiting for the tide? It could be three months. It could be years. There's a statistic about the average American's cumulative time spent at traffic lights, waiting for green, but most of my life has been in a place without traffic lights.

"You're like a piece of driftwood," Luke says, laughing. "Just floating around, wherever the tide takes you."

I guess he's right. Driftwood doesn't resemble its original tree. I'm shorter than average, and I have what people call a year-round tan. Luke looks like Dad. He's tall and blue-eyed, he loves hunting and fishing, and he's competent at handiwork. He would have fit in with our Viking ancestors.

We all originate from the same roots. Like multiple rivers from the same headwaters, we branched apart in all directions. We continue to branch away from each other into smaller streams and tiny twigs, reaching farther and farther away from the trunk, but sometimes those branches twist and intertwine.

It's why our stories are intertwined more than we realize, even after they fall and drift with the tide. Odin breathed life into driftwood and brought life to Ask and Embla, the first people. As they multiplied, he watched people through his messenger ravens. Then, at Ragnarök, the demise of all people and gods, just a tree and a serpent were left unscathed. In a new beginning, Adam and Eve tasted the tree's forbidden fruit, tempted by a serpent. Their descendant, Noah sent a raven from his ark as a messenger. The raven never returned.

Maybe the Bible never resonated with me because it never mentions the tide — but maybe it is just lost in translation. In the beginning, the ocean covered the surface of our planet, and the entire ocean was murky with particulates. There was no light below the surface and almost no oxygen. Then, as the tide repeatedly turned upon the surface of the ocean, it cleared and allowed light to penetrate into further depths. Meanwhile, land strengthened into a solid, firm structure, or *firmamentum* in Latin, as a barrier between parts of the ocean.

Maybe Jesus didn't walk on water but a mudflat. Maybe Moses and the Israelites arrived at the Red Sea at the end of the ebb, and the Egyptian army arrived just before the flood. Maybe the story of Noah's Ark took place over the course of six hours. Maybe the firmament is the shoreline. Maybe God is the tide.

The Anglo-Saxon word, *tyd* developed from the word *tidi* of the ancient Germanic tribes. *Tidi* developed from *di-ti* from the Proto-Indo-European language. Perhaps its similarity to *deity* is no coincidence. Time and tide are unchangeable, inevitable, and unavoidable. Time and tide stayeth for no man. Time and tide are divine.

Before the first Wilsons, the term wasn't specific to the ebbs and floods of the ocean. A tide was an era, an age, an epoch, or an event. A tide could be a season, an hour, or a day such as the Yuletide — the darkest day of our planet's orbit around the sun. A tide could be the nineteen years it takes before another full moon on a solstice. A tide could be the time it takes for a heart to beat, the time it takes to inhale and exhale, or the time it takes me to stride from my right foot to my left.

Run itself developed from *rune*, which referred to any kind of course, such as road, a path, or a trail, but it also could have referred to the course of an orbit, a month, or any specific section of time. Before it was *rune*, it was *ryn* — synonymous with *flow*, as in that of a tidal current. An engine *runs*. We can *run* a business. Blood *runs* through our veins. Salmon make their *run* back to their natal lakes and streams. We *run* out of time.

There is a time, of course, between ebb and flood, when the water is still, that we call slack tide. When salmon spawn, they die before their eggs hatch new fry. Between heartbeats, there is silence. Between breaths, there is pause. Between footstrikes, I go airborne. When these moments merge, my perception of time changes.

As I flow through the current of time, I'm not the son of Will. I'm not even the son of the son of Will. I'm not like Will at all. I'm quiet and non-confrontational. Will was a conqueror and a bastard. History specifically calls him *Will the Conqueror* and *Will the Bastard*. Without mercy, he invaded the Anglo-Saxons the Romans had left in England as their empire was falling. Then so happened the merging of the Anglo-Saxon language with Latin, giving us our words for running and the tide.

Julius Caesar himself had used ebbs and floods to conquer Great Britain for Rome. Predicting the placement of the shoreline helped strategize attacks — but as I sit, waiting for the tide, without a single splash in the net, I feel less like a conqueror and more like Brutus in Shakespeare's *The Tragedy of Julius Caesar.*

"There is a tide in the affairs of men," says Brutus, "which taken at the flood leads on to fortune. Omitted, all the voyage of their life is bound in shallows and in miseries. On such a full sea are we now afloat. And we must take the current when it serves, or lose our ventures." In other words, the tide waits for no one.

This quotable line appears as the army of Antony, Lepidus, and Octavius approaches their camp. Cassius argues that they should stay and fight the enemy well-rested and in familiar territory. Brutus, however, believes that they need to be on the offense as soon as possible, as their army shrinks due to rumors of corruption. Brutus is more compelling in his argument, but the strategy fails, and before the end of the play, Cassius and Brutus have died.

History tells us that Octavius would become the first emperor of Rome, which would rise and fall just like the tide. As Rome ebbed, and it lost control of the British Isles, it was Will who took the opportunity to invade. The Romans had never forced Latin upon the Anglo-Saxons, but Will's language merged with it. In this new language, the Venerable Bede wrote about the ebb and flood of the ocean using the word *tide.*

We have included the ocean in our affairs, but there is a tide beyond the affairs of men. There is a tide beyond the affairs of women, children, flowers, furbearers, and fish. I've been told that all matter, energy, and time in the universe was compressed into a sphere too tiny to see. Then that sphere exploded, and it hasn't stopped exploding. Galaxies, solar systems, black holes, subatomic particles, and dark matter keep expanding away from the center of the universe.

I often wonder, while running, or sitting as I wait for the tide, if once the universe has expanded to its maximum capacity, it will reach stillness, like the mouth of the Naknek River before the flood when no bubbles or twigs move on the surface. I wonder if there is an ultimate slack tide before the flow begins to turn the other direction, compressing once again into a sphere too tiny to see. Maybe the universe expands and contracts over and over again as an ultimate ebb and flood through eternity.

If the universe truly does work this way, and existence is indeed infinite, any event, and no matter how small and insignificant, has already happened an infinite number of times and it will happen an infinite number of times again in an infinite number of variations. In this universe, somewhere out there is a Krypton. Somewhere out there is a version me with scales, gills, and fins, living in the ocean with the other salmon people. If the universe is not forever, I've read enough comic books to wonder if there is a multiverse.

Then there is my favorite story that explains the tide. It is a story about an old woman who held the ocean from falling off the edge of our planet with a line of braided twine. Raven and his people had always hunted and gathered their food on land, but people had been fruitful and multiplied, and soon there were too many to feed.

Raven, hungry and weak like his people, summoned the strength to fly to the edge of our planet to the old woman. He knew there was food beneath the surface of the ocean, and if she let go of the line, it could feed him and his people.

"If you let go of the line," Raven said, "I will give you the stars that I kept before releasing them into the sky."

"No," she said. "Everyone knows you didn't keep any."

"I have them right here," Raven said.

She leaned over to see what was in his hand, and Raven flung sand into her eyes. As she brushed at them frantically with her hands, she dropped the line, and the ocean began spilling over the edge of our planet, dropping into infinity.

Raven flew home and began plucking clams from the mud. He collected fish from the exposed floor of the ocean. He and his people feasted for days, weeks, months. Soon, there was more food than they could eat, and when they were full, they realized the fish and sea creatures left uneaten were rotting, going to waste. The smell wafted against the shore.

Raven sighed and flew back to the edge of our planet where the old woman was still blind with eyes full of sand. The line was still laying at her feet. Raven placed it back into her hands.

"You tricked me," she said.

"You're right," Raven said. "I hope you will forgive me. My people were starving, and we needed the food from the ocean."

Raven wiped the sand from the old woman's eyes.

"Thanks, I guess," she said. "I suppose I forgive you."

"I do have one thing to ask of you," Raven said.

"Now what?"

"With you holding the line, the ocean will fill again, and my people and I will starve. Can you agree to release it on a regular basis?"

"Oh, all right," she said. "I can do that, but how will I know when it's time?"

"Let the sun and moon guide you," Raven said. "Use their alignment to time the ebb and flood."

As the tide begins to turn again, the skiff turns around, and the corks on the surface curve in the opposite direction. Fish are starting to splash. It's time to check the nets again.

In Marquette, crisp breezes rustling red and yellow leaves down the trail had given way to blistering cold and heavy, drifting snow. Mountain biking and trail running had turned to cross-country skiing and snowshoeing.

"First beer for first place," Brian said as he passed me the silver can of Grand Rabbits Ale from Blackrocks, a house on Third Street converted into a brewery. I'd been chased from that house by police even after I'd turned 21.

I'd won the Noquemanon 15-mile snowshoe race for the second time, but it was the first time since the last time I was living in Marquette. The second and third beer were with dinner at the Vierling, the brewery on the corner of Front and Washington since the 1800s. Four, five, maybe six, were at the Ore Dock Brewery, the spot that opened the night before I left for Winnett. The final drink was a tall can of PBR at Remie's, the dive bar with a low ceiling, worn pool tables, and no door on the men's room. It was always a place that left a bad taste in my mouth.

When I woke up face down in my pillow, cigarette smoke didn't saturate my clothes, my hair, or the cash in my wallet, and I was still ever-grateful for Michigan banning smoking indoors. My scattered recollections had less to do with fog in my brain and more to do with my scattered timeline with this town.

The hangover was not as profound as the soreness in my legs, but my car was parked at Lower Harbor behind the old Ore Dock and I knew the walk would clear my head. I sat up on the inflatable mattress in front of an empty wall. Most of my belongings were hundreds of miles away in a storage unit in Oregon.

The night before, Brian, his work friend from Lacrosse, Wisconsin, and I had meandered along Washington, stomping in the snow like six-year-olds. They stopped at the Staybridge Suites, a massive new hotel where a bakery used to be, where they were staying. From there, I continued to my apartment behind ShopKo, hiccupping all the way. Now I had to walk back.

Outside was dark, eighteen degrees, and snowdrifts hadn't yet been plowed. As I walked by Subway, I recalled one more time when Alice asked me to drive her to Milwaukee. After I left her at the airport, as many roads as I took, and as many times I was lost, I still made it back to this town, like my entire adult life had been a series of trips to Milwaukee. I looked across the street and figured the last time I was there was probably the last time Grandpa took me and Erica there for Happy Meals.

Some of the establishments on Washington had been the same forever, but others had changed several times since I first lived in Marquette. The Citgo station, like all Citgos in the UP and northern

Wisconsin, had become a Krist. The Recovery Room used to be the Rover, but I couldn't recall what it was before that. The 906 used to be the Blue V after it was the Mixx, after it was the Matrixx. I went there once when I was 21 and walked out disgusted by sweaty, wiggling bodies, stale air ridden with hormones, and the overall depravity of Marquette's attempt at club culture.

Long before my time, people used to ride the train from all over the UP to see the latest movie at the Delft Theater. I was old enough to have seen *Underworld* there, but now it was closed, being converted into a bodega. The empty building on the corner used to be a Snap Fitness, where I spent many an hour during my training for the Philadelphia Marathon. Sometimes, if it was late enough in the afternoon, I'd look out the window from a treadmill as patrons of Remie's peered in at me, blowing cigarette smoke, seemingly bewildered by my decision to partake in such an activity.

Hundreds, maybe thousands, of times I'd parked my truck, my car, or one of my bikes, and stepped into Book World, Donckers, Aubree's Pizza, or the Portside. Seeing the length of this street at this pace was such a rarity that the spacial relationship between these places had been lost on me. I knew they were all on the same street, but in which order, I would struggle to remember. Maybe the cannery workers walking on the side of the Alaska Peninsula Highway knew Naknek better than me.

I'd often run on Washington, but when I ran, the windows on either side of the street received a glance before time and space pulled me into the next moment. It's not something I did often, because people wandered on the sidewalk with no idea a runner might plow them down at any second. I may as well have been driving. This time, here I was walking, with no sign of another person, a car, enjoying the slow movement of time and my surroundings. By the time I reached the Savings Bank Building at the end of the street, with its copper-coated clock tower on top, I realized that I wanted to find this experience while running. It was never about racing time. No one can win that race. It was about reaching what was beyond the end of the road.

When I arrived at my car, I looked over Lake Superior. The dark reached forever beyond the old Ore Dock, and all I could see were ripples lapping against the shore. Soon, beyond Washington

Street, beyond the ripples, the sun would rise over the horizon and reveal a lake that looked like the ocean.

Waves aren't crashing against us, but an onshore wind always makes it more difficult to work. There are more fish in the nets than we had expected. It's too early for it, but Keegan, the new guy, doesn't know the difference. He's seventeen years old, and Dad found him in Wisconsin. When he picks fish, he stares at them, fumbling with the head, trying to yank it out from between the corners of a square hook, but blood and scales splash his face with no success. He'll get better. They always get better, but right now Keegan doesn't realize the stress of the situation. The Naknek-Kvichak District is about to close, but fish keep splashing.

We pull three of our four nets. Keegan learns how to roundhaul quickly enough.

One of the nets, however, remains in the water with twenty minutes left, and it is sinking with heads and tails.

"There is only one way out of this," Dad says.

I know what he's thinking. I don't like it, but he's right. He doesn't like it either. Keegan really won't like it. I have to untie the outside end of the net and let the whole damned thing flag against the beach. We have to let the net go high and dry with the ebb, fish gilled in the mud. There are at least two-thousand pounds there. Most of them are still splashing as the corks nestle against the shoreline.

"Keegan, you stay here," Dad says. "Pick as many fish as you can before we get back. Try to keep the seagulls away."

He jumps into the water and Dad and I leave him. When we return, Keegan is on his hands and knees, covered head-to-toe in mud, and fish are piled along the net, now at least twenty feet above the shoreline. Dad and I leave the skiff anchored out before we wade in and walk up the slope of the mud. Keegan's face and glasses are splattered with mud, sweat, and blood. A pile of fish is behind him. Keegan has gotten better, but there is plenty more.

Through the hours of the ebb, sometimes all three of us pick. Then sometimes two of us pick while the other one of us hauls fish down to the skiff, rinsing them in the water, and tossing them into the brailers. There is no intended order or pattern to our distribution of tasks, but we settle into one. Soon it's just me making trips to the water with two or three fish on each hand. Every few trips, I move the anchor to keep the skiff from going high and dry. I'm the only one with the endurance to sustain it, even without stopping for lunch, dinner, or a snack — even water— in almost an entire day. If I could get through a day like this one, I'm sure I can run 100 miles. Maybe this fall, I will take on that challenge.

First, I have to get through this season and this day. The mud is soft and sticky, and there isn't one trip down to the shoreline where I don't sink to my thighs. Every time I head down to the skiff, I go a different route since making a path makes mud softer. Never do I walk a straight line or go the same way twice, and each trip takes a little longer. Then I realize once again that the shoreline is never the same. It shifts and changes, but so does anywhere on our planet as it spins and orbits and expands farther from the center of the universe every moment. My fingers start to fatigue, and fish fall before I get to the water, so I start leaving them near the shoreline ready to rinse later.

By the time the fish are out of the net, all three of us start walking up and down the slope of the mud, carrying them. Then the skiff switches directions from its anchor. The flood has begun. Now we have to toss fish up the beach before they are washed away. Keegan, Dad, and I keep bringing them down, but not too far down, rinse them, and throw them into the skiff, but we are no match for the tide. It waits for no one, and it's moving fast. The tide brought these fish. Now it's going to take them.

Our moves become hurried. We become frantic in our process. Hurrying is all we know how to do now. Then a skiff approaches us knee-deep in water, sliding fish uphill onto the mud. It takes me a second to realize it's Luke with Kayla. He has been working as a project manager in Naknek. His plan has been to fish on weekends when he isn't constrained to a day job. At first, I'm confused, because it's not a weekend. Then I remember it's the fourth of July. People who workday jobs get holidays as breaks. The fact that he's here means fishing is about to open again. It had been closed for six hours.

I look at Dad and Keegan, and they look how I feel — wobbly, muddy, and dreary-eyed. Luke and Kayla see it too, and they help us with our fish so we can make our delivery in time before we set our nets again.

On a cool day in November, inside a sleeping bag, flat on a camping pad in the back of a van on I-94, I drifted between dreams and my surroundings — scattered sweat-soaked clothes, Mom and Dad in the front seats, the sky a gray blur on the other side of the windows, and a commemorative belt buckle for running 100 miles in under 24 hours.

For some stretch of mileage, I managed to stay awake long enough to call Mandy, cellular signals between towers navigating between my phone and hers. When she knew I was drifting away again into dreamland, we said our goodbyes one more time before my next flight to Sun Valley. Like one booth after another on the road through Chicago, running 100 miles took its toll. Like any section of life, it was one more part of the course with both challenge and reward between a start and finish, a finish and a start, or however you want to look at it.

The course was on Tunnel Hill State Trail, in Illinois, a corridor of crushed limestone gravel where trains used to transport passengers along tracks no longer there. The event began at Vienna City Park and went to a southern turnaround point in the town of Karnak for a return to the start. Then participants ran in the other direction to Tunnel Hill, the steepest hill on the course, which we didn't run up and down, but through it. Then we kept going to a northern turnaround point. The next arrival at the start was the completion of the first 50 miles. 100-mile runners repeated everything one more time — all the way south, all the way back and then north, and then south again to the start. In other words, the run was divided into a back-and-forth and another back-and-forth, and then it repeated both back-and-forths.

Mom and Dad took me to the start, and at 7:00 AM, I took my first steps of the race, around the parking lot and onto the trail. It seemed everyone was passing me, and I cringed as I kept a close eye on my watch, keeping my pace at about a nine-minute mile. I knew fatigue would later force me to slow even more, but if I slowed any more in the moment, too much energy would be lost in the restraint. With my ego screaming, I let runner after runner blaze by me and then do it again from the opposite direction after reaching the northern turnaround.

By 26.6 miles, at the first return to Vienna Park, temperatures had risen to the 50s, and I ditched my jacket. I stopped at every station, chugging water, scarfing down bananas and potatoes. Mom and Dad met me along the way with words of encouragement. At the Tunnel Hill station, 36.3 miles into the race, they brought me my drop bag from the pile of them. I refilled my vest with RX Bars, Munk Pack Oatmeal Pouches, Panda black licorice, and boxes of dried cranberries. I drank half my growler of cold brew coffee.

By the time I turned around and returned to Tunnel Hill again, my first watch had died, so I handed it to Dad. Then I drank the rest of the coffee. The caffeine helped reduce my rate of perceived exertion. It also started the urge in my bowels. There was a portable toilet every few miles, but every few miles, someone was in there. My next action was inevitable. I ducked into the trees to my left, did what I needed to do, and used the fallen leaves to wipe.

Trusting my pace in autopilot, I waited until the second return to Vienna Park to turn on my other watch. I ran the 50-mile course in seconds within eight hours, and it was so much fun that I decided to run it again. The location of the halfway point is the reason for a high dropout rate of the 100-mile race, but of 3,000 salmon eggs, 800 hatch, 80 make it to the ocean, a few become adults, and one or two spawn. I had to have a better chance than that.

100 miles was no easy task, but it was Illinois, and relatively flat. Instead of running over the steepest hill on the course, participants ran straight through it. Peripheral vision was black. There was light at the end of the tunnel, but after reaching it there were 62 more miles.

The second time through the tunnel, I didn't know it until my feet hit the concrete, the walls illuminated by my headlamp. The sun had set by the time I reached the southern turnaround again, and I ran the rest of the way in the dark. Mom and Dad helped me put on my jacket the second time through Vienna Park, and then the struggle began. First, I thought my jacket was inside out when it wasn't. Then I couldn't go faster than ten-minute miles, and soon, twelve-minute miles. My second watch died just after the northern turnaround when I was clocking 14-minute miles. With ten miles left of the course, I handed my watch to Dad and ran in the dark the rest of the way.

I had begun passing runner after runner after mile 50, but now it was all-the-more apparent. After the speedsters whipped by me, every time someone shuffled from the opposite direction, headlamp shining, I knew they were behind me and not ahead. Most of the time it was just me, surrounded in black, just a short stretch of trail in my headlamp. I was competing with no one but myself, having a conversation with darkness alone. After all, that's what much of these endeavors are about.

What I think about when I run is the same as what I think about when I don't run, but it's amplified, magnified, scrutinized. I analyze and criticize my life, my choices past and future. I think about the flaws and functions of society. I contemplate the wisdom of the universe and wonder how systems upon systems work in harmony inside of chaos. I think about what I'm going to do after the next fishing season. That day, I thought about Mandy and how much I missed her.

Then I thought about the creeping fatigue and soreness, as much as I try not to. I thought about how at any moment, any body part could break, and the run could come to a screeching halt. Then I thought that if I can spend the night in the bottom of a skiff in the rain and wind, and then pull nets and pick fish with cold, dysfunctional fingers, I can keep running. I thought about how salmon are an elite anadromous fish with an ability to forge against currents for miles and miles, and I have their nutrients swimming through my blood.

One foot strode in front of the other foot, and the other foot strode in front again. Breath flowed in and out. Electrical signals surged to nerves, contracting fibers, relaying back to the brain before surging again in an instant. Like salmon smolt hatch in fresh lakes and streams, swim brackish channels to the salt of the ocean, and return as adults to spawn, blood pulsed through vessels, carried nutrients to muscles and returned again to ventricles ever beating.

A journey forward is a journey inward, reaching outward as our planet rotates around the sun, its moon pulling the tide from one shore to the next four different times. I ran the four sections of the Tunnel Hill 100 and crossed the finish line in eighteen hours, thirty-nine minutes. Then I collapsed into the back of the van.

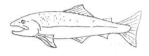

It's five minutes to midnight on a cloudless, mid-June night on the Alaska Peninsula Highway. The rearview mirror of Shoosh's car reflects the Aleutian Range, tiny on the horizon behind cottongrass expanding across the tundra. I'm in the passenger seat, controlling the music the way I did when Shoosh and I were teenagers.

Soon those mountains disappear, and we drive into Naknek. Without any fish yet to process, workers are walking toward the Barmuda Triangle. As Shoosh parks on the gravel, we hear their hooting and hollering as they walk from the open yellow gate to join the rest of the hordes — but the air is as still as slack water, and despite all the ruckus, Naknek is quiet. The quiet is amplified when Shoosh's engine stops, and I listen to the slow sound of gravel crunching beneath our shoes.

We're not at the same house of my childhood, but the memories here have accumulated. Dad built this house, and I was here to help him. The first summer we slept here, the walls were bare sheetrock and we walked on plywood subfloors. Then it became more like home every summer. I still expect, when I turn the metal doorknob, to hear Chrissy's high-pitched yip of a bark until someone lifts her and gives her a pet on her lightbulb-shaped head. Then her bark should fade into a soft growl until her gigantic marble eyes shut. Now when I open the door, there is no bark, because she was hit by a van years ago in Washburn. Murphy is gone, too — buried on the corner of this property behind the spot where the skiffs are parked during the winter.

Mom and Dad are outside on their metal chairs by a fire in the rock pit inside a circle platform of bricks we gathered from fallen canning stoves at Libbyville. They're drinking Busch Ice out of cans and throwing scrap two-by-fours from the greenhouse into the flames. Shoosh and I grab our cans and meander to the fire. Beyond the line of bushes on the edge of the gravel, fourwheelers hum by us in the dirt trail below the side of the pavement. Dad planted those bushes when they were a foot high. I watch as faint shadows projected from those bushes stretch as the sun hovers above the horizon. They reach across the gravel the way I have reached toward my different goals outside of Naknek — get this job, go to that place, run this far. The shadows are like the branches themselves. They grow, but the shadows are like a movie, a representation of another reality projected with light.

On TV, I've seen flying cars, time travel, more than one war, school shootings, environmental catastrophes, and the teenage sex-capades that Shoosh and I misguidedly idealized. When we were kids, the flickering and changing pictures on the screen had enchanted us. We wanted to be part of it. Both of us left Naknek at age eighteen, but his repeated return is more frequent than mine. He lives two weeks here, two weeks working in the Arctic. He has even built his own house in Naknek.

The only house that has ever felt like home to me was the one Dad built on the tundra with wooden, knotty walls, its colored bedrooms, the sounds of it settling at night, and the carpet of hot lava. It was TV, internet, and stories on the page, however, that had brought me to the world outside of that house, outside of Naknek, outside of the tundra and water surrounding it. When we moved out of that house, it was one less attachment to this town.

In my adult life, familiar things have become strange. The dining room table, paintings, framed photographs, and the dishes are all the same, but the house is different — but home isn't just a house or a town. It's along the Naknek River pouring from Naknek Lake into Bristol Bay. It's on the Kvichak and out at Graveyard. The hospital at Graveyard has outlasted any other roof over my head in the course of my life. I'm home again with Mom, Dad, Luke, Erica, and my friends like Shoosh.

Around the fire, there is no reason to say anything. All of us, with this place in common, can stare into the flames and think our different thoughts. Shoosh is always quiet, and it's probably the reason we're good friends. I call it a comfortable silence, like the still air surrounding us.

Of course, with this comfort and familiarity comes a level of suppression, too. When I was a teenager, I wanted nothing to do with this place, and I still want nothing to do with it 46 to 48 weeks out of a year. I knew I needed to get away from this town, this region, and even this state. Alaska is big and vast and open, and people like Mom and Dad left the cities and the concrete in their youth to come to places like Naknek, but to me, places like Naknek are the trap. I want to live in a land of infinite interconnected roads, where I can get anywhere that I desire. It started in Marquette, but that place only took me on both Mom and Dad's paths. I became both a teacher and a fisherman just like them, but I had no special talent in either of these endeavors.

Fleeing from Naknek didn't divert from the road back here. I am still back every year for the commercial fishing season. Although I'm a setnetter, I have become somewhat of a drifter — moving from one place to the next. I went from Marquette to my travels in Europe to the basement in Washburn to a weird little town in the middle of Kansas. I lived in Latin America, middle-of-nowhere Montana, and Oregon just north of the California border. Then I was in Idaho. There is the running, skiing, teaching, driving from one coast to the next coast. I have made wrong turns and wrong decisions, and I have had failed relationships. The person in my successful one encourages me to find my own way.

I don't know how much longer I want to keep fishing, or whether I am done when Dad is done, but I hope the return remains strong for future generations. The future is unclear, but just as it was when I was a teenager, in the solitude of a long run, I put ideas together. It's in an activity most people don't understand where life makes sense. It's where the confusion is gone, because there's nothing to understand. It's where I feel peace inside chaos, elation inside of pain, and direction inside of endless possibilities. I learn about myself through my wrong turns, mistakes, and my failures. When I run, I reflect on the past, even though I can never travel back to it. Looking back, some of these answers seem so simple that they seem stupid. Then there are the answers I still seek and the ones I have abandoned, knowing they are unknowable. I know I am never going to be a complete person, because the person I am becoming is always re-created as deep as the molecular level.

The biome of my digestive system, the wiring of my synapses, and ideas perhaps engraved deep into my gene pool affect my decisions, but every experience I have is of my own doing. My lack of direction exists because I find so much direction in a race — and I don't even get that right all the time. I am aware of it, and I accept it. Life will never reflect a race, because as deep as the molecular level, I don't want to see life as the distance between a starting point and a finish line.

As the sun remains in the sky even as the time approaches midnight, the Busch Ice buzzing around my brain by the fire enhances these thoughts of my choices. I'm in my thirties now — too young to be wise, but too old to feel like a teenager itching to leave his hometown. Salmon have one single drive to return to their natal streams to spawn and die. Almost none of them make it there, but they serve a purpose in the end, even if it is just to serve as fertilizer. Maybe we are as simple as salmon after all. I don't find comfort in this thought, nor do I need to find comfort in it. Comfort is sitting on a fluffy couch with my eyes glued against a TV screen, my heart and lungs docile.

No person's life is a straight line of progress. There is not some finish line we reach, where we can take a breath, sit down on a big fluffy couch, and relax. The finish is seldom when we want it to be, and if it were up to me, it would not exist — but I find it best not to think of it as a finish line. I take my last swallow of beer. Dad looks up from the fire and says we have to launch the skiff at about 5:00 tomorrow morning. The tide waits for no one.

When Galileo Galilei first noticed the tide in Venice, he realized that it was evidence of our planet and its moon revolving around the sun. His ideas, of course, were considered blasphemy by the Catholic Church, and in the end, the power of the Inquisition placed him under house arrest for the remainder of his life. He never saw an ebb or flood in the canals again. Someday, I would learn about Galileo's theories as conventional science, but the tide didn't wait for Galileo. It seems like nothing in Venice ever does.

The first time I was in Venice, I was 23. I had reserved a bunk at a hostel in Vigonza, a town ten minutes away from the city by train. The train didn't stop as much as it slowed barely enough for doors to fly open and passengers to disappear. I stepped out of those doors with those passengers, onto a concrete platform that was an island shrouded in fog. I had transcribed directions to the hostel onto a crumpled receipt for a can of sardines I had bought in a supermarket in Ravenna.

I walked onto an empty street, fog concealing anything outside of a stone's throw. When I saw the sign for the Magic Venice 2, I walked inside to see empty tables and a woman behind a counter flipping uncooked pizza crusts. She was pierced in one eyebrow and she wore a bright pink bandana. I'd walked into the wrong building.

"Le capiche l'inglese?"

"Yes," she said. She did speak English.

"I'm looking for the Magic Venice Two."

Pizza Lady slapped the dough onto the counter and looked up, sternly. "Do you know how much it costs to stay there?"

"Ten Euros, I think."

"No," she said. "They will charge you 100 Euros."

"The website says ten."

"It's ten Euros per person for ten beds," she explained. "It's a trick. A scam. "

"Are you sure?"

"I am absolutely sure," she said. "I have argued with the owner many times about taking advantage of tourists."

Two other employees, a girl and a guy about my age, appeared from behind the counter and joined her in an Italian dialogue I couldn't decipher, but I could tell they were discussing what to tell me. They knew a cheap place in Venice I could stay, where there was a vacancy. The next train was the last one for the night, but it wasn't arriving for another three hours.

I ordered a pizza with anchovies and mushrooms from Pizza Lady, and the other guy and girl sat with me, drinking an Italian pilsner. Then, instead of one pie, four of them arrived on the table. The four of us ate and drank together, speaking in English and in the universal language of pizza and beer. Pizza Lady had a sudden realization and pointed to the clock. The train would arrive in less than five minutes. She rushed me to her car, we drove less than two minutes, and she slammed her brakes at the familiar concrete platform. I dug into my pockets, found a wad of cash for the pizza and beer. I tried to hand it to her, but she shook her head.

"Get on the train!"

"Well, thank you for the pizza and beer," I said.

"Go!"

The doors were opening. With one backpack strap over my shoulder, I bounded up the stairs and jumped aboard the train. The doors shut, and I rode back into Venice to find the place Pizza Lady had called on my behalf.

The second time I was in Venice, I was 33 and I was with Mandy, and I shared with her the places I'd visited all those years ago — the Vatican, the Coliseum, the Uffizi, the David, the Leaning Tower of Pisa, and Venice. When I was by myself, I'd decided it was too tacky to take a gondola ride by myself. When I was with Mandy, a driver paddled us through canals as she asked him about the city. He explained almost no one lives in the bottom floors of any of the buildings because the humidity, mold, and mildew destroys them. Sometimes, he told us, the tide rises into them, the way it fills the square of San Marco when servers wear hip boots.

As the sun was setting, I asked Mandy when our train to Milan left. She told me 21:40, as she told me already, but I kept asking because it didn't seem right. Again, I counted on my fingers to convince myself it translated to 8:40. Again, I had thought we were leaving earlier. We wandered, we had dinner, we got our backpacks at the hotel, and we went to the train station. I didn't see our train on the monitor, so I asked to see the ticket. Then gut sunk.

"This says 18:20," I said. "That's 6:20."

Both of us looked at the monitor.

"Oh no," she said. "I was looking at the arrival time."

The arrival time was 21:40. It was 21:35. Our train had left hours ago.

Mandy's eyes began to water. I tried to remind her of all the times I'd missed a road sign or taken a wrong turn on the freeway. She was the brains of the relationship. One mistake didn't change that. It didn't help.

We went to the ticket office and Mandy asked if there was anything else leaving for Milan, where we had a room reserved near the main square for the New Year. Our flight was at 10:00 on New Year's Day. Fireworks or not, we had to get to Milan. There was a train to Verona at 22:15 and then another to Milan at 5:45 in the morning. It was New Year's Eve, and there were no hotels available. We had no choice but to take the itinerary the agent had suggested.

Then we lay our scene in fair Verona. Montagues and Capulets loitered with bottles of liquor. Security was throwing them out of the station, but they lingered in the parking lot. It was not a safe place to be. Mandy found an expensive hotel on her phone and concluded we should bite it and pay for it given the circumstances. There was a cab driver in the parking lot, but he did not take credit cards, and I'd spent the last of my cash on the gondola ride. The train station had no ATM, or at least not in the section still open.

We wandered up to the platforms and found our way to the security office where guys in uniform were walking out for frequent smoke breaks and to chase away the riff-raff. We stood nearby until we confirmed they didn't care we were there. Every time someone walked out, they looked right through us, like we didn't exist. We put our backpacks against the wall, added layers of clothing, and leaned against each other until midnight. We watched fireworks in the distance, from behind the platforms.

One of the officers, a bearded, portly guy, walked out with two plastic cups of sparkling wine and handed them to us. He invited us into their quarters, and we all watched Italy's cable network television celebration on a laptop in front of the security monitors.

"Where do you think that is?" Mandy asked.

"Milan," I said, but she didn't laugh.

One of the officers told us it was Naples. None of them spoke English other than small pleasantries. Like gremlins, the riffraff in the monitors would appear in the peripheral for fractions of seconds, and the guys would, as we gathered, discuss whose turn it was to go take care of it. Most of their attention, of course, was on the laptop screen displaying fireworks, champagne, and dancing.

When we felt we had worn out our welcome, we nestled back into our spot. Like before, no one seemed to recognize our existence, let alone acknowledge us.

Then an older gentleman in a yellow vest crouched by us and handed us a bottle of sparkling wine. He wished us a happy New Year and asked where we were from.

"Alaska," I said, my way of avoiding saying the United States.

After he walked away, it was mere moments before he returned a second time.

"Winter is cold," he said. "Follow me."

I got up right away. Mandy was reluctant.

He dialed a number into a console by a door, led us up some stairs, and took us into a breakroom. He showed us reclining chairs, restrooms, and vending machines. He was disappointed when no one had any coins. When he left, he told us to be out by 5:00. I went straight for one of the recliners and fell asleep instantly.

It was only a few minutes later when he returned with some coins and bought Mandy a snack and some coffee from the machine. I was sound asleep, and I was still sound asleep when two men in conductor uniforms were at the door a while later, but still hours away from 5:00. Mandy woke me as they walked over to us, asking us one question after another in Italian.

"No capisco l'italiano!"

"Who gave you the number for this room?"

"I don't know," I said. "Some nice guy."

He had told us his name, but there was no way I was repeating it and ratting him out.

We gathered our things, and once again nestled in our spot by the security office. Mandy said she hadn't slept a wink the entire time we were in there, too worried about this exact thing happening. It was still only 2:30. We bided time by reading aloud, and by 5:00, I decided it was time to go look for our platform. According to the chart on the wall, it was platform number five.

People were lingering in the station, which meant the indoor section was open, so we went down there where it was warm, and I validated the tickets.

"Keith," Mandy said. "Look."

She was pointing up at the monitor in the corner. Next to the word *Milan* with the 5:45 departure time was another word in big, bold letters. *Cancellato*.

I did not, by any means, speak or understand fluent Italian, but I was pretty sure that *cancellato* meant we were out of lucko. I paced back and forth, wondering what the hell to do next until Mandy stopped me with her arm.

"Keith, listen," she said.

A group of police officers were talking to a twenty-something guy and his dad. We heard that familiar word, *cancellato*, and we gathered that they were supposed to be on the same train. Then the dad and son walked away into the parking lot, and Mandy and I looked at each other.

I said to the officers, "Same problem."

"Maybe you catch ride with them, pay petrol."

Mandy and I darted after them, into the rain that had begun pouring down.

"Scuzi!" I yelled. "Le capsische l'inglese?"

The dad didn't understand English, but the son did.

"Are you driving to Milan?" Mandy said.

They were.

"Can we have a ride?"

They let us put our bags in the trunk and we sat down in the backseat. Both of us were asleep minutes into the drive. Then we arrived at the airport with plenty of time for our flight from one side of the ocean to the other.

Another fishing season is over, and the water level is low. There are no skiffs on the Naknek River except a few that belong to South Naknek residents, and maybe some Levelockers, ready to take groceries from Naknek Trading home. Eagles and seagulls peck at bare spines on the beach until dogs chase them flying to the next closest one. The mouth of the Naknek River is reduced to a thin flow between mudflats.

Soon it will be slack tide, and the Naknek River will as still as the town after the gate in front of every cannery has closed and padlocked with a chain. There are no cars on the road, and foot traffic is no longer people. If it were, they could walk from driftboat to driftboat in the yards of canneries.

As I bide my time before my trip out of the King Salmon airport, I tie my shoes and run along Alaska Peninsula Highway again. When I run past Leader Creek, there are hundreds of square miles of tundra to my left, without obstruction. With Bristol Bay behind me, I look ahead to the mountains. Their snow-capped peaks and jagged edges shine in the sun as they rise from the horizon.

Now I know why I run toward the mountains instead of toward the Bay. Mountain peaks are symbolic. We imagine them as the pinnacle of physical prowess, financial success, or the ultimate truth. On the top of a mountain, perception changes. Trees, cities, rivers, and roads look small and insignificant. In Greek stories, Zeus and eleven other gods and goddesses reside on the peaks of Mount Olympus. Shiva lives on the peak of Mount Kailash. Moses attained the Ten Commandments on Mount Sinai. Mount Katmai is the largest of the mountains on the horizon, but it has no peak. It imploded when Novarupta imploded in 1912.

At the end of the Alaska Peninsula Highway, the mountains are far away. Their peaks are virtually unreachable. In my experience, I've run far enough to learn that after the miles, pain, elation, injuries, and the destroyed muscle tissue, through rain and snow and cold and heat, but I don't need to reach a mountain peak to know a mountain doesn't care. My impatience to leave Naknek, my failed relationships, my successful one, or what I want to be when I grow up affects Katmai not at all — but even the largest mountain will flatten someday. Katmai's caldera is a reminder of it.

Everything and everyone passes through existence. We are all driftwood, floating back and forth with the tide, our physical material and our energy transferred elsewhere. The universe, after all, is made of matter and energy, neither of which is created or destroyed. Perhaps consciousness works this way, too — brought out to the ocean and washed again to shore, over and over again.

The surface of the ocean moves like muscle, but underneath it is the pulse of the ebb and flood, like my heart urging the movement of blood and limbs over a distance through space. When I run a long enough distance, it is all-the-more-clearer that I'm just a vessel of consciousness constructed of cells and bacteria.

Then my pulse beats harder, urging further this ancient movement — one that is more crucial than the traditional dance of any culture. I surrender to it, allowing muscle fibers to fire hotter, propelling me forward faster. I wait and absorb the potential energy like the string of a bow pulling back. It has built for millennia, as primates moved this way before words were written, before fire was controlled, before distances were measured in standardized units.

In a race, I am surrounded by other primates in rubber shoes, visors, and shorts as revealing as loincloths. Each of us has a number safety-pinned to a shirt. Each number is an arbitrary combination of digits, but we are all together among the trees, under a banner, behind a mass of cords under a mat waiting to activate the computerized chip hidden behind your number bib. Despite moisture-wicking material, a GPS watch, Oakley sunglasses, and a meticulous training plan, we are still just primates. We were fish once, and before that, we were mere molecules.

When I run, whether or not it is among other people, my pulse beats faster, and my breath flows deeper. Heat rises, pores open, and sweat pours. Breath steadies as each foot falls into the grasp of gravity for an instant, another instant, and another. Moments between footstrikes, moments between heartbeats, and moments between breaths, no matter how brief, merge and become one stillness. Consciousness surges through thousands of miles of synapses, both toward the sky and down to the dirt. Absence and presence are synonymous as they are stillness within movement, where distance doesn't matter, because distance is infinite.

Pain receptors bring me back to my body soon enough, and I feel my feet thud into the ground. The force shoots up my legs, my spine, all the way into the brain. My mind shakes. When I finish, I might feel worn down and broken, but soon the cells replace themselves, making my body new again.

A driver in the right turn lane sign motioned for me to open my passenger-side window. His hair was long, and his eyes were concealed by opaque lenses. He looked friendly yet mysterious, as I'd imagine Raven incarnate.

"Where in Alaska are you from?"

It must have been the Alaska license plates and the anti-Pebble Mine sticker that had grabbed his attention.

"Bristol Bay."

"I lived in Naknek a year," he said without pause.

"Hey, I'm from Naknek," I said. "What's your name?"

He just smiled and said, "Oh, it was a really long time ago."

Then traffic cleared and he turned, disappearing southward. I had just turned out of the post office in my current adopted hometown of Hailey, Idaho, where Mandy and I were remodeling a house. I'd just picked up boxes of tubing and metal plates. Dad had just traveled from Wisconsin to install an in-floor radiant heat system.

Installing this system, I had learned, was a delicate process of weaving polyethylene tubing back and forth and back and forth through the crawlspace in holes drilled into floor joists. Then we stapled the tubing inside those metal plates and added layers of insulation. Dad spent another week fitting together copper pipes, valves, thermometers, and pressure tanks — all connected to the boiler in our garage. Four of the tubes looped in four different zones beneath the house, circulating water, and I thought of them like an intricate river system or blood through vessels in the body's limbs. The contraption mounted on the wall of our one-car garage was the heart.

At last, I was becoming settled in one place, but I didn't think of the mystery man as a mystical guide telling me that I had made it to the finish line. I didn't think of him as a trickster character either. He wasn't Batman, just as clueless in his direction as me. As often as these encounters have happened throughout my life, I thought of him merely as a fellow traveler. Even when the pace seems to slow, we are all still on a journey.

What brought me to Idaho, of course, was the fellow traveler with whom I wanted to share my life. Early in our relationship, Mandy and I began climbing Mount Shasta as the sun ascended into the sky. Shale crumbled beneath our shoes, and as we gained altitude, the wind blew harder. My lips were blown open, exposing my teeth to pebbles. Gusts pushed us repeatedly onto the rocky trail. I'd gotten ahead of Mandy, and while my stubbornness kept me climbing, she stayed hunkered behind a boulder out of the wind. As gusts blasted dust into my sunglasses, I was knocked down again and again, scraped by shale. The peak was so close that I felt like I could reach out and touch it if not for the wind.

We lived in Klamath Falls then, where I could see Mount Shasta from across the California border when I ran. It had allured me the same way Katmai has always allured me from the Alaska Peninsula Highway, but now I was actually climbing. While the draw of reaching the peak at over 14,000 feet was overpowering, Mandy remained hunkered behind a boulder. Zeus wasn't up there. Shiva wasn't up there. There was no ultimatum up there. There was, however, a draw even more powerful. It was more powerful than a mountain peak or finish line. She was hunkered behind a boulder a few hundred feet below me. While I had gone ahead of her, and while she remained angry at me for continuing to risk our lives, when I turned around and found her behind that bolder, it was the first time I told her that I loved her.

Several years later, we were working on our house in Hailey near the Big Wood River, a tributary of the Malad River, which is a tributary to the Snake River and the Columbia. Before dams and other human development, salmon used to run even thicker and even more abundantly into these rivers as they still do in Bristol Bay. They would enter the mouth of the Columbia and forge upstream into Washington, Oregon, and even Idaho as far as Red Fish Lake, not far up the road from our house. Although the salmon population here is all but extinct, a trivial number of them still find their way here.

As generations return to the same places, but they haven't always been there either. Somewhere in their anadromous pattern, some of them have found new places to be. Some evidence suggests that the first salmon evolved near the shores of Norway and in the Baltic Sea. As temperatures have changed and glaciers have melted into lakes, salmon have found new places to live and new patterns to follow, bringing them to Naknek, and bringing them to Idaho.

There is, of course, a story that explains the patterns of salmon. It's about a time when the gods had become tired of Loki's mischief, and they were going to gather to kick the snot out of him. Loki fled from Asgard and hid by taking the form of a salmon. When Odin received a message from his ravens about how he was staying hidden, Loki coerced millions of salmon to swim into their birthplaces with promises of love and companionship. Then Odin created people from driftwood, and they wove nets, and they set these nets all along the coasts, catching salmon for sustenance. Loki was never caught. It was Thor who at last found him, still in the ocean. He grabbed Loki and tightened his grip around his slippery scales. As his salmon form propelled forward in Thor's grip, his tail took a tapered shape. The salmon continued their anadromous pattern.

Then there is evidence. Evidence suggests that salmon are brought back into their natal lakes and streams by an incredible sense of smell. With or without evidence, however, it might also involve a sense beyond our understanding. Maybe it involves a larger form of consciousness that can't be observed, existing through millions of slick, silver-scaled bodies. Who is to say that the anadromous pattern of salmon isn't the result of a trickster character? Whatever the explanation happens to be, young salmon always leave, and older salmon always come back to spawn — but without deviation from this pattern, salmon would have disappeared from the water completely a long time ago.

I don't know how much we are all connected or if there is such a thing as fate or destiny or meant-to-be, but we do find ourselves swimming with others similar to us in the same streams. I don't know whether or not there is a universal consciousness. All I can observe is that most of us have, unlike salmon, have different, specific ambitions. Unlike salmon, most of us spawn.

Of course, I didn't always think Mandy and I were headed in the same direction. When we spent six nights squashed into a tent somewhere outside Squamish, British Columbia, my evening ritual after a day of hiking, biking, and running was shedding clothes and dunking in the stream downhill from our campsite, splashing away dirt and sweat before scurrying to the fire in nothing but sandals and a towel. Mandy shivered, shook her head no, and resorted to a bottle of dry shampoo.

During another trip, nine nights in a tent between Denali National Park and the Kenai Peninsula, neither of us had showered besides one time during a stop in Anchorage. We took turns, keeping the steam accumulating, shrouding us, and melting away the residue of the trails, the mountains, the Salty Dog Saloon, and the halibut we had caught in Cook Inlet. Unlike salmon, we humans love hot water.

I do, however, know that Mandy can take the cold and brutal weather and wind and days of fishing that never seem to end. She has since been onboard the skiff with me, but I also think of a time before she fished, on a mountain bike ride we once took on trails near our home. The ride had begun clear and warm, but at the first crack of thunder, trees began falling all around us. Rain poured and wind howled as trees cracked more frequently than the lightning. We had to climb over trees on the trail, as their branches scratched us open, before we could keep riding. Hail pelted our exposed skin. Our shoes splashed at the bottom of every pedal stroke. Both of us exhaled battle cries as we forged against the gushing river that the trail had become. In the parking lot, we stripped our muddy clothing, shivering as we got into the car. We had survived.

   It was a different time when I knew for sure that I wanted to share my life with her. We had gone down a winding dirt road outside of Sun Valley, where we followed the slight scent of sulfur in the steam rising from the hot springs. The air was frigid as we stripped into swimwear, but the water was almost scalding as we soaked. Muscle tissue and fascia and inhibitions softened. Our sweat no doubt made the spring brackish until I stood and walked over to the stream on the other side of the rocks. I submerged my feet, ankles, thighs, waist, torso, and head all at once. Then I surfaced, and Mandy was walking barefoot across the cold, slippery rocks. I watched as she took a breath and submerged her entire body. For the first time, we were together in the oxygen-rich rush of a cold, freshwater stream.

Special thanks go to Jon Billman, Matt Frank, Katrina Myers, Chad Casper, and Luke Donkersloot.

Keith Catalano Wilson has competed in 25 marathons and over 40 ultramarathons. He is the winner of such races as the Salt Flats 50-Miler, the Boise Foothills 50K, and the Sun Valley Endurance Run. He is a cross-country coach, English teacher, and a commercial fisherman. His regular column appears in *Mountain Running Magazine*, and his work has been featured in *Wanderlust Journal* and the *Young Fishermen's Almanac*. Both his bachelor's and master's degree are from Northern Michigan University in Marquette. He currently lives in Hailey, Idaho with his wife, Mandy. Together, they sell fish via their business, Wilsons' Wild Salmon.